Bridging the Foreign Policy Divide

Bridging the Foreign Policy Divide brings together twenty leading foreign policy and national security specialists—some of the leading thinkers of their generation—to seek common ground on ten key, controversial areas of policy. In each chapter conservative and liberal experts jointly outline their points of agreement on many of the most pressing issues in U.S. foreign policy, pointing the way toward a more constructive debate.

In doing so, the authors move past philosophical differences and identify effective approaches to the major national security challenges confronting the United States. An outgrowth of a Stanley Foundation initiative, this book shows what happens when specialists take a fresh look at politically sensitive issues purely on their merits and present an alternative to the distortions and oversimplifications of today's polarizing political environment.

Derek Chollet is a senior fellow at the Center for a New American Security, a non-resident fellow at the Brookings Institution, and an adjunct associate professor at Georgetown University.

Tod Lindberg is a research fellow at the Hoover Institution, Stanford University, and editor of its journal, *Policy Review*.

David Shorr is a program officer at the Stanley Foundation, focusing on national security strategy and the U.S. role in the world.

Bridging the Foreign Policy Divide

A Project of the Stanley Foundation

Edited by
Derek Chollet, Tod Lindberg, and David Shorr

Routledge
Taylor & Francis Group

NEW YORK AND LONDON

First published 2008
by Routledge
270 Madison Ave, New York, NY 10016

Simultaneously published in the UK
by Routledge
2 Park Square, Milton Park, Abingdon, Oxon OX14 4RN

Routledge is an imprint of the Taylor & Francis Group, an informa business

© The Stanley Foundation 2008

Typeset in Transitional 521 by
Keystroke, 28 High Street, Tettenhall, Wolverhampton
Printed and bound in the United States of America on acid-free paper by
Walsworth Publishing Company, Marceline, MO

Library of Congress Cataloging-in-Publication Data
Bridging the foreign policy divide : a project of the Stanley Foundation /
edited by Derek Chollet, Tod Lindberg and David Shorr.
p. cm.
1. United States–Foreign relations–2001– 2. International cooperation.
3. United States–Military policy. I. Chollet, Derek H. II. Lindberg, Tod.
III. Shorr, David. IV. Stanley Foundation.
JZ1480.B67 2008
327.73009'0511–dc22
2007033995

ISBN10: 0–415–96226–9 (hbk)
ISBN10: 0–415–96227–7 (pbk)
ISBN10: 0–203–93320–6 (ebk)

ISBN13: 978–0–415–96226–1 (hbk)
ISBN13: 978–0–415–96227–8 (pbk)
ISBN13: 978–0–203–93320–6 (ebk)

Contents

Acknowledgments

Before *Bridging the Foreign Policy Divide* was a book, it was a project of the Stanley Foundation, and like all foundation projects, it depended on key staff members to make it run smoothly. Amy Bakke and Margo Schneider ushered the text of all ten essays through copyediting and production with great care and alacrity. Natasha Wilson Boland coordinated a punishing schedule of events, making us look highly organized in spite of ourselves. And Michael Schiffer played a key role as a matchmaker for the initial planning.

We are grateful to a number of colleagues for serving as early readers and commentators on the essays: Benjamin Wittes, Joshua Muravchik, Michael Kraig, Matt Martin, Michèle Flournoy, Johanna Mendelson Forman, Steve Clemons, and Michael Lind. We were encouraged by John Oakes' confidence that this series deserved to be published as a book and thank our editor, Michael Kerns of Routledge, for making that happen.

Any collaboration of twenty highly opinionated policy experts from different political perspectives requires a degree of patience and a spirit of openness that is too often rare in Washington. Yet that is how every author engaged in this project, focusing not only on their own chapters, but providing constructive comments to others. As the coeditors of this motley band, we deeply appreciate our colleagues' willingness to join us, for the commitment they showed to this enterprise and to each other, and for the camaraderie the group shared.

Derek Chollet and Tod Lindberg wish to thank their respective institutions for supporting their work on this project. Kurt Campbell and Michèle Flournoy of the

Center for a New American Security and John Raisian, director of the Hoover Institution, Stanford University, graciously viewed this project as complementing rather than conflicting with their regular duties. Several review sessions took place in the Hoover Institution's Washington office, and we thank Sharon Ragland for her work to make that the pleasant experience it was.

While this book would not have been possible without help from the many individuals and institutions mentioned here, the views and opinions expressed in the pages ahead are the authors alone.

Preface

David Shorr

Many of the challenges that the terrorist threat poses for America's democratic system have drawn extensive attention and controversy. Questions of the separation of powers, privacy rights, and the handling of terrorist suspects have all been thoroughly aired, though far from resolved. The essays in this volume speak to a component of the American body politic that has received less focus, yet is equally vital: the quality of our debate on foreign policy and national security.

By definition, no consequential policy choice is ever self-evident. Whether the issue involves sending our military into battle or a diplomatic or economic step, whether the forum is the Congress, the White House, or a local town hall discussion, the interplay of arguments and the weighing of alternatives are essential. Especially for a superpower that sits at the center of the international system, and whose every move ripples out through the globe (and then reverberates back), the need for well-considered foreign policy decisions should be compelling.

Such collective wisdom should also be easily within the capacity of a society with a high degree of education, myriad links to the world beyond our shores, and a history of social-political self-renewal (the civil rights movement, for example). In other words, the United States has at its disposal a wealth of perspectives to help navigate rapid global change. For any challenge we encounter, the nation can draw on the counsel of the widely traveled, battle-tested, shrewd-bargaining, street-smart, folk-wise, business-savvy, and incisive philosophers of all stripes—any and all of these, as applicable. Our political discourse need only open the marketplace of ideas for business. Except that it doesn't.

The fact of bitter political division in contemporary America is well known. The associated cost to US foreign policy is the subject of this book, at least indirectly. Politics today leaves little room for deliberation over issues; by and large, it is total war between sworn enemies. Rather than winning arguments on the particular merits of a matter, each side seeks to thoroughly discredit the other. As a result, what the public sees primarily are the caricatures that both parties draw to define their counterparts.

The authors in this collection are all foreign policy and national security specialists. Policy debates are our professional domain and arguments on the merits are our bread and butter. Each of us has been directly involved in foreign policy deliberations as government officials, military personnel, issue advocates, commentators, or scholars— many serving in multiple roles over time. (Most have been citizens of what one participant called "Thinktankistan.") We are also aligned on one side of the political divide or the other, in equal numbers actually.

What unites the group is its commitment to constructive debate and concern over the corrosive effect of partisan rancor. Its motto might be: "policy wonks coming together for the good of the country." One additional criterion for participants should be noted, a generational one. All coauthors are members of the "rising generation," neither at the outset nor the apex of their careers. In practical terms, this means that nearly all the writers are under the age of 50.

This project is essentially an experiment in revealing common ground that has been obscured by the political power struggle. What would happen if matched pairs of conservative and liberal specialists jointly wrote about their points of agreement in different areas of foreign policy? The mission of the Stanley Foundation is to contribute new ideas to debates on international policy, which throughout the organization's half-century history it has done mainly by convening in-depth dialogue. The idea to build consensus between the right and left, the brainchild of project coeditor Derek Chollet, thus seemed like a natural.

As with any experiment, our intuitive hunch about underlying common ground had to be tested empirically. And so Derek and I set out with Tod Lindberg to recruit pairs of authors to address different topics. Before starting work, each duo had to confirm that they were operating from shared premises on which they could build. After all, they would be agreeing in advance to agree.

Likewise, the selection of topics had to match up with our goal of building bipartisan consensus. The Iraq war is too politically sensitive and complex to ask two colleagues to cut the Gordian knot for us. An even greater number of issues, on the other hand, do not have a discernible right-left split to begin with.

Therein lies the editorial guideline of the project. Each chapter contains some points that readers will be surprised to find a conservative endorsing, and others that are not usually put forward by liberals. Ideally, the careful crafting and weaving of these points was the creative tension that molded each piece. Because some of us may be judged guilty of heresy by colleagues on the same side of the aisle, one project participant started referring to Bridging the Foreign Policy Divide as the "twenty sell-outs on ten topics" project.

For some topics, we urged authors to address questions we viewed as clearly the most interesting. For others, we merely identified a major area of policy and gave them latitude to choose their own focus.

Drafts of every essay were circulated for review and comment to the entire group of authors. We met a total of six times to discuss each draft, which the coauthors used as the basis for their revisions. Not only did this process improve the resulting products, but it also helped strengthen our sense of bipartisan solidarity and our commitment to look for the most effective approaches to international challenges, rather than the most politically advantageous.

This isn't to say that Bridging the Foreign Policy Divide resolved all political differences between the left and right, far from it. No political epiphanies or conversions took place. Despite any charges of selling out, the authors have reached across the political divide rather than met in the middle. This project was an encounter between worldviews, not the creation of a synthesis.

That said, some consistent strains can be noted for the conservative-liberal common ground that emerged, as well as for the trenchant differences of outlook. As a shared frustration with the low level of political discourse, many of the essays set aside the false choices that many politicians have sought to use as domestic political wedges: international law or power realities, China as partner or adversary, arms control regimes or the direct disruption of some nations' efforts to acquire the bomb, preservation of due process or the aggressive pursuit of terrorist suspects. In the place of these either/or choices, the authors stress the importance of managing inherent tensions and striking careful balances.

Given that all of the authors are writing from a certain political, even philosophical, outlook, we took pains to keep those worldviews from functioning as blinders. As the chapters describe the challenges that US foreign policy confronts, the depictions are sober assessments rather than projections of ideology onto reality. An early reader commented that you don't get to pick your reality—you either deal with what is real or you fail. Hence many of the chapters try to draw lessons from recent successes and failures.

The coauthor pairs were asked to specify not only their points of agreement but also the remaining differences. Which leads to the inevitable question of the nature of the split between right and left. This question must be handled with care for two reasons. First, the entire point of this project is to break down the stereotypes that the partisan sides toss at each other like hand grenades. Conservatives, for example, do not necessarily reject international law or the United Nations, nor do liberals place their whole faith in them. Second, no matter how we move from caricature to genuine exchange, it is still difficult for a representative of one camp to describe the essential differences between conservatives and liberals with thorough evenhandedness.

But I'll try anyway. What distinguishes these schools of thought in the arena of foreign policy is how they view, and handle, American exceptionalism. As with so many issues treated in this volume, it is a difference of emphasis rather than a clash of polar opposites. For liberals and conservatives alike, the United States has a special mission as an upholder of ideals and an important role as the powerful guarantor of international order. They differ, though, over whether it is imperative for the United States to step outside of itself and exercise a degree of critical self-awareness, or whether the priority should be to stand on principles and guard against their being watered down.

The question here is the extent to which the United States must accommodate the views of others that are at odds with our own. In other words, is it more important for the United States to remain firm in its particular outlook as consistently as possible, or to defer to other perspectives and interests to avoid being seen as imperious? Where the liberal sees international resentment, the conservative sees the jealousy and self-interest of other nations. For the conservative, if you give others an inch, they'll take a mile; as a liberal sees it, if you don't give an inch, you won't move forward an inch, never mind a few yards. Yet even with this difference in outlook, liberals and conservatives share many of the same "redline" positions that are nonnegotiable— some matters of national self-interest, and others matters of principle and ideal.

Readers of this book will judge for themselves whether the areas of agreement reached by our liberal and conservative writers are significant. Again, this is the very nature of the experiment we have undertaken. The coeditors and writers view their work as the basis for a much more constructive debate over foreign policy and national security. Rather than starting with a clean slate, we have taken the debate as we find it. That said, however, the chapters that follow contain many proposed shifts in approach, reformulation of goals, and action steps that will break some issues out of the tedious back-and-forth in which they have been stuck.

Some early readers found the remaining differences between coauthors more significant than their points of consensus. This critique charged that the writers merely agreed on the easy stuff. It is certainly true that our project failed to resolve the foreign policy dilemmas of our time. At the very least, though, we can help cut down on some of the wastefulness in policy debates—the false choices that consume a distressing amount of attention, time, and energy.

When this volume is published, the 2008 presidential campaign will be at full throttle, and foreign policy is expected to be a major focus. We offer the enclosed contributions in the hopes that the campaign will shed more light than heat. After all, whichever party wins in November, it must move from the challenges of campaigning to the demands of governing. They will face the question asked by Robert Redford's character in *The Candidate*, on learning he has won, "What do we do now?"

Introduction

Derek Chollet and Tod Lindberg

At a moment when nearly every aspect of American politics seems hopelessly gnarled in partisan polarization, it is unusual to find policy professionals from different political perspectives come together to seek common ground—let alone find any.

But that is exactly what the essays in this volume set out to do. Usually, when thinkers from the right and left meet to embark on a common enterprise, it is intended to sharpen the differences and stoke a debate—and the uglier, the better. This has been especially true during recent years, when the "with-us-or-against us," 51 percent mentality of the Bush administration has combined with an increasingly insular and angry political left to leave little room for shared perspectives. Even if there might be areas of agreement, there are often very powerful political (and career) incentives not to express them. So when the two sides do exchange ideas, the results usually leave each side bruised and often self-satisfied, and the way forward for the issue at hand is rarely clearer. Things just end up where they started.

There's clearly a booming market for such spectacles—as the audience for the cable news channels, talk radio, and the blogosphere illustrates. At times, many contributors to this book engage in such contests, and they are quite good at it. But this book rejects the premise that those on each end of the political spectrum should *only* be brought together to fight. It is an exploration of what happens when analysts from the political right and left join forces to try to tackle a major challenge: when the task is not to reveal what divides, but what unites.

We believe that this is important because we are living during a unique political moment. It has often been noted that the next presidential election is the first since

1

1952 (or, by some counts, 1928) when no sitting president or vice president is running to be on the ticket, leaving the 2008 race wide open. There are strong signs that, while the political wings are energized, many Americans have grown tired of partisanship and disillusioned with the debate in Washington. These political trends are colliding at a time when the world only seems to be getting more complex and, most believe, more dangerous.

This enterprise began with a shared belief that, regardless of which political party the president who enters office in 2009 belongs to, he or she will inherit an array of global problems unlike any since the end of World War II—from the economic, political, and military rise of powers like China and India and the negative trajectory of Russia to the challenge of a nuclear North Korea and a possibly nuclear Iran, an unstable Iraq and Afghanistan, a festering conflict between Israel and the Palestinians, a Muslim world in crisis, climate change and global pandemics getting worse, global poverty deepening, and alarming energy insecurity—all coming at a time when many around the world are questioning the purpose and legitimacy of US leadership. Meanwhile, domestically the confidence of many Americans in their leaders and institutions has been shaken. Therefore, it is incumbent upon all of us to help try to find a way forward.

Of course, complaints and concerns about the influence of political divisions in foreign affairs are not new. There have always been those who have warned that too much debate is in fact a bad thing for US foreign policy, that we would be better off if the experts could be left alone to divine what's in the nation's interest and act on it. Yes, as Madison reminded us at another pivotal moment in American history, factionalism can go too far. Yet the openness of our debate and the competition of ideas is also an instrumental part of what makes America unique—and we believe, is a source of its great strength.

Some years ago, the legal theorist Cass Sunstein wrote an influential law review essay about what he called "incompletely theorized agreement," a process in which people come to the same result for different reasons. He was writing chiefly about judicial decisions, but the connection between what he described and democratic politics more broadly is easy to see. If everybody had to agree on *why* to do something *in order* to do anything, democratic politics would be impossible.

This insight resonates with our project here in two ways. First of all, it opens up the possibility that *what to do* is a matter on which people might come together even if they remain divided on precisely why to do it. It may not be necessary to settle disputes over first principles in order to settle on a course of action. The perspectives that yield the same answer or at least similar answers to a question need not be identical. You might take your case to the UN Security Council in the hope of hastening the day when the United Nations becomes the "parliament of man," per

Tennyson's lofty vision, recently reaffirmed in a book of that title by the noted historian Paul Kennedy. Or you might take your case there for reasons entirely cynical and instrumental, in order to "give futility a chance," in the words of one commentator describing the Bush administration's willingness to take the case of Iran's nuclear program to the Security Council. Yet you can agree that there is value in going to the United Nations, which yields a course of action. In some of the chapters that follow, readers will find instances of "incompletely theorized agreement" of this sort.

More basically, however, the term *incompletely theorized agreement* opens the door to another possible condition of the debate over foreign policy, namely, incompletely theorized *disagreement*. What if the various incentives that come into play in public discourse are actually leading us to view ourselves as farther apart than we actually are? For anyone involved in the political process, there is little to be gained from downplaying differences with one's partisan opponents or giving fair consideration to the other side's proposals. On the contrary, the incentives are to overstate disagreement in order to draw (presumably) favorable contrasts.

What is true of political campaigns is often true as well of Op-Ed pages and talking-heads programs on cable television and politically motivated Web sites (where one typically sees aired only one side of the issues, left or right). The proof of this propensity can easily be found in the rhetoric of successful presidential candidates of both major parties running when the Oval Office is in the hands of the other party. The differences are sharp: The incumbents have been coddling China instead of speaking up for human rights, it is charged, or the incumbents have been engaged in dubious tasks such as nation-building and international social work. Yet upon taking office, the purpose is no longer to draw contrasts and paint a portrait of failure, but to deal with the problems at hand—the very same and often vexing problems that your predecessor faced. As one Democratic wise man once said, "campaigning is a matter of raising expectations, while governing is a matter of lowering them." In the halls of government, freedom of action is no longer a matter of the anything-goes sphere of rhetoric but is constrained by the real world. And expressions of deep disagreement give way to the measure of continuity one might expect when people of goodwill try to cope with difficult questions, sometimes of life and death, as best they can.

So let the pairs of coauthors of these essays begin with little more than the assumption of goodwill of each with regard to the other. That was, indeed, the threshold test for participation in the project: a willingness to see how much agreement is possible. And let the pairs proceed then to see how much of the disagreement they might have expected between themselves proves real, and how much of it is superficial—having been insufficiently thought through, or "incompletely theorized." Let us then see what kind of agreement can emerge. In some areas, and especially with regard to basic questions about the common good in US foreign policy, what emerges is an astonishing convergence on first principles that lay buried beneath layers of partisan vituperation. In other areas, no such common principles emerged, but agreement on a course of action did: incompletely theorized agreement. And in some cases, profound differences remain, the virtue in which instances is a greater degree of clarity.

The authors here consider themselves either liberal or conservative (some with a "neo" prefix). But all believe that, at a moment of tremendous global challenges, the United States has a vital leadership role to play. In this sense, this book is firmly rooted in internationalism. While there are differences of style, substance, and priorities, no one here believes that the US can or should withdraw from the world stage. With few exceptions, the essays do not engage with the arguments commonly referred to as isolationist—in fact, if anything, this work shows how truly isolated such arguments are in the American debate.

Also, this is not a "centrist" book. The authors do not try to convert one another, disavow past positions, or show a third way (or necessarily endorse the book's 18 other contributors). No one checked their political loyalties at the door, and no essay represents 100 percent agreement. Nor do these essays serve as a showcase for high-minded banality in the form of watered-down ideas, which would be unsatisfactory both intellectually and as a matter of policy. Each essay seeks to get into uncomfortable territory for either political perspective, and the authors were challenged not to shirk dealing with the hard questions (like the advice one might get from a therapist, they were encouraged to "go to the pain"). In doing so, we hoped the authors would achieve two goals: to demonstrate that when given the task to be solution-oriented, those from the left and right could work together; and importantly, to show that such an unusual collaboration could produce work that would stand as a significant contribution to the policy debate on its own.

The topics covered here represent ten major challenges for future US national security and foreign policy. None of them has easy answers, but then that was the point. Yet this volume does not purport to offer a comprehensive blueprint for future US policy. Some of the authors tackle very specific sets of questions, like how the United States should approach China, while others address broader subjects like the possibilities and limits of international institutions. Few will miss that several important subjects—the future of Iraq, first of all—are not addressed by a chapter in this book. There are several reasons for this. The first is pragmatic: while Iraq remains the single most polarizing issue in our political debate, we did not see what our comparative advantage would be in tackling it head-on, especially when compared with such explicitly bipartisan efforts as the Baker-Hamilton Study Group. But the more powerful reason will be evident in the pages ahead: Iraq touches every subject covered in this book. How we got into Iraq, what we did while we've been there, and how we eventually will get out (and what's left behind) establishes the strategic context for every major foreign policy decision ahead.

These essays think beyond Iraq, but in the context of having been thoroughly informed by the experience of Iraq, a subject about which all of the contributors to this volume have thought deeply and written elsewhere. For example, of the three editors of this volume, two supported going to war at the time (Chollet and Lindberg) and one opposed it (Shorr). Oddly enough, this breakdown was not far out of line with public opinion at the time. Four years later, in 2007, one of us supported the Bush administration's "surge" strategy (Lindberg) and two opposed it (Chollet and Shorr). This, too, broadly reflects the distance public opinion (and for that matter expert opinion) has traveled. We have made no formal survey of the other contributors to this volume, but they are mostly on the record. We do, however, respect each other's *bona fides*. No one, we agree, had in mind or has in mind anything but doing what was and is best for the United States and the broader good. Those who wish to see taking a particular position then or now as somehow discrediting one from further participation in the debate about America's role in the world seem to us more interested in the cultivation of disagreement than in the conduct of policy.

We presume that this book will be of interest to readers in the United States and abroad not only as an illustration of the ability of partisans from opposite sides to come together but also for the window it provides on, if we may immodestly say, state-of-the-art thinking on several major foreign policy questions.

Ivo Daalder and Robert Kagan assess the question of legitimacy and the use of force and the problematic question of where legitimacy resides internationally and how the United States can best ensure that its actions carry the broadest possible mandate. Mark Lagon and David Shorr consider the role of the United Nations in the international system, both its positive aspects and areas in which it has problems, in an effort to help policymakers and readers understand what the institution can be expected to do and what it should not be expected to do. Kenneth Anderson and Elisa Massimino argue that whatever its strategic utility, the notion of a "war" on terror does not work well as a legal framework and needs to be rethought, with a willingness to provide a legal grounding for the difficult times ahead in the only form appropriate for a democracy, namely, a legislative process that makes the tough decisions. Peter Brookes and Julianne Smith offer some general principles and specific proposals for counterterrorism policy. Frederick Kagan and Michael O'Hanlon argue that given current and future international commitments and the inability of precision munitions ever fully to replace "boots on the ground," the time has come for a major increase in the size of US ground forces.

Stephen Biegun and Jon Wolfsthal think the time has come to shed what remains of outdated Cold War thinking about nuclear weapons and offer a vigorous program for reducing their salience and numbers in an effort to avoid nuclear anarchy. Michael Schiffer and Gary Schmitt offer guidance for the United States as China continues its ascent as a power and a player on the world stage, a hedging strategy that encourages China's peaceful development and integration into the international system while keeping a clear eye out for less benevolent developments. Andrew Erdmann and Suzanne Nossel lay out a program for the sorely needed improvement in the ability of the United States to engage in, for want of a better term, the *nation-building* that likely lies in our future. Francis Fukuyama and Michael McFaul reassert, post-Iraq, the ongoing strategic and moral case for the pragmatic promotion of democracy and liberalization. Finally, the authors of this Introduction, Derek Chollet and Tod Lindberg, write in defense of the broader case for a foreign policy grounded in principle and dedicated in part to the spread of values Americans hold dear, but whose appeal extends far beyond our shores.

These essays were written over the course of a year, and ours was one of the last. It therefore had the benefit of the insight of the other pairs of coauthors, and the chief argument it advances is broadly reflective of the common themes that emerge from the other chapters. The United States is a powerful country, one with global responsibilities. But it is not so powerful that it can do as it pleases. And US foreign policy will be on its soundest footing when it is informed by a vision of the good that is not confined to consideration of what is good for the United States, but reflects the broader principles the United States claims to represent, and needs to live up to.

America and the Use of Force: Sources of Legitimacy

Ivo H. Daalder and Robert Kagan

Many American and foreign observers believe that the painful and so far unsuccessful intervention in Iraq will make the United States more reluctant to go to war in the future. Three powerful factors, however, suggest that, to the contrary, the United States may resort to military action more, not less, often in the future. The character of US foreign policy, manifested over two centuries, is that of a nation willing to use force with relative frequency on behalf of both principles and tangible interests and generally believing in the justness and appropriateness of military action in international affairs. The distribution of power in the world since the collapse of the Soviet Union—not very different today, despite the rise of powers such as China and India—invites military intervention by a dominant military power unchecked by the deterrent power of any nation or grouping of nations with roughly equal strength. Finally, the contemporary international system presents an array of circumstances in which the use of force will be seen as both necessary and proper. Indeed, the number of such challenges—be they to curb proliferation, counter terrorists, curtail gross human rights violations, or counter some other threat requiring military action—is likely to increase, not decrease, in the years ahead.

These three factors have already produced a 15-year post-Cold War period in which the United States has taken military action with greater frequency than ever before and with far greater frequency than any other nation during that time. From 1989 to 2003 the United States intervened with significant military force on nine occasions—Panama (1989), Somalia (1992), Haiti (1994), Bosnia (1995–96), Kosovo (1999), Afghanistan (2001), and Iraq (1991, 1998, 2003), an average of one large-scale military intervention every 18 months. This interventionism has been a bipartisan affair—five interventions were launched by Republican administrations, four by Democratic administrations—and regardless of often-alleged, but in fact largely mythical doctrinal distinctions. The supposedly "realist" administration of George H. W. Bush, for instance, launched two interventions aimed at purely "humanitarian" purposes (Somalia) or to remove a dictator and effect a change of regime (Panama). The supposedly "liberal internationalist" Clinton administration carried out three military interventions without the approval of the UN Security Council and two (Kosovo and Iraq in 1998) over the public objections of one or more of the council's permanent members. At least one intervention, in Haiti in 1994, was undertaken explicitly to remove a dictatorship, reinstall a democracy, and effect a change of regime. But its two interventions in the Balkans also aimed in part at undermining the power of Slobodan Milošević and eventually unseating him, as the Kosovo war ultimately did.

Some argue that the failures in Iraq may temper these impulses. Perhaps. But history suggests that any such tempering may be short-lived. It was only a few years after the US defeat in Vietnam—an even more unpopular and divisive war—that the United States returned to a foreign policy with military power as an essential component and "regime change" a primary objective. If the Reagan administration, which led this return to pre-1970s orthodoxy, used direct military force only sparingly, that hesitance was because it faced a rival superpower: the Soviet Union. Today, in the continuing absence of such a constraint—even a rising China is a long way from replacing the Soviet Union as a rival power—the US willingness to use force to alter the status quo may return even more quickly than it did after Vietnam.

International conditions provide US leaders with abundant potential uses of force to consider. Unlike in the 1990s, when the first Bush and Clinton administrations launched several military interventions despite the lack of any obvious, direct threat to US security, in this decade, following the September 11, 2001, attacks both political parties agree that a variety of foreign actors could present a threat. The new, post-September 11 perspective has cast some old problems in a new and more ominous light. The problem of failed states, for instance, once categorized as largely a humanitarian issue, has now acquired strategic significance given the terrorist infiltration into Afghanistan and Somalia. North Korea's acquisition of nuclear weapons presents a heightened threat because of the prospect that such weapons or technologies may fall into the hands of terrorists willing to use them against the United States and other nations. A sturdy political consensus opposes Iran's acquisition of nuclear weapons on similar grounds.

In this respect, the attack on the American homeland on September 11, 2001, has had much the same effect as the attack on Pearl Harbor did six decades earlier. It has provided justification for an active, and at times even aggressive, defense of American interests far beyond America's borders. To be sure, the change of course was much sharper in the 1940s than it is today. In important ways, September 11 merely confirmed the need for an interventionist approach that had already been adopted after the end of the Cold War.

Beyond the prominent issues of terrorism and proliferation of weapons of mass destruction, there are a number of other, more traditional conflicts that could escalate into military confrontations—some of which might even involve a clash with other great powers. The determination of Taiwan's future could lead the United States and China into a limited military confrontation that might well spiral into a more significant clash, even though neither nation would desire such a confrontation. A war between Russia and Georgia is not beyond imagining and could pit Moscow and Washington against each other, along with some European powers that might feel obliged to come to Georgia's defense. The United States could again find itself in a military confrontation with Syria over Lebanon, as in the early 1980s. In the Western Hemisphere the United States has a 200-year history of using force, including quite recent interventions in Panama and Haiti. There has scarcely been a decade in the past century when the United States did not send troops to Latin America for some purpose. Who knows what catalyst for intervention the next decade might bring? Violence and chaos in Cuba following the death of Castro could prompt a US-led international intervention both to avert a humanitarian disaster and to ensure a desirable transition from the US point of view.

Meanwhile, a significant US military buildup continues and may be accelerating. The US defense budget has risen substantially since the late 1990s and is now approaching $500 billion a year. The percentage of GDP devoted to defense has risen from just over 3 percent to more than 4 percent—not high by Cold War standards, but higher than what most expected after the Cold War ended. The striking thing is that this buildup has proceeded without any domestic opposition. Both political parties have agreed that forces needed to be improved and augmented, and now both parties seem to agree that the size of US ground forces, until recently thought to be too large, must now become even larger. This military buildup occurs at a time when almost every nation in the world, except China, is cutting defense spending. As in the 1990s, the increased military power will affect how Americans view the utility of military force for resolving international problems. For Americans, more power, and especially more power relative to others, will likely produce, as it has in the past, a greater temptation to use it.

The increased willingness of the United States to use force has already generated much unease around the world, especially among traditional allies in Europe, and will continue to do so. In the wake of the Iraq war, the United States is suffering from a crisis of legitimacy. Part of the reason lies in America's actions in recent years and, especially, the way it has carried out those actions. But a large part of the problem transcends Iraq, and stems instead from the major geopolitical shift since the end of the Cold War. Nations that once depended on the United States for security, particularly the nations of Western Europe, no longer depend on American power and have instead become suspicious and wary of it. The legitimacy of American power and of American global leadership has encountered growing skepticism from a majority of Europeans, especially Western Europeans, who generally accorded the United States legitimacy throughout most of the Cold War. Most of the rest of the world withheld support for American global leadership, of course, except when it served their particular interests, and now continues to question the legitimacy of American primacy. There are, of course, significant exceptions to this trend: Eastern European and Asian and Pacific powers who worry about the rise of Russia or China still look to the United States for protection and are therefore more inclined to accord it legitimacy and to support its actions, even in Iraq.

Still, the hostility of many Europeans and others around the world to the United States' use of force poses a problem. Americans have not and will not be able to ignore this problem. Legitimacy matters, if only because the American people like to believe they are acting for legitimate purposes and are troubled, sometimes deeply, if other peoples accuse them of selfish, immoral, or otherwise illegitimate actions. The experiment of attempting to invade and then reconstruct Iraq without the blessing of Europe has been discomfiting, and will be even if the United States were eventually to succeed in Iraq.

There are sound reasons why the United States needs the general approval of allied democracies—reasons unrelated to international law, the strength of the Security Council, and the as-yet nonexistent fabric of the international order. Such allies, including those in Europe, matter because they are the core of the liberal, democratic world, and the liberal, democratic essence of the United States makes it difficult if not impossible for Americans to ignore the concerns of its fellow liberal democracies. US foreign policy will inevitably be drawn by American liberalism to seek greater harmony with Europe and with other democracies around the world, if Europeans and other democratic peoples are open to such harmony. The alternative posture of stolidity will be difficult for the United States to sustain, for it is questionable whether the United States can operate effectively over the long term without the moral support and approval of the democratic world.

This is not only for the reasons that are usually cited. The United States does need the material cooperation of allies, of course, when it intervenes around the world. In particular, the United States needs to pool its resources with allies for reconstruction and development of countries in which the United States has intervened. In military terms, the United States can and does almost "go it alone" when it intervenes, even when allies are fully on board, as in Kosovo in the first Persian Gulf War, and even a half-century ago in the Korean War, despite its international sanction by the UN Security Council. But the American people's willingness to support both military actions and the burdens of postwar occupations in the face of constant charges of illegitimacy from close democratic allies is more doubtful. The steady denial of international legitimacy by fellow democracies will eventually become debilitating and perhaps even paralyzing.

If Americans are compelled to build up their legitimacy reserves, where should they look to find it? How can the United States ensure that its actions—especially the use of military force—are seen as legitimate? In answering this question, we need to consider three aspects of legitimacy: the substance of the contemplated action, the procedure for deciding the action and, third, the normative basis that underlies both.

Self-Defense and Preemption

The legitimacy of using force depends importantly on the intended purpose as well as on whether that purpose is militarily achievable. It has long been a central tenet of international politics that the use of force by states in self-defense is a fully legitimate exercise of military power. Indeed, the UN Charter speaks of the "inherent right" of states to use force to defend themselves against an armed attack—i.e., a right of all states *as* states, and not one granted to them by the Charter or any other treaty.

One issue that has been long debated, and which has reemerged in recent years, is whether states may take defensive military measures in anticipation of an attack—that is, whether the preemptive use of force can ever be justified on self-defense grounds. International lawyers have long argued (at least since the *Caroline* incident of 1837) that such anticipatory use of force in self-defense is legal and legitimate so long as the threat of an armed attack is clearly imminent. Or, as US Secretary of State Daniel Webster put it, when the "necessity of self-defence [is] instant, overwhelming, leaving no choice of means, and no moment for deliberation."[1] This general principle of anticipatory self-defense was most recently reaffirmed by UN Secretary-General Kofi Annan, as well as by a high-level panel of former senior officials Annan appointed to examine these issues in the wake of the UN disagreement over the Iraq war.[2] In an age of catastrophic terrorism, the legitimacy of striking terrorists preemptively is no longer in question.

In the wake of 9/11, the Bush administration pressed the issue of whether the "imminence" standard was adequate, arguing that the new threat environment required modifications to the standard. "We must adapt the concept of imminent threat to the capabilities and objectives of today's adversaries," the president's *National Security Strategy* released in September 2002 stated.

> The United States has long maintained the option of preemptive actions to counter a sufficient threat to our national security. The greater the threat, the greater is the risk of inaction—and the more compelling the case for taking anticipatory action to defend ourselves, even if uncertainty remains as to the time and place of the enemy's attack. To forestall or prevent such hostile acts by our adversaries, the United States will, if necessary, act preemptively.[3]

What was new about this argument was not the notion of using force preemptively. The United States has done so in the past, in efforts to forestall terrorist attacks (e.g., the Libya bombing of 1986 and the Iraq bombing of 1993) and respond to the threat of weapons of mass destruction (e.g., the Iraq bombing of 1998 and the Sudan bombing that same year). Rather, the novelty lay in the argument that such preemptive uses of force could be justified on self-defense grounds even when the threat was not clearly imminent. Indeed, the Bush administration argued that the United States could use force preemptively even without knowing whether a threat would materialize at all or, if it did, whether it would pose a direct threat to the United States.

This argument raises two issues—both of which go to the heart of the substantive and normative legitimacy of using force. The first concerns how, under these terms, to distinguish force used for self-defense purposes from force used for aggressive purposes. The administration acknowledged this difficulty when it warned that other nations should not "use preemption as a pretext for aggression." But if the imminence of an attack isn't the point of reference, how can one distinguish between these two uses of force—one clearly legitimate, the other clearly not? The second, related, issue concerns how one determines which of these nascent threats will emerge as palpable threats against specific states and which will threaten international security more broadly—for example, by shifting the regional balance of power or giving a state the ability to intimidate others. The former example gives a basis for preemptive action with a potentially legitimate argument on self-defense grounds. But such an argument is more difficult to make in the second instance, when the potential threat to one's own national security is less certain or real.

These theoretical issues came to a practical head in the debate over the Iraq war. Supporters of the war, including the Bush administration, argued that the invasion of Iraq was justified because Baghdad's development of weapons of mass destruction, combined with Saddam Hussein's record of past aggression, made his regime an emerging threat that had to be defeated before it had the chance to fully materialize.

"We don't want the smoking gun to be a mushroom cloud," as Condoleezza Rice famously put it.[4] For that reason, the preemptive use of force was justified not only on prudential grounds but also as a legitimate form of self-defense. In contrast, many of the war's opponents maintained that in the absence of a threat that was truly imminent, alternative means (including beefed-up sanctions and continued international inspections of Iraq's weapons programs) must be pursued before the resort to force. They also argued that because Iraq did not pose a direct threat to the United States, any use of force required international support and authorization.

There can be little doubt that if the Iraq war had confirmed that Saddam's Iraq possessed the kinds of weapons programs many believed it did, and that if the postwar situation had been more peaceful and stable than it has been, judgments about the overall legitimacy of the war would not be what they are today. While the war is now seen by many as lacking legitimacy, a different outcome would have produced a different assessment of its value and validity. This underscores that the legitimacy of using force is at least in part related to the efficacy of force in achieving its stated purpose.

Who Decides?

Substance, however, is only part of the basis of legitimacy. Procedure matters as well. And the critical issue, underscored by the preemption and Iraq debates, is who decides? Who decides whether a threat is sufficiently real or probable or grave to warrant preemptive action? Who decides whether the emerging threat is directed against a specific state or whether it threatens regional or international security more broadly? These questions point to the importance of procedural considerations for the legitimacy of using force—at least in cases without a traditional self-defense claim.

The longstanding answer to the question "who decides," endorsed by the United States and others in theory if not always in practice, is that the UN Security Council decides. Under the UN Charter, the use of force is prohibited except in cases of self-defense or when explicitly authorized by the Security Council to deal with threats to or breaches of international peace and security. In the past 15 years or so, the Security Council has interpreted this prerogative to authorize the use of force evermore broadly—including to deal with internal conflicts and large-scale human rights abuses that it viewed as threats to international peace and security. And this broad mandate to authorize coercive action, including the use of force, was reaffirmed by Kofi Annan's high-level panel, which in its 2004 report argued that the Security Council may authorize force against a state "whether the threat is occurring now, in the imminent future or more distant future; whether it involves the State's own actions or those of non-State actors it harbors or supports; or whether it takes the form of an act or omission, an actual or potential act of violence or simply a challenge to the Council's authority."[5]

The reality, however, is that the Security Council is deeply divided over these issues and in many, if not most, instances will not authorize any coercive action, let alone the use of force. Among its five permanent members there is no consensus on what constitutes a threat to international peace and security and no agreement on how to respond even to those threats on which it does agree. From Rwanda to Kosovo to Darfur, and from Iraq to North Korea to Iran, the Security Council has failed to act because it was split over whether and how these situations constituted threats and what the appropriate response should be. Even strong advocates of the United Nations have admitted that the Security Council has often fallen short. ("The Council's decisions have often been less than consistent, less than persuasive and less than fully responsive to very real state and human security needs," acknowledged the high-level panel.) And proposals to reform the Security Council—by making it more representative of the UN membership, expanding its numbers, or taking the veto away from the permanent members—are not only doomed politically, but even if miraculously approved would hardly facilitate the search for consensus or decisions on timely and effective action.

The paralysis of the Security Council is thus both a reality and unlikely to change any time soon. From the United States' perspective, the central problem is its membership, which, among the five permanent members, includes two countries that are governed in ways that are antithetical to everything America stands for. While the interests of the United States, Russia, and China may occasionally coincide—as in the early 1990s, when the Security Council united in response to threats from Iraq, Somalia, Bosnia, and Haiti—on today's most pressing issues, their interests diverge. America and its democratic friends are deeply concerned when governments engage in the wholesale slaughter or ethnic cleansing of groups of their people or when regimes passively allow others to engage in such horrific behavior. In contrast, Russia and China have given priority to maintaining good relations with such regimes—be it Milošević's Serbia in the 1990s or al-Bashir's Sudan today—abandoning those who are being "cleansed," raped, mutilated, and murdered by the millions to their fate. America and its democratic friends care deeply when rogue regimes flout international treaty obligations and set out to build a nuclear bomb with which to threaten and intimidate countries around the region and the world. Again, Moscow and Beijing are more interested in maintaining good relations with Pyongyang and Tehran, thereby thwarting efforts by America and its allies to prevent and reverse the nuclearization of these unstable regions.

Sovereignty as Responsibility

These differences reflect the very distinct natures of authoritarian and democratic regimes, which also differ in their conceptions of sovereignty, the issue on which UN members are most divided. Russia, China, and a host of developing nations continue to view sovereignty as the defining principle of international affairs, and they steadfastly maintain that a country's borders demarcate an international no-go zone. What happens within the borders of a state is strictly the concern of the regime that governs that territory, not of anyone else. Others, including the United States and its democratic friends, believe that insisting on absolute sovereignty ignores a basic reality of our increasingly interconnected age: i.e., that the principal threats to security today come from within states rather than from their external behavior. Indeed, the last three wars the United States has fought were provoked by internal conditions and actions—Serb ethnic cleansing of its Albanian minority in Kosovo, the Taliban's harboring of Al Qaeda and Osama bin Laden in Afghanistan, and Saddam Hussein's purported development of weapons of mass destruction in Iraq. Clearly, when developments within one state can profoundly affect the security and well-being of peoples in other states, the only practical way for countries to safeguard their security is to interfere in the internal affairs of those states.

We must adapt our standards for intervention—as well as the decision-making structures for questions of whether to intervene—to the transformation in the nature of sovereignty. Rather than conceiving of sovereignty as a government's inherent right to do as it pleases, we must recognize that it entails real responsibilities—both with respect to those who live within the state and with regard to internal developments that can affect those who live outside it. This changing conception of sovereignty—from conceiving sovereignty as a right to conceiving it as a responsibility—has become more widely accepted in recent years. There has been growing recognition that states have a *responsibility to protect* their own citizens from genocide, mass killing, and other gross violations of human rights.[6] But states also have a *responsibility to prevent* the emergence of security threats within their territory—such as developments relating to weapons of mass destruction (like their acquisition or the failure to secure weapons, materials, or deadly agents against possible theft or diversion); the harboring, supporting, or training of terrorists; or environmental dangers (like allowing the spread of dangerous diseases or the destruction of the rain forest).[7] Because in each of these instances what happens inside a state has consequences beyond its borders; they are a legitimate, sometimes vital, concern of any nation that is or could be affected by a sovereign government's actions or inaction.

The emergence of a new norm of state responsibility raises the important question of what should happen when states fail to meet their responsibility. The world's leaders, meeting at the United Nations' 60th anniversary summit in 2005, made clear that when a state is unable or unwilling to fulfill its fundamental responsibility to protect its own people, then the onus for action shifts to the international community. "We are prepared to take collective action, in a timely and decisive manner, through the Security Council," the leaders declared, "should peaceful means prove inadequate and national authorities are manifestly failing to protect their populations."[8] Similarly, when a state fails to meet its other major responsibility, to prevent the emergence of threats within its borders that pose dangers beyond them, that responsibility falls to others. And the most effective way for doing so will often involve preventive action. Indeed, the best time to defeat many of the new threats is before they become imminent—*before* enough fissile material has been produced to make nuclear weapons, *before* weapons in unsecured sites or deadly diseases in laboratories have been stolen, *before* terrorists have been fully trained or are able to carry out their plots, *before* large-scale killing or ethnic cleansing has occurred, *before* a deadly pathogen has mutated and spread around the globe.

Of course in many of these cases, military intervention is not the only, or even the preferred, means for dealing with the emerging threat. There often are good alternatives. At the same time, force will sometimes be necessary to address these new threats. And when it is, it often is best used early, before threats have been fully formed, since timely use of force will likely reduce the associated costs and enhance the probability of success.

The Democratic Alternative

Who, then, should decide when intervention is warranted? Until the UN members, particularly the Security Council's permanent members, fully embrace the logic of state responsibility, leaving the decision-making authority solely with the United Nations is a recipe for indecision and inaction—and increased insecurity. Instead of the United Nations, the decision to intervene promptly to keep small threats from turning into big ones must lie with those who take seriously the notion of sovereignty as responsibility: the world's democracies (including in particular the United States and its major democratic partners in Europe and Asia). Democracies know—in a way that non-democracies do not—that real sovereignty, like real legitimacy, resides with the people rather than with the states. That is why the decision of states to intervene in the affairs in another state can be legitimate only if it is rendered by the people's democratically chosen representatives rather than the personal whims of autocrats or oligarchs.

Of course, there is no guarantee that the democracies will always agree on the circumstances and manner of an intervention. Regional differences, historical experiences, and power differentials all influence democratic states' perspectives on questions of intervention. Disagreement is therefore possible, if not likely. At the same time, democracies are undoubtedly more likely to agree among themselves on these issues than would a group that included nondemocracies. That much is clear from recent history. Within 24 hours of the 9/11 attacks, NATO invoked Article 5, thereby committing itself to the collective defense of the United States—including, were Washington to decide, by conducting the military operation in Afghanistan (which is currently under NATO command). While the Security Council also responded swiftly to the attack, it only implicitly endorsed the Afghan campaign, and more than a few UN members subsequently questioned its legitimacy. More to the point, perhaps, is the Kosovo campaign of 1999, which demonstrated that there are indeed circumstances when the NATO democracies can agree on the use of force even when the UN Security Council cannot.

The NATO precedent, we believe, suggests that for all their differences, democracies are more likely to agree on the use of force in certain circumstances than any larger grouping of states that included nondemocracies. Indeed, for that reason we strongly support the creation of a global organization of democracies to cooperate on matters of common concern. Such an organization would include not only Western democracies that have long cooperated within NATO and other security alliances but also India, Brazil, South Africa, and other democracies from around the world.[9] Of course, creating a Concert of Democracies will take time; so until a new organization uniting the world's true democracies has been built, decisions on using force for reasons other than self-defense would have to rest with the North American and European democracies united in NATO—augmented, we would hope, by other critical partner nations like Australia, Japan, South Korea, Sweden, and similar like-minded allies. Many will object to this proposal as drawing the decision-making circle either too narrowly or too broadly. But their proffered alternatives are worse, which is why it is very much in the interest of the United States as well as the other major democracies to make the proposed structure work.

One set of critics, coming mainly from the left and from abroad, argues that decisions on the use of force by a small number of the world's nearly 200 countries are by definition illegitimate. But this argument equates legitimacy with universality, a common conceit of UN spokesmen and all too many of the world's countries. It reduces the concept of legitimacy to a procedural question—the number of states or votes one can marshal in support of a given action will determine whether it is legitimate. Under this approach, the nature of the action itself or of the states consenting to it matter little, if at all. This is a deeply flawed conception of legitimacy. Surely, the rightness or wrongness of a proposed course of action inheres, at least in part, in the nature of the action being contemplated. Indeed, the lack of broad support for forceful action that is necessary to reverse a terrible wrong such as genocide or widespread humanitarian atrocities would hardly render inaction legitimate. Similarly, it surely matters as much for legitimacy *which* states support an action as *how many* support it. Would anyone seriously argue that an action supported by authoritarian regimes would, by garnering more votes, be legitimate in a way that an action supported by the world's democracies would not? If so, that is a notion of legitimacy that we cannot accept as, well, legitimate.

Another set of critics, mainly on the right, argues that it is unacceptable to give other democracies, even our longstanding friends in Europe and Asia, a say (let alone a possible veto) over decisions to use force, both because it would wrongly constrain the United States and because it would render the use of force ineffective. According to this argument, under our Constitution, the ultimate decision on whether or not to employ the armed forces rests with the commander in chief, and there it must remain. Moreover, these critics argue, from Kosovo to Afghanistan to Iraq, the application of military power has proven most effective when the United States is in complete command and control of all the forces and least effective when other nations have a voice in their strategic, operational, and tactical use. With very few exceptions, our allies hesitate to commit their military forces. Even when they finally agree on the need to use force, they don't bring much to the table, and what they do bring often comes with a requirement of national approval for how the forces are used, as well as other caveats. In most instances, these critics contend, it's just not worth it.

We don't disagree. We don't expect, nor would support, any president handing over his ultimate authority as commander in chief to another body or country. But as a matter of prudence, we believe any president would be well advised to gain the support of US democratic allies when deciding to employ force in situations that are not strictly for our self-defense. For reasons stated earlier, the United States needs the legitimacy that such support confers, and we should always work hard in such situations to obtain that support before embarking on a major military operation. Making clear that we want NATO and its global democratic partners to be involved in decisions on using force in these instances will help set a new standard for legitimacy.

Of course, Iraq showed that our partners will not always agree with our proposed course of action. There may come times when we will have to use force over the objections of some, many, or even most of our partners. The fact of their disagreement should weigh heavily in our decision making—at the very least prompting us to re-examine our assumptions and assessments carefully. But such differences cannot constitute a definitive veto over our actions any more than our own qualms about actions a partner nation (or nations) is contemplating should constitute a veto over theirs.

At the same time, our history of cooperation in NATO makes clear that having a strong organizational structure for debating and reaching decisions on matters as important as the use of force is often more of a help than a hindrance. When an action or issue is thoroughly debated, assessed, and reassessed, it only enhances the quality of the ultimate decision. We rely on such debate domestically to make our democracies healthy and dynamic, and we have relied on debate within NATO over the decades to chart a wise and effective course to fight and win the Cold War. We should continue to look to partners within and beyond this institution to help us reach wise and effective decisions on the use of force in the future.

Of course, if the United States commits itself to working with its democratic partners on these central issues, that gives allies, too, a major responsibility. They must come to the table prepared not only to debate with Washington but also fully prepared to implement the decisions that are reached. And by "prepared" we mean both capable of deploying a significant force to the most likely loci of conflict (i.e., far away from Europe) and demonstrably willing to employ force when necessary and appropriate. The essential deal to be struck between the United States and its democratic partners on the use of force must be a true bargain—a two-way street. While Washington would commit to involve NATO and its global partners in decisions, the NATO and global partners would commit to bring real capabilities to the table and a willingness to use them when a decision to do so is reached.

The viability of this bargain depends on how well it works in practice. NATO has worked well because the allies have long valued what that institution does for them and for their security. For most members, maintaining the unity and effectiveness of the Alliance became at least as important as winning the debate on a particular issue. The Alliance even devised mechanisms for members that wished to express reservations on a particular course of action but that did not want to block an action supported by a large majority. The silence procedure and the footnote are two such mechanisms; an agreement to endorse the action but not participate in it (as Greece did, for example, during NATO's Kosovo war) is another. In each of these instances, alliance members with a minority viewpoint placed the value of the institution and collaborative decision making above having every decision come out to their liking.

When it comes to the use of force, the American and global debates often present a narrow choice between going with the United Nations or going it alone. This is a false choice. There is an effective and viable alternative to multilateral paralysis and unilateral action—working with our democratic partners in NATO and around the world to meet and defeat the global challenges of our age.

Notes

1 *http://www.yale.edu/lawweb/avalon/diplomacy/britain/br-1842d.htm*

2 *In Larger Freedom: Towards Development, Security and Human Rights for All*, Report of the Secretary General of the United Nations (New York, September 2005), *http://www.un.org/largerfreedom/contents.htm*, para. 124; and *A More Secure World: Our Shared Responsibility*, Report of the Secretary General's High-level Panel on Threats, Challenges and Change (New York, December 2004), *www.un.org/secureworld/report3.pdf*.

3 *The National Security Strategy of the United States of America* (Washington: The White House, September 2002), *http://www.whitehouse.gov/nsc/nss.pdf*, p. 15.

4 *http://archives.cnn.com/2002/ALLPOLITICS/09/08/iraq.debate/*

5 *A More Secure World*, p. 63.

6 Evans-Sahoun Commission.

7 For a similar argument, confined to weapons of mass destruction, see Lee Feinstein and Anne-Marie Slaughter, "A Duty to Prevent," *Foreign Affairs*, Vol. 83, January–February 2004, pp. 136–150.

8 "2005 World Summit Outcome," United Nations General Assembly, A/60/L.1, September 2005, p. 31.

9 Cf. Ivo Daalder and James Lindsay, "Democracies of the World, Unite," *The American Interest*, Winter 2007, pp. 5–15.

2

How to Keep From Overselling or Underestimating the United Nations

Mark P. Lagon and David Shorr

The policy choices that the United States makes regarding the United Nations and other intergovernmental organizations rest on a set of assumptions on whether our aims in the world can be achieved through sheer power, set international structures, or a combination thereof. The bedrock for policy, therefore, is an assessment of the capacities and limitations of these structures. In other words, our appraisal of the United Nations' potential impact helps determine what we seek there. These questions raise others about the very nature of the international system and whether it is a brutal Hobbesian struggle or subject to some sort of regulation.

International organizations are premised on their ability to make the realm of nations more, rather than less, orderly. In US domestic politics, this is often portrayed as an all-or-nothing proposition. The United Nations' treaties are worthless, goes the argument, because they cannot stop those who are bent on ruthless destruction. So what's the use of such bodies?

US policymakers will always face controversial and difficult decisions for the US stance at the United Nations. But if some of the rancor can be drained from the surrounding political debate, it would be easier for officials to focus on the merits of the proposed courses of action. The place to start is with a set of realistic expectations that neither oversells nor underestimates the value of international organizations.

Former United Nations Secretary-General Kofi Annan wrote in his March 2005 report on UN reform *In Larger Freedom* that "sovereign states are the basic and indispensable building blocks of the international system."[1] Sovereignty no longer gives national governments license to commit grave abuses within their borders, and nonstate actors have grown in their impact, both harmful and beneficial. Nonetheless, the secretary-general's point stands—even in the networked 21st century world, nation-states remain the essential constituent elements.

Is the System Legal or Political?

In what sense, then, are international organizations supranational? There is some truth to the skeptical view of international organizations' ability to enforce compliance. They are not able to halt and punish transgressors in the same way governments can enforce laws within their own borders. This statement is not a claim about the standing of international law and treaties; it is instead a practical observation that international norms work differently and have limits.

Lacking an extensive justice system such as the United States has domestically, the international system's judgments and sanctions are not based as directly and consistently on the presentation of legal argument and precedent. Some international mechanisms function in a legal mode. The International Court of Justice, for example, operates in its recognized sphere of jurisdiction. The World Trade Organization, likewise, adjudicates disputes between nations on the basis of agreed trade rules, and its verdicts have met with remarkable compliance. By and large though, the court of world opinion is not actually a court.

Despite this, the concept of international law tends to loom large in the debate over multilateral politics, which points toward the need for a more realistic working concept of the international system—namely the realm in which nations clash, cooperate, and establish mutual expectations. The international system does not feature over-arching judicial authority, but it can often function as a rules-based order that defines some boundaries for commerce, military action, and respect for human rights. A depiction that squares these realities could help focus the policy debate on appropriate expectations for international organizations and what the United States seeks from them.

The domestic rule of law itself, it is worth noting, is not completely mechanistic. Its rules and precision serve as a gyroscope for law, order, and liberty, yet it must also be flexible to deal with new situations, resolve internal tensions, and adapt to shifting political realities. What differentiates the international level is that it has less of the former and more of the latter.

Domestically, statutes, their legislative history, and judicial precedents form a dense web of rules, keeping latitude and discretion to a relative minimum. There are also explicit norms at the international level, to be sure, but order is maintained in a more dynamic way. As noted, the international system lacks an extensive judicial apparatus; instead, diplomatic interchange is necessary and prevalent. Rather than being adjudicated by jurists, then, international norms are given effect through formal intergovernmental decision-making bodies and the underlying political interests and commitments.

Just because the collective decisions of governments are mainly political in nature, this doesn't mean they are always merely advisory. The United Nations Security Council has a legal as well as a political function. Chapter VII of the UN Charter establishes the Security Council as authorized to establish binding international legal obligations needed for international peace and security, with the authority not only to compel actions by member states but also to mandate military action or other sanctions to give force to its decisions. Of course the council will only act according to the decisions of the national governments that comprise it, subject to the veto power of the United States, China, France, Russia, and the United Kingdom.

The lack of consistent enforcement of Security Council resolutions and other international norms that we consider important is a shortcoming of today's international system, due largely to a current political fractiousness among nations that hinders progress toward greater security for all. Politically, the United States is often the most insistent voice diplomatically that some norms be enforced. Nonetheless, even with its indispensable and preeminent military assets, enforcement is still difficult without the legitimacy that stems from broad international support.

The challenge is to steer a course that avoids either precipitous confrontations with violators or paths of least resistance; the pressure applied to states at the center of international attention must be serious and sustained. The difficulty for the United States is the inconclusive drift that occurs when pressure is not maintained. From the Darfur genocide to the prewar economic sanctions against Saddam Hussein, the approach of going along, getting along, and papering over differences has allowed problems to fester rather than be resolved.

The coauthors differ in their diagnoses of the obstacles to stronger enforcement and on the question of whether the United States bears a special onus to surmount them. For David Shorr, overcoming international suspicion and mistrust of the United States itself is essential. He views international resistance to the US calls for stronger enforcement steps as stemming from a perception that the superpower is driven by its own likes and dislikes rather than on behalf of the global community. Therefore, the United States must persuade others that enforcement is not merely a pet concern.

Alternatively, Mark Lagon believes that other countries resist enforcement because of their economic and political interests, and will support enforcement of norms when there is a cost or penalty for not doing so. He does not take at face value that other nations are truly concerned about US proposals for multilateral enforcement being self-serving, but instead views those nations as merely motivated by their own perceived interests. Lagon believes that where consensus cannot be achieved in the United Nations, US efforts to enforce norms constitute leadership rather than "license." Both coauthors agree, however, that the United States will be better off with a broader and more united front to bring defectors into better compliance with norms.

The broad-based representation and inclusiveness of the United Nations can help bolster international norms. In other words, the specific form of rules and institutions is not what elicits confidence and support. Norms are strengthened when, through the international community, they are viewed as broadly beneficial, responding to the concerns of member states and meeting their needs. In those instances where nations' interests coincide, the United Nations can catalyze the political legitimization so as to strengthen international cooperation.

And just as the political dynamic is related but distinct from the legal, so too the global political agenda is broader than just the regulation of actions by states. However the world's nations arrange themselves and conduct their affairs, the world community must not only establish and preserve order but also promote progress and further prosperity and freedom—i.e., the global "general welfare" (a good in and of itself and also a foundation of greater peace and security). Accordingly, the world's intergovernmental bodies offer mechanisms to set agendas, agree on fundamental approaches, and decide courses of action and implement programs to deal with the entire range of international problems. The mandates, focus, and priorities of these bodies may not be optimal, but any deficiencies are not essentially architectural. Confidence in the system is a function of its performance in channeling effective action across a wide agenda of needs and concerns.

Both coauthors believe in the importance of an inclusive multilateral agenda that ranges across development and poverty reduction, the threats of weapons of mass destruction (WMD), and terrorism. At the same time, the coauthors have different views of the relationship between such baskets of issues. When the Secretary-General's High-level Panel on Threats, Challenges, and Change issued their sweeping reform platform, it could be seen as a kind of global grand bargain in which developed and developing countries exchange support for their respective concerns. Yet such a view undercuts the idea of shared commitment by all for all of the goals. The coauthors differ over whether nations' support for the goals on this broad global agenda is essentially a matter of principle or whether it has a quid pro quo dimension to it.

For Mark Lagon, each area of policy has its own principles and norms that serve the collective good, and they are not open for bargaining between areas. In development, the Monterrey Consensus reached in 2002 recognizes the mutual obligations of developed and developing nations alike and among them emphasizes the importance of market reforms, rule of law, attraction of private capital, unfettered trade, and development assistance (without a rigid target level). In the area of security, keeping WMD from being acquired anew by states (especially those with illiberal governance) or by terrorist networks is a crucial norm. Likewise, halting terrorist attacks on civilian populations is a norm—with no exception for national liberation or attacking Israel. A bargain whereby the North transfers official aid to the South in exchange for cooperation in fighting proliferation and terrorism ignores the basic interest the South itself has in the aforementioned principles and norms.

As David Shorr sees it, the nations of the world can share an interest in all of the world's many problems, but not the same levels of interest in the various challenges. In Ethiopia, for example, the government faces a much greater threat from the spread of AIDS than the spread of WMD. Shorr would thus approach the tension over development versus traditional "hard" security not as a matter of principle but an opportunity for nations, at an especially fractious time, to build bridges through mutual support. Over time, he expects that such exchanges of help will build rather than undermine a sense of common purpose. The coauthors' different approaches to diplomacy and persuasion extend to other contexts, which will be addressed below.

The term *international system* is a broad category extending beyond the United Nations as a particular organization. Even though the United Nations itself is a system made up of various organs, it is not the only vehicle through which nations can cooperate. There is an abundance of intergovernmental fora with diverse memberships and portfolios.

The availability of multiple outlets for international cooperation is highly useful as we seek a more secure nation and world. Indeed, this diversity both reflects and helps with the broad 21st-century security agenda. There are instruments of a political, financial, legal, or technical nature to deal with arms control, health and disease, poverty reduction, terrorism, telecommunications, trade, air traffic, meteorology, and more. Some of these fora are more inclusive, while others are less so. Regional and subregional organizations focus on the challenges of "the neighborhood."

US policy toward international organizations should always draw on the strengths and avoid the weaknesses of these various bodies. Complementarity among intergovernmental organizations is not only possible but also vital. We should always look for the "right tool for the job" in pursuing our aims—based on capacity, legitimacy, and membership—and should continually push for greater effectiveness and impact on real-world problems.

The comparative advantage of the United Nations, for instance, is the universality of its membership and the range of issues and mechanisms it encompasses. As the sole global political forum in which every nation has a voice, it enjoys the greatest breadth of participation. Whatever its shortcomings and dysfunctions, the United Nations will not be replaced without a radical reshuffling of the geostrategic order, a shift that cannot and should not be anticipated. The Community of Democracies, for example, can serve as a complementary or catalytic caucus within the United Nations, but is unlikely to replace it as a forum for action.

The presence of so many authoritarian regimes in the community of nations should not be taken complacently; it is a serious problem, both for the capacity and even legitimacy of the United Nations, and even more so for the people who live under their repressive rule. With all the work still to be done to promote democracy, it is worth noting that as a result of the global spread of democracy in recent decades, democracies now constitute a majority of the UN membership, with the organization itself playing an increasing role in democracy's spread.[2] Let us hope this trend continues.

Meanwhile, efforts to position the Community of Democracies as a potential replacement for the United Nations are unlikely to bear fruit. To begin with, the negotiation of a new global constitutional order, even just among democracies, would be an enormous and complex undertaking. The failure to reach agreement in 2005 over changes to the composition of the UN Security Council is an indication of the difficulty. Nor should it be assumed that democratic allies would be supportive; even many of the United States' friends would be resistant to any effort to ostracize nondemocracies in framing a new construct. That said, an effort by democracies to function as a strong coalition within the United Nations would be highly constructive as an effort of those governments that rest solidly on the rule of law to strengthen the United Nations' ability to achieve its noble goals. Furthermore, over time, if the Community of Democracies proves to serve particular functions (such as in areas of human rights and democracy promotion) with greater capacity or legitimacy than the United Nations, then the United States should welcome it.

Sovereignty and Responsibility

The United Nations' universal membership is both a source of its legitimizing role and a hindrance to its problem-solving role. All member states have a voice and sovereign equality. They formally have equal say on budgets and programs. At the UN's founding, the realist victors of World War II, with eyes wide open, decided that universality permits an all-inclusive, accepted forum for dialogue that would promote peace, prosperity, public health, and pluralism. In practice, though, such international deliberation, with all voices equal, can make for more brakes than engine, and more heat than light.

By wise design, the founders created a key exception to pure equality of members states to deal with the most sensitive issues of war and peace: the UN Security Council. There is persistent tension within the United Nations about enlarging both the Security Council's permanent and elected membership to be more inclusive and to better fit the power realities of the early 21st century more than the mid-20th century. Hopefully, deserving candidate nations that have been true to UN ideals will eventually be brought into the council (e.g., Japan) without it swelling to a size that would make it even more difficult to forge agreement on situations—like Iraq or Darfur—over which it has struggled in recent years. Yet this battle is unlikely to be resolved soon. In the short run, the existing council should reinforce its credibility, particularly through taking effective action regarding situations such as those in Iran and Sudan. Meanwhile, fora such as the G-8+5, G-20, and Asia-Pacific Economic Cooperation can be key gathering points for major, middle, and rising powers.

The UN Charter begins with the words "We the peoples," thereby indicating the organization's obligations not only to member states but also to their citizens. While the UN General Assembly is more broadly representative than the Security Council, the universality of the General Assembly and some other bodies is not inherently democratic since sovereign equality takes no account of democratic governance or the popular will of the citizenry. Universality allows for dialogue and for less powerful nations to air real or perceived grievances. However, in some arenas, equal standing for repressive governments with free ones undercuts the organization's purposes. To have non-free states on the new Human Rights Council standing hypocritically in judgment of others does not serve the aim of advancing what the UN Charter calls "fundamental freedoms." In this particular respect, the design of the new council has by no means corrected the failures of the discredited body it was fashioned to replace, the Commission on Human Rights. David Shorr views the reforms as incremental improvements at best, and in Mark Lagon's view, not even that. Both regard the early regular and special emergency sessions of the council as entirely too dominated by focus on and criticism of Israel and a cause of great concern for the future. Even a progressive such as Shorr would question the usefulness of the council if the pattern persists; conservatives like Lagon are that much closer to reaching a conclusion.

Conceived as a responsibility, sovereignty is not solely a matter of status in the world body but also the upholding of the fundamental ideals affirmed in the UN Charter within a nation's own borders. There is a presumption in favor of noninterference in the United Nations, yet this is not as absolute as Star Trek's "Prime Directive" against interference in the strange new worlds visited by Captain Kirk and his crew. It is a positive development indeed that the United Nations now recognizes situations in which national sovereignty loses its legitimacy: most notably, when a government commits or allows genocide, war crimes, or other mass atrocities.

One of the great successes of the UN 60th Anniversary World Summit of September 2005 was the affirmation of the principle of the Responsibility to Protect (RTP).[3] RTP has two noteworthy parts: (1) states must protect their citizens from genocide, war crimes, and other mass atrocities and (2) the Security Council should act to fill the protection vacuum. Seen as a political norm rather than a mechanistic legal trigger, the second dimension is a significant step forward in the United Nations preparing itself to better address future cases of the man-made bloodletting seen in Cambodia, Rwanda, the Balkans, and Sudan. It still will require political will, as slow Security Council action on Darfur demonstrates, but RTP will encourage that will.

Such human rights atrocities are the focus of a relatively new international mechanism: the International Criminal Court (ICC). The coauthors differ over the likelihood that Americans might be prosecuted through the ICC and whether the court has sufficient safeguards against politicized prosecutions. Lagon considers it necessary to seek alternative venues for prosecution that have greater political accountability and oversight—domestically or via prudently constituted international tribunals. Shorr believes the safeguards built into the ICC, including deference to capable domestic justice systems, are sufficient and that there is greater legitimacy and efficacy in a permanent court compared with ad hoc tribunals. In any case, the United States did not stand in the way of the Security Council's referral for prosecution of Sudanese genocide perpetrators when no other avenue was available, and the coauthors agree that referral had the benefit of a Security Council trigger rather than a self-starting ICC prosecution. The United States has an enormous stake in continuing to be at the forefront of accountability for atrocities as it has been since the Nuremberg Trials.

Another dimension of domestic governance, the promotion of democracy, has also been a growing area of UN activity. The Secretariat's Electoral Assistance Division does useful work to monitor elections and train people to conduct them. The UN Development Programme embraces democracy promotion, considering political liberalization not just a product of economic development but an enabler of it. The UN Arab Human Development Reports authored by Arab scholars have been landmark assessments of deficits of political freedom, knowledge, and women's rights in the Arab world. The new UN Democracy Fund proposed by President Bush helped fill a void within the United Nations by fostering vital civil societies through grants to nongovernmental organizations. Former UN Secretary-General Kofi Annan and his deputy secretary-general, Malloch Brown, realized that democracy facilitates both peace and economic prosperity as two major aims of the United Nations and has to be a focus of its work. It is to the credit of the United Nations that it balances non-interference in sovereign affairs not just with a concern for extraordinary catastrophes but with more steady efforts to nudge along democracy. This is very helpful with some of the steps that can be pursued more easily under a UN umbrella than through bilateral efforts.

Working Within the System—Doing Business at the United Nations

The United States has been a long and consistent champion of UN reform since its earliest days. By now, "UN reform" is itself a hackneyed phrase. For some, it evokes images of our CPA-style concerns about funding, and suspicion that the United States seeks to radically rein in the United Nations. But the best objective for reform is a United Nations that better lives up to its founding aims and its potential. It should be aimed at a United Nations that delivers not *less* for its member states, but *better*; "renewal" is thus a more apt term than "reform." Developing countries are often at the front lines of ground-level programs to promote peace, development, and human rights, and thus have a large stake in a United Nations that delivers more reliably.[4] Americans and the rest of the world community should look at reform in this larger sense of institutional renewal and tangible progress on the ideals of the Charter.

The question of how often the United States should press its positions insistently in international negotiations offers a window into the diverging diplomatic approaches mentioned above. Progressives and conservatives alike seek effective outcomes and appreciate the need to stand firm on priority bottom-line needs and forthrightly wield American influence to achieve them. But what about the steady flow of issues that arise in international organizations—should consensus building or tough bargaining be the primary mode of American diplomats?

From David Shorr's vantage, it is possible on most issues to accommodate the reasonable concerns of others while preserving the essentials. The goodwill accrued along the way yields leverage to seek support on other matters or to fend off pressure on bottom-line US concerns. Shorr is concerned about the best as the enemy of the good and sees value in the decisions that can be reached by compromise, imperfect as they may be. For one thing, he views decisions with broad and genuine ownership as more durable than those reached through grueling diplomatic struggle.

Mark Lagon's approach is to be ambitious in reinforcing the United Nations' own ideals, be frank, uphold standards, and aim high, as a higher priority than moving to forge confidence-building consensus. Reluctant to lower our sights, he prefers to hold out in negotiations, a strategy he believes will improve final outcomes. While both coauthors share an impatience with lowest-common-denominator diplomacy, as seen in the General Assembly and elsewhere, Lagon as a conservative is especially on guard against watered-down decisions. Vigilant on a wide array of issues, he is reluctant to make compromises he views as flawed that would severely undercut the value of an agreement.

These diverging approaches extend to the coauthors' differing assessments of US influence at the United Nations. Mark Lagon believes the one-country-one-vote system in a body of 192 nations diminishes American clout completely out of proportion to our power and our financial support of the United Nations. Lagon believes weighted voting based on stakeholders' economic strength and contributions would be the more appropriate procedural basis for a greater range of multilateral decisions; it would promote stronger resource stewardship as well as policy prudence. As David Shorr sees it, the United States is never viewed by others as just another country. Whatever the voting system, the United States' preponderant power is palpably apparent, and pressing for further advantage only provokes resistance. Moreover, the permanent US veto in the Security Council is more than fair compensation for the more egalitarian General Assembly. There is likewise a split between the coauthors about putting increasing portions of UN financing on a voluntary basis, a move viewed by Lagon as promoting accountability and efficiency and seen by Shorr as unilateral cherry-picking.

Despite these differences, though, it is clear to both that requiring consensus among the 192 nations obstructs optimum administrative *and* policy decision making. The administrative micromanagement of the UN staff by the entire membership is merely the absurd extreme. The broader problem is the lowest common denominator for policies and programs set by the member states when there is no accounting for their qualitative differences (regime-type, population-size, and level of economic contributions).

But to suggest that promotion of structural changes is not the most fruitful course is not tantamount to throwing up one's hands in resignation. Beyond current earnest efforts to work within existing structures to improve oversight and accountability, administration and personnel practices, and the regular review of whether programs have outlived their usefulness, the most important matter is to tackle the poisonous *politics* of the United Nations. The tensions between the North and South in the United Nations are pronounced. The divide takes many forms: debates about the centrality of aid to development, political versus economic rights, Security Council enlargement, and disarmament by nuclear haves versus nonproliferation to nuclear have-nots.

These debates may or may not be made more acute by US unipolar power, squabbles over Iraq, and globalization. Still, much could be achieved if the rigid alignments in place since the Cold War era changed. The problem is not so much that the UN *institutions* have not kept pace changing with the world's problems, but rather that *political groupings* within the world body have not. The United Nations works like a legislature, with individual actors (states) often developing their positions within blocs and caucuses. To the degree that the bloc system of the G-77, the Non-Aligned Movement, and the regional blocs freeze in place arguments, it must be loosened. If this could be accomplished, the developing world might see the United Nations' reform and renewal as a benefit rather than a threat to its equities.

The United Nations' nature as a political body is the source of both its strength and weakness. States remain the central actors in world politics, and they are in the strongest position to mobilize resources and make a positive difference for the world's people. The United Nations and its Charter call on states' leaders to use their collective political power for the highest ideals. Yet too often it is political games-manship in the United Nations that distracts from this vital work. The United Nations is an arena to air real and perceived grievances, with developing nations accorded an equal voice to great powers, and dictatorships an equal voice to democ-racies. Moreover, a number of member states that are cooperative partners of the United States at a bilateral level use the United Nations as a stage to showcase their independence from the United States, safe in the knowledge that such grandstanding will not elicit the retribution that vital bilateral matters would.

Realizing the United Nations' Potential

It is silly to deride the United Nations as "politicized," because it is inherently a political body. The United States should energetically engage the players in this legislature-like body. Successes depend on seeking support diligently and adroitly and forming different groups of partners on different issues. Yet marked success will involve working overtime to improve the mindset and conduct of politics at the United Nations. States' leaders face a basic choice regarding the United Nations' role and future: is the United Nations an instrument for cooperative problem solving or a debating society? Cooperation depends chiefly on political will, rather than changes in institutional arrangements unlikely themselves to alter international politics. For all of its difficulties, a great deal can be accomplished through the United Nations when governments close ranks behind it: pressuring Syria over the Hariri assassination, caring for millions of refugees, providing a mandate for a coalition to drive Saddam Hussein out of Kuwait, improving airline safety and security, immunizing children and helping assure they receive education.

The simple fact is that the world community needs vehicles for actions on which they can agree. But they have to muster the political will to agree. So in addition to being a vehicle for implementing solutions based on common interests, states should muster the political will to use the United Nations as its founders intended: as a forum to explore where their interests intersect. A frank expression of nations' interests to each other without facilitators speaking for them will help the United Nations play that role, if the temptation for polemics can be set aside.

Progressives and conservatives can agree on a compromise course in multilateral policy involving two key dimensions. First, instead of focusing on structural changes, a more effective United Nations requires a change in the "culture" of the United Nations and its rigid blocs and caucuses. The politics of the United Nations could be more flexible. It would be helpful to ask questions like: Why do developing nations allow a few prominent bloc leaders to speak for them all despite their diversity of economic conditions, cultures, and interests? Why are some transregional blocs in the United Nations far more cohesive than the transregional democratic bloc? Why do regional blocs all too often shield their most repressive states from frank appraisal by the international community? Why is the Warsaw Pact still intact as a bloc in the United Nations? Why are Near Eastern, South Asian, and East Asian states all part of the same bloc? Here is where the Community of Democracies could play a role, not by replacing the United Nations, but by joining an expanded array of alternative caucuses within the United Nations.

Second, while renewal of the United Nations to better serve its founding purposes and deal with 21st-century problems is crucial, expectations for the United Nations need to be adjusted. Ardent proponents and critics of the United Nations both make the mistake of suggesting we should expect it to do what it cannot. Some problems will be endemic to universal membership or divergent political, economic, and military interests of member states. Other multilateral institutions will at times serve some functions better. "Minilateral" solutions might be preferable to multilateral ones when an organization narrower in membership or mission offers better capacity to solve problems, be it the African Union, the Organization of American States, the World Trade Organization, the Association of Southeast Asian Nation, the North American Treaty Organization, the Organization for Security and Co-operation in Europe, or any number of others. The United States should examine alternatives, not to retire or replace the United Nations, but to turn to them when they offer comparative advantages.

In short, the United Nations is unique in breadth. We should work hard to make it more legitimate and deliver better. But the United Nations is part of a rich fabric of multilateral options that are not mutually exclusive. Multilateralism is not an end in itself. Yet multilateral means can often best serve the common good.

Notes

1 Kofi A. Annan, *In Larger Freedom: Towards Security, Development and Human Rights for All*, Report of the Secretary-General of the United Nations (New York: United Nations, March 2005), document A/59/2005, para. 19.

2 Freedom House, *Freedom in the World 2006* (New York: Rowman & Littlefield, 2006).

3 "2005 World Summit Outcome," United Nations General Assembly, A/60/L.1, para. 138–139, p. 30.

4 Stanley Foundation, *Delivering Coherence: Next Steps for a Unified United Nations System*, 38th United Nations Issues Conference (Muscatine, IA: The Stanley Foundation, March 2007).

The Cost of Confusion: Resolving Ambiguities in Detainee Treatment

Kenneth Anderson and Elisa Massimino

The treatment of detainees—interrogation, detention, and trial—has been among the most controversial policies in the Bush administration's global war on terrorism. Indeed, many of the questions that have arisen in the detainee treatment debate are fundamental to counterterrorism policy, and the next administration will have to provide its own answers as a basis for whatever approach it adopts. What has been the import of declaring a "war on terror"? Is this a wise or sustainable organizing principle for counterterrorism policy? What are the respective roles of the three co-equal branches of government in establishing and enforcing the rules? What is the relationship between national security and respect for human rights? Are security and rights competing interests in a zero-sum game?

We believe that there are some general principles that can be shared across progressive and conservative lines on which national counterterrorism policy should be grounded. We do not aim to examine all aspects of counterterrorism policy, which would require us to address a wide array of issues of national security, civil liberties, and human rights—surveillance, seizure of asserted terrorist assets, use of force short of armed conflict, assassination and targeted kidnapping policies, and many other matters. We focus instead on three specific and closely related issues—interrogation, detention, and trials of detainees—as sources of the principles that should guide counterterrorism policy. We start here because issues of detainee treatment raise profound questions of American values.

Should Counterterrorism Policy Be a
"War" on Terror?

Within days—hours, even—of the Al Qaeda attacks on September 11, 2001, the Bush administration was characterizing it and the US response as a war. While some argued that the attacks simply constituted criminality on a mass scale, bipartisan opinion in the United States largely coalesced around the view that the United States was at war, and at war with a transnational, nonstate actor that had declared war upon the United States. This view gradually was transformed in the rhetoric and policy of the United States into what the Bush administration dubbed the "global war on terror." Although the administration—in an effort to recall the Cold War idea of a long struggle against a persistent enemy—recently sought to rename the effort the "Long War," the original moniker persists.

Why does the terminology matter? At one level, using the war framework helps build public support for confronting terrorism; the images, analogies, and metaphors that are used to justify the national response shape what kind of action the public supports and its perception of how long and how deep the struggle might be. The invocation of war can justify a great many measures that would not otherwise be contemplated in a peaceful constitutional democracy—emergency powers, strictures on civil liberties, the use of force outside of ordinary domestic police powers, a sense of national unity in a time of crisis that transcends politics, and a heightened expression of presidential and commander-in-chief power, potentially at the expense of the other constitutional branches of government. All of these measures were evident in the response following September 11; it would be accurate to say that despite some misgivings of civil libertarians, in the immediate aftermath of the attacks, there was broad sentiment across party lines and across American society that all of these options for a national emergency were appropriately on the table and that *war* was a good way of summing up the situation.

Six years on, unsurprisingly, this unity has evaporated. Questioning government and the policies of the party in power is deeply ingrained in our political DNA. In the case of a war that is today more ideological and metaphorical than "hot"—resembling, in this regard, the Cold War—fundamental questions of policy are bound to arise. Thus the very idea of a "global war on terror" is today seen as the policy of a particular presidential administration in a way that it was not immediately following September 11. At this point, the war on terror no longer serves as simply a synonym for US counterterrorism policy. The very question of whether US counterterrorism policy should be conceived as a *war* is precisely what is at issue; to refer to it as a war on terror is to presume the conclusion to a fundamental and contested issue. Hence, in this paper, when we refer to *counterterrorism policy*, we mean it in a generic sense of the set of issues on the table, and when we refer to the *war on terror*, we mean the specific and actual, contested and contestable policies of the Bush administration.

We agree that in the moment of crisis and its immediate aftermath, the president exercised extraordinary powers appropriate to the executive role, including the power to use force to prevent and disrupt further attacks. Moreover, just as we agree that the moment of crisis occasioned extraordinary executive powers, we also agree that over time, those powers must diminish in a return to ordinary constitutional order. As a democracy, we must fashion a response to the ongoing threat of terror in a constitutionally democratic way. Heightened executive power eventually must give way to democratic, majoritarian procedures. The legislature, as a co-equal branch of government, might understandably be sidelined in the moment of crisis but, we agree, must reassert itself if it is to remain a constitutional co-equal. Likewise, the courts must ensure that individual rights under the Constitution and obligations under international law are observed. Such rights are a constitutional obligation of the legislative and the executive branches to protect (although they may well have their own views as to the content and meaning of such rights), but it is the province of the courts, finally, to determine and enforce them.

The characterization of counterterrorism policy as a war on terror affects how domestic political and constitutional processes come into play and is, therefore, far more than simply a matter of public motivational rhetoric. It is language deeply imbued with legal implications. We believe that over time, the characterization of counterterrorism policy as a war must be limited to its use as a strategic paradigm for dealing with nonstate actors that have arrayed themselves as enemies of the United States, but it must be carefully confined to make clear that this is a strategic, rather than legal, use of the term. Otherwise, the United States risks going down the road of authoritarian anti-Communist states in the Cold War—Chile, for example, or Guatemala—using the threat of communism as a justification for a permanent state of emergency and emergency presidential powers. This is not to say that the threats posed by terrorism are not real and that the strategic conception of war was not useful—only that the responses must be crafted within constitutional democratic processes and that war, within those processes, has a highly specific legal meaning that is not applicable to most matters of counterterrorism policy.

Domestically, the executive branch strengthens its powers insofar as the immediate crisis is characterized as a war because the Constitution gives special powers to the president and commander in chief. More precisely, few question the enhanced powers of the president in a moment of crisis such as September 11; when the crisis is converted into a war, those powers become the powers of a commander in chief for as long as the war goes on. It has long been apparent that the strengthening of those executive powers has been an independent goal of the Bush administration, apart from the war on terror itself and sometimes at considerable cost to it. We disagree about the breadth of the president's powers in war, but there is little doubt that those powers depend on how broadly *war* may validly be defined for legal purposes of the laws and customs of war. But we are in agreement that as a legal matter, the administration's definition of the war is unacceptably broad.

Characterizing counterterrorism efforts as a *war* has quite different implications, however, for actions taken by the United States abroad.[1] The Bush administration has wanted quite inconsistent things from its characterization of these actions as a global war on terror. There is, first of all, an inconsistency in strategic vision in the characterization of war. The administration has wanted to make clear to the American people, as well as to the world at large, that the United States is willing to pursue terrorists wherever they seek to hide—to deprive them, in the language of the 2006 national counterterrorism strategy, of safe havens—and to do so using all the tools of war. Under this view, the entire world is a battlefield. And yet, even as a matter of strategy, the idea of a global war is more metaphor than reality; the world in its entirety is not—not even potentially—a battlefield. The strategic engagement with terrorists is partly in Afghanistan, but it is also even more so in Pakistan—and the United States, for political reasons, at this moment is plainly not willing to make Pakistan a battlefield. It is also, from a strategic standpoint, an engagement with ideologues and radicalized clerics and their followers in such places as Hamburg, Birmingham, and Paris—but they obviously will not be battlefields except in an entirely metaphorical sense. In our view, insofar as counterterrorism policy requires *all* of the tools of government, most of those tools will *not* in fact be the tools of war in the actual meaning of armed conflict. Instead, they will involve surveillance, interdiction of terrorist financing, intelligence gathering, diplomacy, and other methods. Thus the language of global war is necessarily metaphorical. It should not diminish the national resolve to defeat the enemy to acknowledge that actual war is only one tool in that struggle.

Thus trying to apply the term *war* to the entire effort when it is only intermittently a war *operationally*, and therefore *legally*, in particular times and places creates significant problems. The Cold War was strategically well-considered as a war; yet only occasionally and in certain places around the world did it operationally and legally constitute war. Such is the case with the war on terror. Calling global counterterrorism policy a *war*—not only as a strategic concept but as a global operational fact that invokes a specific legal characterization—has profound legal implications and anomalous legal consequences.

Invoking the Law of War in Global Counterterrorism

Invoking war as the strategic policy frame has the virtue of recognizing the way that our enemies see their actions with respect to us. Likewise, from the viewpoint of the administration, invoking war as the policy frame has the virtue of rhetorically separating the current response to terror from policies of the past that essentially treated terrorism as a matter of organized crime gone global, appropriate for law enforcement and the criminal justice system, not the military and war.

But the *legal* invocation of war against a nonstate, transnational actor or actors creates many anomalies in the application of the law of war, an essentially state-centric legal regime. Counterterrorism is a global struggle against an enemy which, while obviously real, cannot be identified by the usual indicia of victory or defeat—the end of a regime, the occupation and control of territory, the destruction of enemy forces. It is therefore hard to know when, if ever, the war will be won for legal purposes, a question that is critical for prisoners, who have a legal right to be released at the end of fighting. One might as well say spatially that the entire world is a battlefield, and that temporally, the war will be won when the threat of terrorist violence is banished from the world, which will be a long way off indeed. If correct in any sense, it is only useful as a strategic metaphor, a way of saying that our enemies are not limited to any particular place or people and that they take a long view of their struggle, as a guide to strategic analysis and a spur to our own long-term counterterrorism policies.

Other issues arise, however, when our terrorist adversaries are portrayed as warriors—issues on which the coauthors are divided. Such a depiction can have the unintended consequence, Massimino points out, of elevating the stature of the enemy in the eyes of its own potential constituency by boosting Al Qaeda's mythic appeal as the defender of Islam, its own preferred image. Anderson, on the other hand, believes that how our enemies see the struggle must be integrated into how we see it.

However useful war may be as a strategic concept, it cannot stand as a legal definition triggering the rights and duties under the laws of war, which rightly require a more tangible and operational foundation. It would be like saying that the Cold War, at every moment of its 40-year run, was legally an armed conflict with the Soviet Union and the Warsaw Pact. The fact was, instead, that however much the United States conceived the Cold War in strategic terms as a *war*, it did not treat it as a legal state of war governed by the law of armed conflict. Recourse to the law of armed conflict was then, as should be the case now, limited to active hostilities rising to the traditionally accepted definition of an armed conflict. We must not confuse the important insights of a strategic view of counterterrorism as metaphorical war with the legal implications of invoking the formal laws of armed conflict.

The Bush administration's invocation of the laws of war may be strategically useful, but it is simply at odds with the legal requirement of an "armed conflict" triggering of the laws of war. The operational conduct of counterterrorism to date has involved several armed conflicts and might involve more, but the global war on terror does not meet the legal definition of an armed conflict.

We therefore agree that the Bush administration's global claim is incorrect as a matter of law. The administration has dealt with the lack of fit between the nature of the conflict and the laws of war in radically inconsistent ways—but always, it must be said, in ways that benefit its preexisting desire to strengthen the hand of the executive branch. We examine three issues—detention of individuals as enemy combatants, trials by military commissions of detained enemy combatants, and interrogations—in which this disconnect has had the most profound consequences.

Detention

The laws of war permit belligerent powers to detain captured enemy combatants without charge or trial for the duration of the conflict in order to prevent them from rejoining the fight. The Bush administration embraced the laws of war and claimed under them the traditional legal right to hold detainees, for example at Guantanamo Bay, until the end of hostilities. What is at issue here is not the right of a belligerent in wartime to hold combatants—this is undisputed. The dispute is over the very definition of *war* in the "global war on terror." This is a difficulty of legal definition all on its own on which the coauthors are agreed that the administration was wrong.

While claiming the rights of a belligerent to detain captured enemy combatants, however, the Bush administration at the same time, through the office of the White House counsel, made one of the most legally and conceptually ill-considered moves in its entire counterterrorism strategy. It concluded that, although the war on terror was a *war*, the Geneva Conventions—the laws of war—did not apply to those detained in it. Terrorists are not lawful combatants, it argued, and hence fall outside the law altogether. They could thus be dealt with by the commander in chief at his discretion.

The inconsistency produced by this decision was breathtaking. The United States was taking detainees not only on traditionally defined battlefields such as Afghanistan but also at O'Hare airport in Chicago and Bradley University in Peoria. The administration argued first that the constitutional war powers of the president provided the basis for these detentions; later, it argued that the detainees were combatants who could be held for the duration of hostilities. Invoking constitutional war powers, or alternatively, the laws of war, as a basis for holding detainees without charge or trial in the domestic legal system, while simultaneously denying that the laws of war applied to them, created a legal black hole that threatened to subvert the laws of war altogether.

Indeed, this critique was shared by most of the military's own uniformed law of war legal specialists in the military, who have argued that the Geneva Conventions should apply only to battlefield detainees, no matter how one defined the strategic scope of the "war." Al Qaeda flunked the tests of Article 4 of the Third Geneva Convention on POWs, and hence its members were not entitled to the privileges of POW status. Prisoners of war are held to keep from taking up arms again but are not subject to prosecution or punishment, provided that they have complied with the laws of war. For Al Qaeda's part, though, while its members were *combatants* by virtue of taking an "active part in hostilities," the group's systematic violations of the laws of war rendered them unprivileged combatants individually, i.e., unlawful belligerents under the laws of war. They could be detained under the law of war and, as unprivileged combatants, charged with crimes arising from their acts of belligerency, such as murder and destruction of property. Legal procedures for trials of unlawful combatants derive from the terms of Article 75 of the 1977 Additional Protocol I of the Geneva Conventions.[2]

But this international law of war approach went unheeded by the administration. Instead, the administration sought to hedge against legal challenges to its war-without-law approach by holding detainees at Guantanamo which, it hoped, would be beyond the reach of US courts and habeas corpus. It lost on the substance of that argument in the *Rasul* case, having rested it on a claim of executive power so over-reaching that it failed, on the habeas corpus issue, to gain even Justice Scalia's vote.

We are in agreement that the scope of the administration's global war on terror is legally too broad. There are two wars in which the United States is currently involved: Afghanistan and Iraq. Other armed conflicts may develop, but the world is not a battlefield in its entirety, and the United States may not seize and detain as combatants under the laws of war individuals not directly engaged in these armed conflicts. On this fundamental point we are agreed.

We disagree, however, as to the concept of illegal combatancy. Massimino takes the view that a person who flunks the tests of legal combatancy in Article 4, Third Geneva Convention, becomes thereby a civilian protected by the Fourth Geneva Convention (albeit one who may be charged with violations of the laws of war). The International Committee of the Red Cross (ICRC) also takes this view, along with a significant body of the human rights community. Anderson believes that such an approach effectively rewards combat that violates the laws of war and that a person who fails the tests for legal combatancy is not a civilian, but an illegal combatant, an unlawful belligerent. The disagreement is far from merely academic; it involves fundamental questions of treatment of civilians under the Fourth Geneva Convention (who nonetheless may be detained as security risks, but with considerably greater protections than those afforded unlawful belligerency).

These disagreements between the authors notwithstanding, both agree that the current legal situation is an unsatisfying and unworkable mish-mash of bits of highly contested international law combined with Bush administration policy decisions, Supreme Court opinions that are themselves bits of this and that, and narrow legislative fixes designed to satisfy minimum requirements of the case law. The Supreme Court, in successive cases and with various hedges, has allowed certain domestic law remedies at Guantanamo such as habeas corpus which, while arguably defensible holdings under US domestic law, have no historical or textual basis in the law of war, at least regarding foreign combatants. Yet at the same time that the court has grafted essentially domestic law onto the question of detention, it also has found, in *Hamdan*, that the conflict is governed by Common Article Three of the Geneva Conventions. This legal holding thus puts a certain practical floor under the administration's conduct—prohibiting cruel, humiliating, or degrading treatment of detainees and violence to life and person.[3]

The administration, for its part, has responded to this holding by acknowledging the application of the Geneva Conventions as a largely formal matter, asserting that in any case, the United States is in compliance with Common Article Three. In the Military Commissions Act of 2006, the administration sought and obtained legislation to insulate it from habeas corpus, claims by detainees asserting the Geneva Conventions, or other claims to the contrary.

The most important additional issue with respect to detention policy is who has the power to determine that one is a combatant in the first place and not, say, an innocent shepherd or someone sold into our custody for bounty by the Northern Alliance. The administration has asserted that this is a matter of executive branch discretion. Prior to the Supreme Court's decisions in the *Rasul*, *Hamdi*, and *Hamdan* cases, it based this view on the claim that the Geneva Conventions did not apply to these detainees, hedging its bets by keeping them in Guantanamo, which it hoped would be beyond the reach of the federal courts. After losing, in part, its habeas as well as other claims defended on executive power grounds in *Rasul* and *Hamdi*, it established limited tribunals for detainees, apparently intended to satisfy the requirements of the Third Geneva Convention, Article 5, requiring, in cases of doubt, a tribunal to determine combatant status.

Those tribunals are of a limited nature—and judicial review of them is confined to the question of whether the tribunal followed its own procedures. They have, as a result, been sharply criticized on due process grounds. These combatant status tribunals, however, exist for purposes of establishing the basis for detention, not for the separate question, addressed below, of trials for violations of the laws of war.

Congress has written legislation narrowly designed to meet the requirements of *Hamdan*, and the president has signed it: the Military Commissions Act (MCA). That legislation is an admixture of fundamentally domestic assertions of authority, with one eye defensively fixed upon the requirements of Common Article Three. Among other things, it purports to deprive the courts of jurisdiction with respect to habeas claims by alien unlawful enemy combatants, and deprives them of the ability to allege violations of the Geneva Conventions before any court.[4] It makes the decision to detain someone designated by the president as an enemy combatant—potentially even for life—an executive branch determination, and almost entirely unreviewable by the federal courts.

If one assumes hypothetically that the executive branch is infallible in its judgment as to who is or is not a terrorist, then one might accept such an arrangement. In such an "infallible executive" scenario, Anderson would support such detentions, while Massimino would not. But since neither Anderson nor Massimino regards the executive branch's designations as actually or potentially infallible, we agree strongly that this procedure, as enshrined in the MCA, is unacceptable and not remediated by the provision of limited combatant status review hearings.

Congress has so far agreed that federal court access will not be permitted. Whether the Supreme Court ultimately will defer to the two political branches of government on this legislation's many extraordinary measures is at this point unknown, but no one doubts that litigation will be both lengthy and momentous. Changes in party control of one or both houses, or other political factors, or further court decisions, are highly likely to produce new legislation or significant modifications of existing legislation—already, the new Democratic Congress following the 2006 midterm elections is considering amending the MCA, particularly with respect to habeas corpus.

Yet the pattern of highly reactive legislation is unfortunately likely to continue. Rather than pushing for truly systematic reform (as recommended by the authors of this chapter further below), the US legislature seems content to react either to a specific court decision or to a particular demand of the executive branch.

Trials of Detainees by Military Commission and Combatant Status Review Hearings

Not many months after September 11, the administration announced that it did not intend to submit alleged terrorists to regular trial by the federal courts except in particular circumstances, but would instead submit them to trial by military commission.[5] This procedure is fundamentally different from the combatant status review hearings described in the preceding section. Those combatant status review hearings are not a judgment about guilt or innocence; they are hearings designed to offer a limited review of whether the person being detained should be called an "enemy combatant" at all and whether that person continues to pose a security risk to the United States.[6] The combatant status review hearings are akin to administrative detention hearings, rather than a trial. By contrast, the military commissions, as originally conceived and in the tradition of US military law stretching back to the Civil War, are military trials on charges of violations of the laws and customs of war.

Although possessed of a long history and indisputably part of military law, such commissions have been hotly disputed in their specific application in the global war on terror since they were first promulgated in executive orders following September 11, through to their legislative authorization in the MCA of 2006. The policy objective of the administration following September 11 was stark—to make entirely plain that it was breaking with the criminal law approach to transnational terrorism pursued by earlier administrations. The paradigm would be war and, henceforth, it would operate under the laws of war.

Military commissions were thought to provide a form of justice that is defensible under US law and military custom as well as international law and custom (once the administration had reversed course on the relevance of the Geneva Conventions in establishing unlawful belligerency). The most fundamental objection to military commissions in the global war on terror—one which we share—is that whatever the concept of battlefield detainee arising from either international law or US military law and custom, the invocation of a global war on terror, with the entire world a battlefield encompassing Al Qaeda detainees found in Afghanistan and a US citizen detained in Chicago, is simply too broad to sustain its legal weight.

The *Hamdan* court held that the executive branch exceeded its authority in establishing military commissions that differed from provisions of the Uniform Code of Military Justice, but the court also emphasized that these issues could be resolved through legislation. (It also held, by reason of finding that Common Article Three applied, that the administration had to proceed with trials that fell within the meaning of Common Article Three's language of "regularly constituted courts.")[7] Accordingly, the administration sought legislation designed merely to ratify what it already had designed and put in place. Opposition developed in the Senate, however, with Republican Senators John McCain, John Warner, and Lindsay Graham all insisting on changes to the procedures for military commissions. After rounds of negotiations on the trial issue, as well as the detention and interrogation issues, the White House and the senators reached agreement, and the MCA was signed by the president in October 2006. Democrats largely stayed out of the wrangling between the three Republican senators and administration, although they fiercely attacked the bill as it came to a vote and overwhelmingly voted against it. At this writing, the new Democratic Congress is considering efforts to amend it.

Although we agree, in principle, that military commissions *can* be used to try individuals for violations of the laws of war, and although we further agree that the global war on terror is too broad a definition of *war* to support the *universal* application of military commissions to all detainees that the administration determines to put on trial, we disagree as to the proper "fix." Massimino would require that all those not captured on a traditionally defined battlefield be tried, if suspected of criminal violations, in regular US courts, while limiting military commissions to those captured on battlefields as traditionally defined in US military and international law. Anderson agrees that military commissions should ideally be limited to those captured on traditionally defined battlefields, but does not believe that those otherwise captured should necessarily be tried in regular US courts. He believes, as discussed below, that Congress should create a special, civilian counterterrorism court to try such cases, with limited habeas review by regular US courts; if such reform is (as is likely) unreachable, then he prefers the current MCA approach (modified to include a limited form of regular court review).

With respect to the initial decision to detain and its review through the combatant status review tribunals (CSR tribunals)—as distinguished from any trial that might later follow for alleged crimes by unlawful belligerents—we agree that the CSR tribunals are inadequate as a procedure and put far too much determinative power into executive branch hands—not just in a moment of uncertain security risk, but permanently. To the degree that current legislation gives the executive branch full power to detain a person as an enemy combatant potentially forever (and we disagree about whether the MCA in fact grants such power to the president), it ought to require a far more substantive process of review than reflected by the combatant review status tribunals.

Just as we differed as to the proper fix for the issue of trial venues and procedures, we likewise differ, however, as to the proper remedy regarding the decision to detain and to continue to detain. Massimino believes that individuals who cannot be properly considered combatants in an armed conflict, but who nonetheless are suspected of criminal conduct, should be tried in the regular federal courts. With respect to those who cannot be tried but who pose a serious threat to national security, she believes that in (the unlikely event of) a full-scale reform of counterterrorism policy, there might be limited room for legislative enactment of an administrative detention procedure, outside the laws of war and outside the military altogether, provided that it comported with the strict requirements of international human rights law.

Anderson believes, by contrast, that allowing a backdoor route into the full federal courts through habeas or other mechanisms is neither required for noncitizens nor acceptable from the standpoint of national security. He would prefer the current MCA legislation to full habeas access to federal court. On the other hand, agreeing that the current law lacks sufficient protections, he would prefer comprehensive counter-terrorism reform to create a special civilian counterterrorism court with special rules of procedure, evidence, and review that address the special issues of terrorism. While agreeing that the United States needs a procedure for administrative detention in terrorism cases using a special civilian counterterrorism court as its vehicle, Anderson is skeptical that international human rights law can serve except in a general and hortatory way as the standard to be met. Anderson further believes that a special counterterrorism court should be created but limited to two functions—to review administrative security detention decisions by the executive and to try terrorist criminal cases for specified terrorist crimes, taking over from both the regular federal courts and military commissions.

But there is a significant convergence of views here on a crucial issue, despite other disagreements of approach. We think that, apart from whether these cases should be heard by the federal courts or, in Anderson's view, a special counterterrorism court, any comprehensive reform of counterterrorism should take the military out of the business of detention generally in the war on terror—including detention and the holding of detainees, combatant status review hearings, and military commissions. The "armed conflict" part of the war on terror should be confined as a legal matter to armed conflicts as traditionally defined in the law of war.

Yet the legislation passed by Congress to satisfy *Hamdan*, the MCA, underscores the increasing distance between the law of war and the domestic law definitions applicable to detention and military commissions. The MCA effectively twists itself into a pretzel seeking to reconcile a law of war and military law paradigm with some-thing that, even if it is not traditional criminal law, does not bear great resemblance to traditional law of war. The definition of an unlawful enemy combatant in the MCA, for example, bears very little resemblance to the traditional definition of a combatant in the laws of war. On the contrary, the MCA fundamentally reaches to definitions of persons to be detained that are appropriate instead to administrative detention procedures, using such standards as "material support" for terrorism.

That being the case, it is time to call it what it is (administrative detention), cease applying a military law rationale to it that does not really work, and make it a civilian rather than military jurisdiction. The military, we suspect, would agree. Similarly, on the habeas issue: While no one seriously wants to extend habeas protections to ordinary soldiers taken prisoner on the battlefield, the reason the issue is now under such bitter debate is because we *also* understand that seizing an American citizen at O'Hare airport is scarcely the same thing as the capture of German soldiers in Normandy and that it *does* raise questions about habeas corpus. The pretzel twisting

and creation of more and more domestic law purporting to be military law or international law of war—while having an ever-smaller substantive connection with it
—risks both the integrity of our domestic law and the integrity of our military law and
commitment to the international law of war. While we disagree on exactly how to
redress this, we are firmly in agreement that the limitless legal extension of the war
paradigm exemplified in the MCA does not work. The current jerry-rigged structure
makes little sense now and will not function in future administrations, irrespective,
frankly, of whether and the extent to which the courts bless it or not.

Interrogation of Detainees and the Definition of Torture

Perhaps no issue in the war on terror has aroused greater passions than the interrogation of detainees. While there is widespread rejection of torture as un-American,
citizens of this country are profoundly divided as to the morality of other harsh
interrogation techniques, those that constitute cruel, inhuman, or degrading treatment short of torture. Many believe that we should not be parsing a distinction
between torture and other cruelty; many others believe that refusing to use such
techniques when they could prevent catastrophic terrorist attacks is itself a breach of
morality. The United States is not the first country to grapple with terrorism, and it is
not the first to face the moral and legal dilemmas raised by these questions.

   The administration's initial approach to interrogations was to assert executive
branch power and exploit what it saw as ambiguities in the rules. Where the domestic
criminal law prohibited torture, lawyers at the Justice Department produced a memo
construing the statute so narrowly that "old-fashioned" torture methods—cigarette
burns, breaking fingers—would not qualify as torture, and reassured interrogators that
in any event, the president can authorize violations of the law in his power as commander in chief. Where the Geneva Conventions required refraining from torture,
cruel treatment, and outrages upon personal dignity, administration lawyers argued
that, as unlawful combatants, detainees in US custody were not entitled to those
protections. Where treaty obligations required the United States to prevent the use
of cruel, inhuman, or degrading treatment, the administration reinterpreted a reser-
vation to the treaty to mean that the United States was not bound by the prohibition
on cruelty when it acted abroad. When Congress passed the McCain Amendment
and overruled this interpretation, requiring US personnel everywhere in the world to
refrain from cruel, inhuman, and degrading treatment of prisoners, reports surfaced
that administration lawyers had found a way around that, as well, by interpreting the
prohibition as a flexible standard that would allow cruel treatment in circumstances
that did not "shock the conscience." When the Supreme Court ruled in *Hamdan* that

the humane treatment standards of the Geneva Conventions (found in Common Article Three) were binding on the United States in its treatment of all detainees, the administration sought to replace that standard with its more flexible "shocks the conscience" interpretation. Congress rejected the administration's proposal to redefine Common Article Three, but it narrowed the scope of what constitutes a war crime in ways designed to immunize past conduct. The president nonetheless concluded upon signing the bill into law that the CIA could continue to use a set of "alternative interrogation techniques" beyond those authorized for use by the military.

In the face of these efforts to circumvent the rules, the president's repeated assertions, however sincere and heartfelt, that "we don't torture" ring hollow around the world. And that is not surprising. We have, in fact, tortured detainees in our custody. According to the Pentagon's own figures, at least eight of these were literally tortured to death—beaten, suffocated, frozen, hung. How do we account for this from a country that led the world in drafting the international convention prohibiting torture?

Torture and other forms of cruelty gain a seductive appeal during times of insecurity because of the lure that their use might "work" to protect innocent civilians from catastrophic harm. But what does it mean to say that torture "works"? No systematic study has ever shown that inflicting torture or other such cruelty yields reliable information or actionable intelligence.[8] When the Pentagon released its new Army Field Manual on Intelligence Interrogations last September, rejecting cruel and inhumane tactics, Lieutenant General John Kimmons, deputy chief of staff for Army Intelligence, explained it bluntly: "No good intelligence is going to come from abusive practices. I think history tells us that. I think the empirical evidence of the last five years, hard years, tell us that."[9]

Moreover, even torture that produces accurate information may work against US interests. Longstanding army doctrine cautions that the use of such techniques, if revealed, could undermine public support for the war effort and degrade respect for the standards on which US troops rely for protection. And certainly the abuses at Abu Ghraib were effective only in undermining US moral authority and providing a boon to jihadist recruitment.

But despite all this, the lure of torture—or if not torture, something very close— remains strong. There persists a communal American fantasy that if we are ever faced with a ticking time bomb scenario, we can save the day and avert disaster if only we overcome our squeamishness and "take off the gloves." Indulging in this fantasy has led American policy far off track and away from the values of life and human dignity for which it claims to be fighting this long war. It is time to put the fantasy aside.[10]

We share the view that intelligence is one, if not the most important, tool in combating terrorism today. We also start from the premise that torture is and should remain illegal. While there is a range of conduct that the United States has agreed to—and should refrain from (and we may disagree about where that line should be drawn)—the conduct on that spectrum for which a person can be held criminally liable (war crimes, torture) must be made crystal clear.

The MCA provides some additional clarity. It defines what it calls "grave breaches of Common Article Three," the violation of which could subject a person such as a CIA official to criminal liability. They are: torture, cruel or inhuman treatment, performing biological experiments, murder, mutilation or maiming, intentionally causing serious bodily injury, rape, sexual assault or abuse, and taking hostages. It recognizes that the executive has the authority to define lesser offenses and the terms of their criminal liability, as well as to "interpret" the meaning of the provisions that do not amount to grave breaches. The act provides protection from legal action for government officials engaged in interrogations prior to the act (by making amendments to the War Crimes Act retroactive to its passage in 1997), and provides that the Geneva Conventions cannot be invoked as a source of rights in any court.

Thus, while the law clarifies some matters, it leaves others open for interpretation. Murder, for example, mutilation, and rape are clear enough. But, strikingly, even something as fundamental as torture is not entirely clear under the new law. During debate about the legislation, Democratic and Republican members of Congress in both houses gave examples of conduct that, while not explicitly listed in the statute, would, in their view, constitute a grave breach—waterboarding; forced nudity; forcing a prisoner to perform sexual acts or pose in sexual positions; beatings; electric shocks, burns, or other physical pain; the use of dogs to terrify; induced hypothermia or heat injury; and mock executions. But none of these techniques, some of which had previously been authorized by the administration, were explicitly listed in the statute.

This is a mistake. Anderson and Massimino disagree about many aspects of interrogation procedures, but we agree that it is the obligation of Congress and the administration to be transparent and specific with respect to what constitutes a crime under US law.[11]

Why is this failure to be specific so problematic? Because the people of the United States are deeply divided as to the substance of these issues—torture, not torture, degrading treatment, not degrading treatment, etc.—and because such terms as *humiliating* or *degrading* are not plainly objective in the way that, say, murder is, the only clear democratic means to establish their meaning is through the process of legislation. But to meet this need, such legislation must be specific, transparent— and above all avoid euphemism, generalities, and vagueness. Granted, no lawmaker willingly votes in a way to make him or herself any more accountable than absolutely necessary—but the importance of these issues is such, and the divisions among the public is such, that only public votes on these issues can give the answers democratic legitimacy. There is, of course, a further question as to whether the courts, in their role as protectors of individual rights, would defer to the legislature's judgments, and we likely disagree as to the extent of deference owed. But we do not disagree on the obligation of Congress to legislate plainly on these questions.

We believe this as a fundamental principle of fairness, not because we think that interrogators should seek to walk right up to that line of criminal conduct. To the contrary, we believe that in order to prevent torture, US policy must build a buffer of additional prohibitions, like a fence around the Torah.[12] As former Navy General Counsel Alberto Mora wrote in a memo critical of interrogation policies that permitted the use of cruelty and other force short of torture: "Once the initial barrier against the use of improper force had been breached, a phenomenon known as 'force drift' would almost certainly begin to come into play. This term describes the observed tendency among interrogators who rely on force. If some force is good, these people come to believe, then the application of more force must be better." Although agreeing that the prohibitions against torture require a buffer, we nonetheless would likely disagree with the content of what that buffer zone should be.

Many countries that have faced a terrorist threat have imagined themselves immune from the force drift phenomenon. In Israel, Turkey, the UK in Northern Ireland—every democracy that has tried to walk along the edge of this cliff, by authorizing abusive treatment only in emergencies or only with respect to certain types of suspects, has ended up falling off. Once physical cruelty and inhumane treatment is authorized, it is very difficult to contain and control within preset parameters.

Just as the use of force tends to "drift" upward, it likewise migrates between agencies. For this reason, we also agree that both the prohibition against torture, and the "fence" around that prohibition, should apply equally to all US personnel. In other words, there should be a single standard of humane treatment to which all US personnel—military and civilian—adhere.

This does not mean that all detainees must be treated alike. We are not arguing here that Khalid Sheikh Mohammed must be granted the privileges to which prisoners of war are entitled. But there should be no daylight between the baseline humane treatment standards governing military and CIA interrogations.[13] In wartime, those standards are found in Common Article Three of the Geneva Conventions. Outside of armed conflict, they are found in international human rights and domestic law.

The authors disagree, however, as to the application of international human rights law. Anderson takes the view, for example, that the International Covenant on Civil and Political Rights does not, in accordance with its text and longstanding US views, apply extraterritorially. Massimino believes that such treaties bind US actions wherever they are taken. Our view of how widely human rights law would serve as a check on US action thus differs considerably.

Many have argued that while it is fine to have these standards, we would be wise to keep them to ourselves. Before the new Army field manual on intelligence interrogations was issued, the Pentagon seriously considered attaching a secret annex in which techniques permitted for use only on certain detainees would be listed. The argument for this approach was that transparency about which techniques interrogators could use would aid the enemy in resisting. But our biggest problem now is not that the enemy knows what to expect from us, it is that the rest of the world, including our allies, does not. So long as they believe that we are willing to engage in torture and other cruel, inhuman, and degrading treatment—conduct for which we routinely condemn others—we will continue to pay for past mistakes.

Conclusion: The Choice of Paradigms

This chapter has focused on the three most domestically and internationally divisive issues in the war on terror—detention, trial, and interrogation. There are many other issues of grave importance, but these three capture the fundamental questions of value that must be answered by national policy in pursuing counterterrorism. And our answers on such essential matters—even in the face of polarizing controversy—will help build a coherent and sustainable counterterrorism policy. Our recommendation is that there be a return to basics, a return to the question of fundamental paradigms in US counterterrorism policy.

Counterterrorism has been presented since September 11 as the choice between a criminal law model of counterterrorism and a war model of counterterrorism. That binary seems to us wrong. What we describe as the war on terror represents a strategic view of a long struggle in which strategic war concepts are appropriate to frame the conflict. They do not describe, however, the legal requirements for invoking the law of war in a global war on terror. The contradictions and strains that arise from trying to fit counterterrorism policy into the straightjacket of war, while at the same time seeking to use the law of war as a means to insulate the executive branch from established checks and balances, are nearing a breaking point. The MCA is likely to accelerate political crises as much as defuse them because it is so ill-structured a settlement for the long term—designed, as it was, to meet the narrowest requirements of a Supreme Court decision and make up for mistakes made early in the interrogation and detention process.

The counterterrorism policies of any new administration or new Congress, of whatever party, Republican or Democratic, must start from a view that counterterrorism operates across a wide range of activities. At one end is law enforcement, particularly domestic law enforcement (the kind that breaks up domestic terrorist plots). At the other end is war—actual war, armed conflict involving armies and troops and the weapons of war. War, we can now begin to see, is more often aimed at government backers of terrorists rather than the terrorists themselves. The real action against terrorists themselves takes place in a zone between those two extremes. The tools in this zone include surveillance, tracking and seizure of terrorist assets, co-operation with foreign intelligence and police services, domestic security measures for key infrastructure, protection of air travel, and so on. It also includes detention, interrogation, and the use of force short of war, such as attacks on terrorist training camps, targeted assassinations of terrorists, and other uses of violence that do not always rise to the legal level of "armed conflict."

It is this ground between the extremes that inevitably will be the focus of most of our counterterrorism efforts in the future, and we badly need legal rules to define that zone of action and its limits. The coauthors may disagree over precisely how those rules should be shaped and, perhaps most deeply, over the role of the courts in monitoring and policing the activities of this category of activity. But we are agreed that developing this center category of activities, which are neither pure criminal justice nor war, will be the key to a counterterrorism policy that moves beyond policy binaries that ill-serve the United States, operationally and legally. Comprehensive counterterrorism policy for a new administration and a new Congress will necessarily look beyond the simple alternatives of law enforcement or war.

Notes

1 Or against non-US citizens. The Military Commissions Act of 2006, for example, distinguishes flatly between citizens and noncitizens. We disagree as to whether this distinction of nationality is appropriate or consistent with domestic or international human rights law.

2 Although the United States has not ratified Protocol I, it has accepted that Article 75 reflects customary law binding on the United States.

3 Yet the court seems not to have considered the possibility that by finding that the conflict with Al Qaeda is a conflict "not of an international character" so as to invoke Common Article Three, it arguably cut out application of nearly all of the rest of the Geneva Conventions, including the grave breaches provisions, for example, and the Article 5 tribunal mechanism for determining combatant status, all of which arguably require that the conflict be an Article 2 international armed conflict precluded by application of Common Article Three. We ourselves disagree (as do military law experts) as to the legal consequences of the court's rather sparsely reasoned holding on this vital question.

4 The MCA purports to do more than deprive detainees of a private action under the GCs. It says that no person can invoke the GCs as a source of rights, even in a habeas or other action.

5 We use *military commission* and *military tribunal* here interchangeably; we reserve the term *court martial* for regular proceedings under the full mechanisms available to US soldiers under the Uniform Code of Military Justice.

6 The issue of habeas corpus is most relevant to the detention question, rather than trials under the military commissions, since habeas pertains in the first place to the legal grounds for holding the detainee.

7 What constitutes a "regularly constituted court" for purposes of Common Article Three promises to be a hotly contested issue, which *Hamdan* failed to quiet, and it is an issue on which we likely disagree but will not pursue here.

8 This is not the same as saying that nothing revealed under torture is ever true. But intelligence must be more than simply true in order to be useful. When US personnel beat an Iraqi Army general, bound him, and stuffed him head first into a sleeping bag, the only information he revealed before he died was information already known to his interrogators.

9 Anderson is frankly skeptical of the assertion that torture does not produce useful information, or at least does not produce useful information distinguishable from intelligence "noise." However, he does not argue for making torture legal under any circumstances. The fundamental issue, for Anderson, is not the illegality of torture, but how it and other terms such as *inhumane treatment* or *cruelty* are to be concretely defined so as to make transparently clear what is legal and illegal.

10 Anderson notes that even if, as he acknowledges, the "ticking time bomb" scenario is largely, though not entirely, a chimera that is tangential to the daily toil of thwarting terrorist plots, it enjoys political support that cannot be dismissed out of hand. A significant range of political figures—including Hillary Clinton, Chuck Schumer, and John McCain—have said they might resort to torture if necessary in such a scenario. It cannot, therefore, be viewed purely as a fixation of the Bush administration.

11 A further issue that deserves a clear policy is whether certain techniques are permissible in certain situations. Can more aggressive interrogation be used on a known terrorist mastermind such as Khalid Sheikh Mohammed, as opposed to a person who may still turn out to be the innocent shepherd? We differ as to this general principle—Anderson in favor, Massimino against—but we agree the matter must be clarified in legislation.

12 According to Jewish law, the precepts of the Torah were to be "fenced around" with additional restrictions in order to prevent violation of the core precepts themselves.

13 Anderson believes that while a comprehensive reform of the existing system should establish a single standard across the US government, there are practical difficulties. He believes that the existing US military manual is too restrictive, for instance, in a case like Khalid Sheikh Mohammed. Since revision of the military manual is in Anderson's view not likely, and probably not wise, he would accept two standards today: one applicable to the military, and one applicable to all civilian agencies. Massimino would hold the civilian agencies to the military standard.

4

Course Correction in America's War on Terror

Peter Brookes and Julianne Smith

In the aftermath of the September 11 attacks, President Bush declared a "global war on terror." At the time, it was impossible to predict the transformative effect that the struggle would have on both the United States and the world more broadly. Inside its own borders, the United States witnessed profound changes in the last five-plus years. The very structure of the US government has been radically overhauled through the creation of new departments, new positions, new legal authorities, and resource flows. Daily life for Americans has changed too. Throughout the war on terror, Americans have experienced moments of both tremendous hope and great despair. They have been inspired by acts of heroism, horrified by examples of terrorist violence and hate, and drawn into heated political debates on the war's overarching purpose and strategy. Any time they travel, any time they turn on their televisions, Americans are constantly reminded about their vulnerability to the persistent scourge of Islamic terrorism. To be sure, Americans today look at themselves—indeed, the world—differently than they did on September 10, 2001.

If asked, few Americans would have a hard time explaining how the world and their lives have changed since September 11. But many would struggle to identify the exact source of the current terrorist threat or gauge the war's progress to date. Many complain about threat fatigue, even weariness, with a concept that has proved difficult to define. Against whom, exactly, is the United States waging war? When will we know that this war is won? How much longer will the struggle last? What sacrifices will need to be made? And what changes in strategy and tactics are required as the United States and its allies prepare for what is likely to be a long twilight struggle?

This chapter, jointly authored by two analysts who sit on opposite sides of the political spectrum, aims to build consensus on the nature of Islamic extremism. The essay also will provide an assessment of progress to date, examine the continuing challenges, and outline the way ahead as the United States and its partners fight what many now refer to as the "Long War."

The Nature of the Threat

With past terrorist threats, it was not so difficult to identify the perpetrators, understand what they wanted, and locate their main base of operation. The terrorist groups that were pursued in the days after September 11, though, are different. A collection of loosely affiliated terrorist groups and cells associated with Osama bin Laden's Al Qaeda were quickly identified as responsible not only for the 9/11 attacks but also for the bombing of the USS Cole in 2000 in Yemen and the destruction of two US embassies in Eastern Africa in 1998. While the group's most important operational base was known to be in Afghanistan, Al Qaeda would prove to be an elusive target for US counterterrorism officials. It had and still has a presence in dozens of countries around the world, continually developing new relationships with terrorist groups committed to reestablishing an historic Islamic caliphate.

Al Qaeda's demands of the West have also proved difficult to grasp fully. United by a common ideology that violently rejects "apostate" Muslim states and Western influences, Al Qaeda's leadership has not demanded any single action or policy change that would constitute a satisfying outcome and a conclusion for their quest. Some, most notably President Bush, have described the group as hating freedom. That is certainly a part, but not the entire story. Al Qaeda and other Islamic extremist groups are promoting an exclusionary ideology that fuels a violent jihad seeking the unconditional surrender of both the "near" and "far" enemy.

The terrorist tactics used by Al Qaeda—such as the 9/11 attacks, car bombs, and suicide bombers—have been both innovative and effective. There appears to be no limit to the violence that Al Qaeda and its disciples will employ to meet their overarching objectives. US intelligence continues to collect information that indicates that Al Qaeda and other groups are still attempting to acquire chemical, biological, and nuclear weapons and materials. Osama bin Laden has been clear that his followers should use these weapons, from "dirty bombs" to poisons to nuclear weapons, against their enemies.

Once the 9/11 attacks were attributed to Al Qaeda and the Taliban refused to hand over Osama bin Laden, the United States moved to invade Afghanistan to topple the Taliban regime, eliminate Al Qaeda, and end its sanctuary there. Beyond direct military action in Afghanistan, the Bush administration drew on other instruments of national power such as law enforcement, financial actions, information operations, and intelligence work to pursue Al Qaeda and associated terrorist groups until they were depleted of their resources, arms, and will to engage in terrorism. By fighting terrorism abroad, President Bush argues the United States will prevent terrorism at home. Within merely a few weeks after the 9/11 attacks, Al Qaeda had become public enemy number one.

Just a year after the start of the war on terror, however, the terrorist threat started to evolve. After the military action in Afghanistan and the elimination of the vast majority of Al Qaeda's 9/11 leadership, Al Qaeda began to morph from a centrally controlled organization based in Afghanistan into a slew of loosely associated groups and cells that now form part of a global movement. In some cases, the new adherents never have contact with Al Qaeda's core leadership nor travel to Afghanistan for training but are "homegrown" radicals. These groups, inspired by jihadist ideology and Al Qaeda's zealous sense of global purpose, often display (through evidence gleaned from confiscated laptops, messages left behind at terrorist sites, and the Internet) a mix of both local and global grievances. For example, Mohammed Bouyeri, the young man who killed Dutch filmmaker Theo van Gogh, left behind a note, detailing his frustration both with local Dutch policies concerning Muslims and US foreign policy in Iraq and the Middle East, more broadly. That act highlighted just how attractive the radical Islamic movement can be for a young, second-generation immigrant in Europe who is facing blatant discrimination and humiliation at home and witnessing the "persecution" of his or her Muslim brothers abroad.

Today the terrorist threat remains just as diverse. The challenge of terrorism plagues countries from the Philippines—where the government still is fighting an Al Qaeda affiliate, Abu Sayyaf—to the United Kingdom, where an Al Qaeda plot that originated in Pakistan sought to bring down ten airliners over the Atlantic last year using liquid explosives and homegrown British operatives. Just across our northern border in June 2006, Canadian authorities arrested 17 would-be terrorists who were planning bombings, beheadings, and the seizure of parliamentary buildings. In September, Al Qaeda announced that the Algerian terrorist group, GSPC, and the Libyan LIFG had aligned themselves with Al Qaeda.

Smith believes that, in addition to evolving, the terrorism threat is growing, thanks to Al Qaeda's innovative techniques, the war in Iraq, and a series of unfortunate US actions, including the human rights abuses at Abu Ghraib prison and allegations of torture and the desecration of the Koran at the Guantanamo Bay detainment camp. Smith thus believes that recruitment is on the rise. Brookes, skeptical that recruitment can be measured accurately, is less sure about this point but does believe that misdeeds, misinformation, and propaganda such as that carried on Al Qaeda-associated al-Zawraa television have provided fertile ground for the recruitment of new jihadists. Today, Osama bin Laden and his deputy Ayman al-Zawahiri remain the chief recruiters for Al Qaeda, even while in hiding. Not only does their rhetoric intend to provoke Muslims to undertake jihad, it is also designed to muster new adherents and boost morale. Homegrown terrorists and radical imams cleverly promote this jihadist narrative through the Internet, DVDs, and sermons to audiences in affluent as well as underprivileged Muslim neighborhoods around the world.

Progress to Date

While the United States continues to struggle to identify, understand, and defeat the global threat of Islamic terrorism in its ideology and overarching objectives, there have been a handful of important victories in the war on terror over the last five years. First and foremost, the war in Afghanistan and the toppling of the Taliban regime deprived Al Qaeda of its core operational base, eliminating one of the most dangerous and better-known safe havens. In addition, since 9/11, a number of key operatives— such as Khalid Sheikh Mohammed, Hambali, and Abu Musab al Zarqawi—were killed or captured, weakening Al Qaeda's ability to operate.

Through robust law enforcement, intelligence, military, and homeland security cooperation, the United States has worked with allies to foil dozens of terrorist plots. Despite significant levels of anti-Americanism, domestic legislative hurdles, and resource restrictions in several partner countries, the level of international cooperation has been unprecedented (even with countries that firmly opposed the war in Iraq, such as France and Germany). The near-global coalition has broken up cells and deprived terrorists of safe haven, operatives, resources, and financing. The war on terror also has fostered new counterterrorism partnerships with countries such as Indonesia, Saudi Arabia, and Pakistan, and some new organizations such as the Proliferation Security Initiative, which works to keep weapons of mass destruction out of the hands of rogue regimes and terrorists.

In the United States, one of the most commonly cited success stories is the lack of another attack on American soil. While Brookes views this as a clear-cut achievement in the war on terror, Smith does so with hesitation. Smith acknowledges that the United States has made it far more difficult for terrorists to stage an attack on US soil through a number of homeland security improvements. But she also thinks it is important to note that terrorist attacks can take years to plan and implement. (It took Al Qaeda six years to carry out the attack in Kenya and eight years to strike the World Trade Center again.) Smith also believes that taking the war on terror to Iraq and Afghanistan provided terrorist groups with easy-to-reach targets in the Middle East.

Despite some differences on whether or not to credit the absence of new attacks in the United States since 9/11 as a major achievement, Brookes and Smith fully agree that the United States has made a number of notable improvements in the area of homeland security. The United States has poured massive sums of money into countering biological, chemical, and radiological attacks; strengthening commercial aviation security; improving border controls; and strengthening emergency response and consequence management. The US government also has improved coordination and communication between the CIA; FBI; and other intelligence, homeland security, and law enforcement agencies (although the current system still has its flaws). Many state and local institutions have played a positive and productive role, improving their ability to respond to a catastrophic attack. Gaps remain, but US homeland security is better than it was five years ago.

Continuing Challenges

To be sure, the war on terror is not without its triumphs. Unfortunately, though, moments of success have been overshadowed by missteps, highlighting the well-intentioned, but sometimes ad hoc, nature of the US response. The fact that Osama bin Laden is still on the loose is troubling. While killing or capturing him would not necessarily end the Al Qaeda movement, it could be a key milestone in the decline of Al Qaeda.

It has become clear recently that some of the early gains in the struggle against terrorism are now in jeopardy. Despite the presence of more than 40,000 US and NATO troops on the ground, Afghanistan is witnessing an unprecedented resurgence by Al Qaeda Taliban allies, which threatens to roll back the progress that has been made since US troops first entered Afghanistan in 2001. Elements of Al Qaeda itself may also be present in Afghanistan. Pakistan's inability or unwillingness to tighten its border with Afghanistan, an area that is known to be hosting Taliban fighters, has allowed the Taliban to set up a forward operating base from which to train, equip, and launch new attacks, leaving these two authors deeply troubled about Afghanistan's future.

Pakistan itself is another deep concern. An agreement reached between the government of Pakistani President Pervez Musharraf and tribal leaders in the Federally Administered Tribal Areas (FATA) resulted in the Taliban, Al Qaeda, and other jihadists finding sanctuary in Pakistan along the southeastern Afghanistan border. Intelligence officials now believe that both Osama bin Laden and his deputy, Ayman al-Zawahiri, are holding up in the Pakistani Hindu Kush. This sanctuary for extremists in Pakistan has not only led to a significant rise in Taliban attacks in Afghanistan but also has enabled Al Qaeda to plan, operate, and direct terrorist plots in the West. While Pakistan has been an important partner in the struggle against Islamic terrorism, its policy in the FATA is failing, at a significant danger to global security.

State sponsorship of terrorism is a force-multiplier for terrorist groups—providing training, funding, weapons, and sanctuary. As the most active state sponsor of terror, Iran poses a significant challenge for international counterterrorism, especially considering the anti-American stance of the current Iranian government. While its relationship with Al Qaeda is murky, Tehran's willingness to employ terrorism to advance its policy objectives, especially directly or through terrorist proxies such as Hezbollah and Hamas, is not. Equally troubling is Iran's quasi-ally, Syria, which is also a major sponsor of terrorism and cooperates with Iran in this arena.

Iraq

The biggest challenge, no doubt, is in Iraq. While Brookes and Smith would argue over the value of taking the war on terror to Iraq in the first place, both authors firmly believe that Iraq has now become a major operating base for several types of terrorists. As of early 2007, the conflict in Iraq remains primarily an intra-Arab sectarian struggle for power, and attacks by terrorist groups only account for a fraction of the violence. But this could change. In either case, today, the war affects the threat posed by Islamic terrorism to US national security broadly. Al Qaeda has established a presence in Iraq. In fact, documents captured from an Al Qaeda in Iraq (AQI) safe house revealed plans for conducting terrorist attacks in the United States. The US intelligence community judges that AQI continues to plan for terrorist operations beyond Iraq.

Moreover, AQI, which is the largest and most active of the terrorist groups in Iraq, has been joined by Ansar al-Sunna, assorted foreign jihadists from across the globe, and homegrown Iraqi "self-starters" who have joined with AQI to attack Coalition and Iraqi forces and Shia targets such as the Samarra mosque in Iraq, which heightens the sectarian conflict. These groups and foreign fighters support Al Qaeda's efforts to attack American interests, defend Sunni interest in Iraq, and replace secular Muslim governments such as that in Iraq with theocratic states.

To be sure, the war in Iraq, especially through the jihadists' extensive use of the Internet as a propaganda tool, plays a role in attracting new recruits. What is less certain is the degree to which the foreign jihadists are returning home to establish extremist organizations or carry out acts of terrorism. There is, however, some evidence of spillover from Iraq to Afghanistan, where improvised explosive devices (IED) and IED techniques similar to those found in Iraq, as well as the increasing use of suicide bomb attacks, are being employed by the Taliban and other foreign jihadists against US, Afghan, and NATO forces.

While the intelligence community views Iraq as a motivator for the global jihadist movement, it also concludes, "Should jihadists leaving Iraq perceive themselves, and be perceived, to have failed, we judge fewer fighters will be inspired to carry on the fight." The National Intelligence Estimate goes on to judge that a jihadist success in Iraq would inspire "more fighters to continue the struggle elsewhere." This conclusion, in our minds, emphasizes the importance of reaching a resolution in Iraq that will undermine the jihadist movement both in the minds of its current foot soldiers and in the eyes of potential recruits.

No Grand Strategy?

Smith views the lack of a comprehensive policy roadmap as a major shortcoming in the United States' fight against terrorism. The United States began this fight by declaring war on a tactic and focusing on what appeared to be, at least at the time, two tactical and relatively short-term aims—regime change in Afghanistan and Iraq. Today, with the terrorist threat evolving; the United States' image tattered; and radicalization, in Smith's view, on the rise, the United States is in need of a grand strategy, one that would match its resources to its capabilities and its capabilities to its ambitions. The United States must now move its loose collection of tactics toward a long-term strategy. The country must be mobilized much as it was during the Cold War so that the private sector, universities, and our research labs—together with the US government—can combine their ends, ways, and means to craft common or at least complementary goals. Such a strategy must be constructed in a way that prevents US foreign policy from being dominated by a single global challenge. The United States' fight against radical extremism will remain one of its core priorities, but it should never become the priority at the expense of a long list of other pressing challenges.

While Brookes sees value in Smith's proposal, he believes that the National Strategies that the Bush administration has issued since 9/11 actually do provide adequate guidance for government actors across areas such as dealing with terrorism and its state sponsors, improving the economic and political conditions in societies where terrorism is prevalent, and making terrorism a societal anathema, among others. Tactics obviously will have to change to meet evolving terrorism challenges. Brookes does agree with Smith that the United States should not put all of its resources and energy into the single threat of combating terrorism at the expense of other challenges such as Iran, Russia, North Korea, and China.

The Way Ahead

What is certain is that it will take the United States, its coalition partners, and other states threatened by the current wave of Islamic terrorism years, if not decades, to defeat it. The to-do list for countering the terrorist threat is long: eliminating terrorist sanctuary; curbing terrorist activity; undermining radicalism; discouraging terrorist funding and the recruitment of future generations of terrorists; enhancing good governance; promoting democracy and education, economic opportunity, and social justice; employing finely tuned public diplomacy; providing generous foreign aid; and resolving the ongoing conflict between the Palestinians and Israel.

The authors agree that there is no pure kinetic, that is, military, solution to the challenge of Islamic terrorism. As the causes of terrorism are multifaceted, so too must be the means of opposing it. The long fight against terrorism requires a wide array of tools, tactics, and strategies that address the challenge at both the local and global levels.

Protecting 50 states, 95,000 miles of coastline, and 7,500 miles of land border from terrorism is no small task. Living in a free, open society makes us fundamentally more vulnerable to terrorism. There is arguably no such thing as absolute security in any society. The United States is deeply integrated with the world beyond its borders, and that is to its benefit. Over 300 million visitors come to the United States every year. Nine million seaborne containers enter the United States annually at 361 commercial ports, carrying half of US imports. Many firms depend on the global market for goods and labor to keep their businesses running and prosperous. Parts of our critical infrastructure—including the Internet, aviation, and energy sectors—are integrated internationally. But this openness and integration has a downside as well. The fundamental challenge is to protect the United States without disrupting the American way of life or infringing upon our cherished civil liberties.

While there has not been a terrorist attack in the United States since 9/11, the threat from international terrorism, especially from Al Qaeda, persists. Although there has been progress in developing new (and improving existing) US government counterterrorism programs, much work remains to be done in a number of core areas. In general, it will be critical for the prevention of and response to terrorist attacks for the federal government to further improve interagency and international law enforcement as well as intelligence and homeland security consultation, co-ordination, cooperation, and communications. The same is true for vertical and horizontal relations between the US federal government and state and local governments. Developing "joint duty" tours for US counterterrorism officials similar to the military's efforts after the passage of the historic 1986 Goldwater-Nichols legislation would be helpful too. Furthermore, congressional oversight of all elements of the government's counterterrorism efforts, especially the intelligence community, must be enhanced.

Although the FBI has made progress in developing its domestic intelligence arm, the National Security Bureau, it still struggles to move beyond its longstanding focus on crime and toward intelligence analysis and collection, counterterrorism, and counterintelligence. In addition, the FBI still has too few agents proficient in foreign languages, particularly Arabic. To spur a shift in organizational focus and culture, the FBI should require senior managers to have experience in counterterrorism. The FBI also must do a better job of integrating terrorism-related databases among federal and state law enforcement agencies. In addition, concerns remain about sharing sensitive national security information with state and local authorities while guarding against mishandling.

The Department of Homeland Security (DHS) was an important step in consolidating various homeland security missions under one roof, but the agency remains plagued by turf battles, inefficiencies, and information blockages. Information sharing within the agency has improved in recent months, but DHS's ability to share information with state and local authorities and the private sector is woefully inadequate —not to mention shortcomings in "real-time" communications interoperability at all levels of government. Data mining to detect terrorism-related patterns and relationships from vast quantities of data also must be much more effective.

The visa waiver program, while valuable, can pose risks to US security because of efforts by some to exploit the system, and it must be administered in such a way as to ensure that it doesn't enable terrorists to enter the country. While there is a move afoot in Washington to extend the visa waiver program to certain countries (particularly allies that currently do not meet visa waiver requirements), extension of the visa waiver program must be considered through a counterterrorism lens. For instance, both Richard Reid and Zacarias Moussaoui entered the United States using passports issued by visa waiver countries. The United States must fully implement US-VISIT so that the government can track who enters, when they leave, and how long they stay in the United States. Multiple terrorist watch lists are managed by different agencies, but these must be better coordinated.

There needs to be significant improvements at the Transportation Security Agency (TSA), which provides passenger security at the country's 438 commercial airports. Screener performance has been uneven, leaving open the possibility that dangerous objects or materials could slip through into the sterile areas of airports or into the checked baggage system. TSA also must fulfill its congressional mandate to take over responsibility for the passenger identity-matching process from domestic air carriers in order to improve accuracy and avoid having to share sensitive information on possible terrorists with airlines. Quality assurance of no-fly lists also must be improved.

Intelligence is our first line of defense against terrorism. Good intelligence provided by the intelligence community's 16 agencies helps us track events taking place at home and overseas, delineate trends, predict events and, hopefully, shape the international environment in a fashion advantageous to American interests. Without question, we must have the finest intelligence available in our struggle with terrorism. While the intelligence community has restructured itself three times over the last five years, its analytical and collection capabilities remain uneven. The new leadership post within the intelligence community, the Director of National Intelligence (DNI), is still a work in progress, especially on the issue of effectively centralizing management of intelligence agencies under the DNI's aegis.

The National Counterterrorism Center has done a better job of integrating strategic terrorism intelligence, but information overload across the intelligence community is common. Better analytical tradecraft, which includes "red-teaming" by outside experts and vigorously challenging assumptions, must be incorporated and institutionalized.

Human intelligence (HUMINT) collection capability, now under the guidance of the National Clandestine Service, has vastly improved since 9/11, especially in terms of integrating US government HUMINT efforts and putting more operatives in the field. There is still a need to enhance relationships with foreign intelligence services, while protecting sensitive intelligence sources and methods and penetrating hard targets such as terrorist cells needs to improve.

Controversial programs such as the interrogation of terror suspects and the National Security Agency's Terrorist Surveillance Program are a potential source of important counterterrorism intelligence and should continue, in consonance with our laws, subject to congressional oversight and under the scrutiny of the Department of Justice. Intelligence sharing that puts critical information in the hands of the right people at all levels of government and the private sector as necessary and in a timely manner is also an ongoing struggle within the US government. The top priorities for intelligence must always be to give those on the front line all of the information they need and to put a laser-like focus on the nexus between terrorism and weapons of mass destruction.

Terrorist financing is another challenge. While it does not take much money to stage an attack, terrorists cannot recruit, plan, train, and conduct operations, especially on a large scale, without funding. Fortunately, US and international efforts to cut terrorist financing have been quite successful. Since 9/11, the Treasury Department, along with other US government agencies and foreign governments, have taken a number of steps, including better intelligence collection, enforcement actions, capacity building, and systemic improvements to safeguard the United States and global financial systems. There are a number of areas in which stronger cooperation between the United States and its partners could spur significant further progress: shared definitions of terrorists and terrorist organizations, joint training, deterrence of terrorists' major donors, closure of Muslim charities that support terrorism, and the constriction of cash smuggling and money laundering channels.

The area where the United States has faltered the most in its war on terror is public diplomacy—a capability gap that has limited the effectiveness of other instruments. With the United States' image badly bruised over Iraq and detainee abuse at Abu Ghraib, maintaining the alliances and partnerships developed since September 11 has, in some cases, become challenging. Yes, as President Bush has noted on several occasions, making policy is not a popularity contest. But when political elites in other countries begin to feel that standing shoulder to shoulder with the United States is a political liability, low popularity ratings can indeed hinder the United States' ability to meet global challenges. US policies do not operate in a political vacuum.

More troubling is the failure to pair short-term tactical gains in the war on terror with matching long-term public diplomacy or development strategies that prevent would-be terrorists from walking down the path of radicalization. Many argue that we are losing the battle of ideas. Because we have failed to develop a viable counter-narrative to Osama bin Laden's, many Muslims around the world believe that the United States is at war with Islam itself. Furthermore, the United States has not yet learned how to use today's technologies to win the battle of ideas. Radical extremists cleverly use the Internet and DVDs to promote their ideology, but the United States' efforts in this area remain sluggish and outdated.

What is needed is a major overhaul of the United States' diplomatic tools, starting with US diplomats. Today, Foreign Service officers are encouraged and required to take part in public diplomacy efforts. Few of them, however, have received the necessary training in foreign languages, public speaking, and message development. (The General Accountability Office reports that 30 percent of language-designated public diplomacy posts are filled with officers who lack the required language skills.) Many officers also lack experience in the Muslim world, limiting their understanding of both the nature of the threat and the cultural and historical roots of the Muslim extremist problem we face. The institutions and offices dedicated to public diplomacy also must receive the resources and authorities that they need to do the job. After a sharp decline in funding over the past eight years, federal spending for public diplomacy is once again on the rise. But US government resource allocation in this area does not come close to matching our ambitions.

The United States also should identify and cooperate with opinion leaders and media outlets in foreign capitals to promote a free press and American values and counter the dizzying array of conspiracy theories about US policies and motivations in the war on terror. Washington also should maximize the use of international broadcasting to the Muslim world broadly. Efforts to date—including US government-sponsored Radio Sawa, Radio Farda, and Al Hurra—have been uneven in their reporting and weak in how they are staffed. Furthermore, these stations and other US public diplomacy efforts lost considerable credibility in late 2005 when it was revealed that the Pentagon was paying Iraqi reporters to write pro-American stories.

Of course, even the best-designed and most generously funded public diplomacy programs will fail if the policies that they promote are unsound or unclearly articulated. To that effect, the United States must publicly demonstrate its commitment to human rights and to the degree possible make its policies and strategies transparent and open to debate. While the United States cannot and should not change policy course solely to improve public opinion, the US government should use its public diplomacy tools to assess the likely effectiveness and impact of its policy options, including through consultation with foreign governments. A failure to do so could produce unintended consequences that do not serve US interests.

US cooperation with international partners is also a critical component of combating terrorism. Despite a long list of achievements, international cooperation currently is plagued in some cases with mistrust and deep divisions over counterterrorism strategy, threatening its overall efficiency, effectiveness, and cohesion. We must counter international perceptions that the US-led war on terrorism is tied almost exclusively to Iraq and Afghanistan and is largely anti-Islam.

Allocating more resources toward nonmilitary means of fighting terrorism and focusing on what drives people toward extremism also would help the United States win back the support of its international partners and help counter the overarching threat. For example, since 2002 the United States has spent approximately six billion dollars on supporting the Pakistani military but less than a billion dollars on educational reform and economic assistance in that country.[1] Given the role of the schools and high unemployment in driving the radicalization of many young males, one has to question the long-term viability of the proportion of hard and soft power that we are using in Pakistan. The United States must match its capabilities to its strategy by investing in critical nonmilitary instruments of national power. From agriculture to education to justice, US civilian agencies need more robust, deployable capabilities to build capacity in weak or failing states where terrorism might find a home.

To its credit, the United States has promoted democratization as one of its core nonmilitary instruments in the war on terror. After five years, though, it is hard to point to concrete examples of progress, due to a lack of a recognizable, integrated strategy; a heavy emphasis on Iraq and Afghanistan; poor analysis of the possible consequences; and limited or unclear benchmarks. (Both Brookes and Smith would cite Lebanon as a success, but Hezbollah, Syria, and Iran now seriously threaten it.)

The concept itself, however, is not without value. Democratization remains essential to combating the roots of radical extremism, particularly in weak and failed states. But without the proper planning, capabilities, and resources, elections that are forced too soon, such as those in the Palestinian territories, can actually work against US objectives. While countries' paths to democracy differ vastly, it could be argued that democracy promotion should be "evolutionary" rather than "revolutionary"— promoted as societies develop an enabling environment of legitimate political parties, civil society institutions, anticorruption measures, and a free media. Conversely, the United States should be cautioned against resisting democratic reform indefinitely in the name of short-term security gains.

Finally, the United States needs to build a foundation of international cooperation that extends well beyond the war on terror, one that focuses on the other pressing challenges, including nonproliferation, energy security, climate change, and global health issues. It will also require the United States to redouble its efforts today to foster strong and committed partnerships with friends and allies that can meet the challenges of tomorrow.

Note

1 An estimate from Frederick Barton, director of the Post-Conflict Reconstruction Project at the Center for Strategic and International Studies.

5

The Case for Larger
Ground Forces

Frederick W. Kagan and
Michael O'Hanlon

We live at a time when wars not only rage in nearly every region but threaten to erupt in many places where the current relative calm is tenuous. To view this as a strategic military challenge for the United States is not to espouse a specific theory of America's role in the world or a certain political philosophy. Such an assessment flows directly from the basic bipartisan view of American foreign policy makers since World War II that overseas threats must be countered before they can directly threaten this country's shores, that the basic stability of the international system is essential to American peace and prosperity, and that no country besides the United States is in a position to lead the way in countering major challenges to the global order.

Let us highlight the threats and their consequences with a few concrete examples, emphasizing those that involve key strategic regions of the world such as the Persian Gulf and East Asia, or key potential threats to American security, such as the spread of nuclear weapons and the strengthening of the global Al Qaeda/jihadist movement. The Iranian government has rejected a series of international demands to halt its efforts at enriching uranium and submit to international inspections. What will happen if the US—or Israeli—government becomes convinced that Tehran is on the verge of fielding a nuclear weapon? North Korea, of course, has already done so, and the ripple effects are beginning to spread. Japan's recent election to supreme power of a leader who has promised to rewrite that country's constitution to support increased armed forces—and, possibly, even nuclear weapons—may well alter the delicate balance of fear in Northeast Asia fundamentally and rapidly. Also, in the background, at least for now, Sino-Taiwanese tensions continue to flare, as do tensions between

India and Pakistan, Pakistan and Afghanistan, Venezuela and the United States, and so on. Meanwhile, the world's nonintervention in Darfur troubles consciences from Europe to America's Bible Belt to its bastions of liberalism, yet with no serious international forces on offer, the bloodletting will probably, tragically, continue unabated.

And as bad as things are in Iraq today, they could get worse. What would happen if the key Shiite figure, Ali al Sistani, were to die? If another major attack on the scale of the Golden Mosque bombing hit either side (or, perhaps, both sides at the same time)? Such deterioration might convince many Americans that the war there truly was lost—but the costs of reaching such a conclusion would be enormous. Afghanistan is somewhat more stable for the moment.

Sound US grand strategy must proceed from the recognition that, over the next few years and decades, the world is going to be a very unsettled and quite dangerous place, with Al Qaeda and its associated groups as a subset of a much larger set of worries. The only serious response to this international environment is to develop armed forces capable of protecting America's vital interests throughout this dangerous time. Doing so requires a military capable of a wide range of missions—including not only deterrence of great power conflict in dealing with potential hotspots in Korea, the Taiwan Strait, and the Persian Gulf but also associated with a variety of Special Forces activities and stabilization operations. For today's US military, which already excels at high technology and is increasingly focused on re-learning the lost art of counterinsurgency, this is first and foremost a question of finding the resources to field a large-enough standing Army and Marine Corps to handle personnel-intensive missions such as the ones now under way in Iraq and Afghanistan.

Let us hope there will be no such large-scale missions for a while. But preparing for the possibility, while doing whatever we can at this late hour to relieve the pressure on our soldiers and Marines in ongoing operations, is prudent. At worst, the only potential downside to a major program to strengthen the military is the possibility of spending a bit too much money. Recent history shows no link between having a larger military and its overuse; indeed, Ronald Reagan's time in office was characterized by higher defense budgets and yet much less use of the military, an outcome for which we can hope in the coming years, but hardly guarantee. While the authors disagree between ourselves about proper increases in the size and cost of the military (with O'Hanlon preferring to hold defense to roughly 4 percent of GDP and seeing ground forces increase by a total of perhaps 100,000, and Kagan willing to devote at least 5 percent of GDP to defense as in the Reagan years and increase the Army by at least 250,000), we agree on the need to start expanding ground force capabilities by at least 25,000 a year immediately. Such a measure is not only prudent, it is also badly overdue.

The Decline of the US Military

The US military now suffers from the greatest strain and danger since the elimination of conscription in 1973. At roughly $450 billion a year (not counting an additional $100 billion or more in yearly supplemental appropriations for ongoing operations), today's force is more expensive than during most Cold War periods. However, these levels are driven largely by a more expensive personnel system (compensation that is well-deserved by our brave men and women under arms, given how much we ask of them), rising costs of weaponry, and modern necessities such as good health care and environmental stewardship. In fact, our all-volunteer active-duty military today is about one-third smaller than levels in the 1980s (about 1.4 million versus 2.2 million troops, with just over 500,000 in the active Army; just under 200,000 in the Marine Corps; 375,000 in the Navy; and 350,000 in the Air Force). Army and Marine Corps ranks have been buttressed by the activation of up to 100,000 reservists at a time, but this process has been pushed almost as far as it probably can be, in relation to the activation that can be expected of those willing to serve in the Reserve and the National Guard.

Meanwhile, any hope that we would have received more help from our allies by this point has been squashed. Media headlines focus on transatlantic squabbles regarding the Iraq war, but the overall strategic problem is that our European (and Asian and Latino) allies have dramatically reduced their available military power since the Cold War ended. The combined capacities of our allies are not even on a par with those of the US Marine Corps, just one of our armed services.

Soldiers and marines are facing their third tours in Iraq and Afghanistan—and historical evidence suggests that it is the third tour that begins to erode morale and reenlistment most seriously. Even if that conclusion cannot be proven, we must worry that at some point our remarkable men and women in uniform will begin to crack—the fact that they have been so resilient and dedicated to date does not demonstrate that they will keep going at the same pace forever. Soldiers, marines, and outside experts looking at areas throughout Iraq and Afghanistan declare that even this level of strain is not providing enough boots on the ground. The course of those conflicts bears out this notion: US forces in both countries are unable to provide security to the populations, an essential precondition for almost any successful counterinsurgency operation.

The prospect of defeat in Iraq and/or Afghanistan is daunting, and is exacerbated by the possibility of "breaking" the Army and the Marine Corps in the process (driving out so many people that those who remain lose heart, given the unreasonable demands on their time and their lives, producing an accelerating recruiting and retention crisis that, in turn, leaves the nation with no choice but the draft). These concerns should be at the forefront of any policy discussion about national security strategy today. But the mismatch between our military and our strategic situation is bigger than these immediate problems. Separate and apart from the wars in Iraq and Afghanistan, the US military would still be too small and wrongly organized for the challenges it can expect to face in the years to come.

To understand the full panoply of the challenges we might face beyond the current threats, it is worthwhile considering a number of plausible scenarios and the forces they would require. The purpose of this exercise is not to recommend precisely how they should be handled or how the military should be used. By forcing ourselves to look at what could go wrong in the world, the country can make informed decisions about its defense needs. The reader is cautioned, however, that helping to create any hope of sustainable stability in Iraq and Afghanistan is likely to require the continued deployment of well over a hundred thousand soldiers for several years to come, a fact to be considered when evaluating the additional threats described below.

The Future of the Two-War Planning Framework—and Future Military Contingencies for the United States

US defense planning since the end of the Cold War has been organized around the need to be prepared to fight two overlapping wars. In 2001 the George W. Bush administration modified the two-war concept somewhat, but kept much of the basic logic and the associated force structure (which Kagan has argued was, from the beginning, always inadequate to support the strategy).[1] In the aftermath of the overthrow of Saddam Hussein, further changes are now needed in America's armed forces and their undergirding defense strategy. The deterrent logic of being able to do more than one thing at a time is rock solid. If involved in one major conflict, and perhaps occupied in one or more smaller ongoing operations around the world, the United States also needs additional capability to deter other crises—as well as maintain its forward presence at bases around the world and on the seas, carry out joint exercises with allies, and handle smaller problems. The current conflict in Iraq highlights the limitations of our two-war force structure, since the US military is patently unable to contemplate another "major theater war" at the present with anything other than horror. But our inability to cope with such a scenario only increases the likelihood that one will emerge, as opportunistic enemies take advantage of our perceived weakness and overcommitment.

The scenarios considered below represent the types of possible operations that defense planners will need to consider in the coming years. We treat the need to be ready for war in Korea as a given, either in the less probable form of a North Korean invasion of the South or in the more likely event of a North Korean collapse. Less likely, but hard to rule out, is the possibility of an invasion of Iran—for example, if that country went to war against Israel as it also neared completion of a nuclear weapon. We do not include some missions that seem relatively less plausible—a hypothetical Russian threat to Europe; an American response to a possible Chinese threat against Siberia (even if Russia joined NATO, technically obliging the United States to respond to such an aggression in some way); and a Chinese overland threat to Korea, which seems extremely unlikely and is probably not a sound scenario for force planning purposes. Even if one excludes these scenarios, however, many remain.

Preventing Nuclear Catastrophe in South Asia

Of all the military scenarios that would undoubtedly involve the vital interests of the United States, short of a direct threat to its territory, a collapsed Pakistan ranks very high on the list. The combination of Islamic extremists and nuclear weapons in that country is extremely worrisome. Were parts of Pakistan's nuclear arsenal ever to fall into the wrong hands, Al Qaeda could conceivably gain access to a nuclear device with terrifying possible results. Another quite worrisome South Asia scenario could involve another Indo-Pakistani crisis leading to war between the two nuclear-armed states over Kashmir.

The Pakistani collapse scenario appears unlikely, given that country's relatively pro-Western and secular officer corps. But the intelligence services—which created the Taliban and also have condoned, if not abetted, Islamic extremists in Kashmir—are more of a wild card. In addition, the country as a whole is sufficiently infiltrated by fundamentalist groups—as the attempted assassinations against President Mubarak make clear—that this terrifying scenario of civil chaos must be taken seriously.[2]

Were this to occur, it is unclear what the United States and like-minded countries would or should do. It is very unlikely that "surgical strikes" could be conducted to destroy the nuclear weapons before extremists could make a grab at them. It is doubtful that the United States would know their location and at least as doubtful that any Pakistani government would countenance such a move, even under duress.

If a surgical strike, a series of surgical strikes, or commando-style raids were not possible, the only option might be to try to restore order before the weapons could be taken by extremists and transferred to terrorists. The United States and other outside powers might, for example, come to the aid of the Pakistani government, at its request, to help restore order. Alternatively, they might try to help protect Pakistan's borders (a nearly impossible task), making it hard to sneak nuclear weapons out of the country, while providing only technical support to the Pakistani armed forces as they tried to put down the insurrection. One thing is certain: given the enormous stakes, the United States would have to do anything it could to prevent nuclear weapons from getting into the wrong hands.

Should stabilization efforts be required, the scale of the undertaking could be breathtaking. Pakistan is a very large country. Its population is more than 150 million, or six times that of Iraq. Its land area is roughly twice that of Iraq; its perimeter is about 50 percent longer in total. Stabilizing a country of this size could easily require several times as many troops as the Iraq mission—a figure of up to one million is easy to imagine.

Of course, any international force would have local help. Presumably some fraction of Pakistan's security forces would remain intact, able, and willing to help defend the country. Pakistan's military numbers 550,000 Army troops; 70,000 uniformed personnel in the Air Force and Navy; another 510,000 reservists; and almost 300,000 gendarmes and Interior Ministry troops. But if some substantial fraction of the military broke off from the main body, say a quarter to a third, and was assisted by extremist militias, the international community might need to deploy 100,000 to 200,000 troops to ensure a quick restoration of order. Given the need for rapid response, the United States' share of this total would probably be over half—or as many as 50,000 to 100,000 ground forces—although this is almost the best of all the worst-case scenarios. Since no US government could simply decide to restrict its exposure in Pakistan if the international community proved unwilling or unable to provide numerous forces, or if the Pakistani collapse were deeper than outlined here, the United States might be compelled to produce significantly more forces to fend off the prospect of a nuclear Al Qaeda.

What about the scenario of war pitting Pakistan against India over Kashmir? It is highly doubtful that the United States would by choice take sides in such a conflict, actively allying with one country to defeat the other. US interests in the matter of who controls Kashmir are not sufficient to justify such intervention; no formal alliance commitments oblige the United States to step in. Moreover, the military difficulty of the operation would be extreme, in light of the huge armed forces arrayed on the subcontinent, coupled with the inland location and complex topography of Kashmir.

There are other ways in which foreign forces might become involved, however. If India and Pakistan went up to the verge of nuclear weapons use, or perhaps even crossed it, they might consider what was previously unthinkable to New Delhi in particular—pleading to the international community for help. For example, they might agree to accept international administration of Kashmir for a period of years. After local government was built up, and security services reformed, elections might then be held to determine the region's future political affiliation, leading to an eventual end of the trusteeship. While this scenario is admittedly a highly demanding one—and also unlikely in light of India's adamant objections to international involvement in the Kashmir issue—it is hard to dismiss such an approach out of hand if it seemed the only alternative to nuclear war on the subcontinent. Not only could such a war have horrendous human consequences, killing many tens of millions, and shattering the taboo on the use of nuclear weapons that is so essential to global stability today, it could also lead to the collapse of Pakistan—thus raising the same types of concerns about that country's nuclear weapons falling into the wrong hands that are discussed above.

What might a stabilization mission in Kashmir entail? The region is about twice the size of Bosnia in population, half the size of Iraq in population and land area. That suggests initial stabilization forces in the general range of 100,000, with the US contribution being perhaps 30,000 to 50,000. The mission would only make sense if India and Pakistan truly welcomed it, so there would be little point in deploying a force large enough to hold its own against resistance by one of those countries. But robust monitoring of border regions, as well as capable counterinsurgent/counterterrorist strike forces, would be core to any such mission.

Stabilizing a Large Country Such as Indonesia or Congo

To consider the strategic implications of another scenario, what about the possibility of severe unrest in one of the world's large countries, such as Indonesia or Congo or Nigeria? At present, such problems are generally seen as being of secondary strategic importance to the United States, meaning that Washington may support and help fund a peacekeeping mission under some circumstances but will rarely commit troops —and certainly will not deploy a muscular forcible intervention.

This reluctance could well fade in the face of factors that compound the dangers. For example, if Al Qaeda or an associated terrorist group began to develop a sanctuary akin to Afghanistan in a given large country, the United States might—depending on circumstances—consider overthrowing that country's government or at least helping the government reclaim control over the part of its territory occupied by the terrorists. Or, it might intervene to help one side in a civil war against another. For example, if the schism between the police and armed forces in Indonesia worsened, and one of the two institutions wound up working with an Al Qaeda offshoot, the United States might accept an invitation from the moderate half of the government to help defeat the other half, along with the terrorist organization in question.[3] Or, if a terrorist organization was tolerated in Indonesia, the United States might strike at it directly. Such action might be taken if, say, the terrorist group took control of land near a major shipping lane in the Indonesian Straits, or if it simply decided to use part of Indonesia for sanctuary.[4]

Clearly, the requirement for international forces would be a function of the degree of instability in the country in question, how intact the indigenous forces remained, and how large any militia or insurgent force proved to be. For illustrative purposes, if a large fraction of Indonesia, or all of Congo, were to become ungovernable, the problem could be twice to three times the scale of the Iraq mission. It could be five times the scale of Iraq if it involved trying to restore order throughout Nigeria, though the monumental scale of such an operation might nudge planners toward more modest objectives—such as trying to stabilize areas where major ethnic or religious groups come into direct contact.

General guidelines for force planning for such scenarios would suggest foreign troop strength up to 100,000 to 200,000 personnel, in rough numbers. That makes them not unlike the scenario of a collapsing or fracturing Pakistan. For these missions that do not affect vital strategic interests, certainly as compared with those considered in South Asia, the US contribution might only be 20 to 30 percent of the total, rather than the 50 percent assumed above. But even so, up to two to three American divisions could be required.

Contending With a Coup in Saudi Arabia

How should the United States respond if a coup, presumably fundamentalist in nature, were to overthrow the royal family in Saudi Arabia? Such an event would raise the specter of major disruption to the oil economy. Saudi Arabia, along with the United States and Russia, is one of the world's big three oil producers (in the range of 9 million barrels of oil a day), and is the largest oil exporter (7 million barrels per day, about 20 percent of the world total). It also has by far the world's largest estimated oil reserves (260 billion barrels, or nearly a quarter of the world total). A sustained cutoff in Saudi oil production would wreak havoc with the world economy.

But a coup in Saudi Arabia would raise additional worries, some even worse. They would include the harrowing possibility of Saudi pursuit of nuclear weapons. An intensified funneling of Saudi funds to Al Qaeda and the madrasas in countries such as Pakistan would also likely result. This type of scenario has been discussed for at least two decades and remains of concern today—perhaps even more so given the surge of terrorist violence in Saudi Arabia in recent years, as well as the continued growth and hostile ideology of Al Qaeda, along with the broader Wahhabi movement.

What military scenarios might result in such circumstances? If a fundamentalist regime came to power and became interested in acquiring nuclear weapons, the

United States might have to consider carrying out forcible regime change. If, by contrast, the regime was more intent on disrupting the oil economy, more limited measures (such as seizing the oil fields) might be adequate. Indeed, it might be feasible not to do anything at first, and hope that the new regime gradually realized the benefits of reintegrating Saudi Arabia at least partially into the global oil economy. But in the end, the United States and other Western countries may very well consider using force. That could happen, for example, if the new regime refused over a long period to pump oil or, worse yet, if it began destroying the oil infrastructure and damaging the oil wells on its territory—perhaps out of a fundamentalist commitment to turn back the historical clock to the first millennium. Since virtually all Saudi oil is in the eastern coastal zones or in Saudi territorial waters in the Persian Gulf, a military mission to protect and operate the oil wells would have a geographic finiteness to it. The United States and its partners might then put the proceeds from oil sales into escrow for a future Saudi government that was prepared to make good use of them.

Saudi Arabia has a population nearly as large as Iraq's—some 21 million—and is more than four times the geographic size of Iraq. Its military numbers 125,000, including 75,000 Army troops, as well as another 75,000 personnel in the National Guard. However, it is not clear, in the aftermath of a successful fundamentalist coup, whether many of these military units would remain intact—or which side of any future war they would choose to back, should a US-led outside force intervene after a coup.

Some standard rules of thumb can help calculate the force requirements for this type of mission. Eastern Saudi Arabia is not heavily populated, but there are several mid-sized population centers in the coastal oil zone.[5] In proportion to the million or so people living in that region, about 10,000 foreign troops could be required for policing. Ensuing troop demands would not be inordinate.

However, requirements could be much greater if a robust defensive perimeter is needed to protect against incursions by raiders. There is no good rule for sizing forces based on the amount of territory to defend. Joshua Epstein's classic rule that one division is needed for roughly every 25 kilometers is clearly excessive in this case. Indeed, it took only several brigades of American forces to secure most of the 350 miles of supply lines in Iraq, which passed through a number of populated regions and significant cities. Thus a modern American division could, if patrolling an open area and making use of modern sensors and aircraft, surely cover 100 to 200 miles of front. Combining these missions would call for a total of some three American-sized divisions, plus support, for a sustained operation to secure the coastal regions of Saudi Arabia. The resulting total force strength might be 100,000 to 150,000 personnel.

The Forces We Need

As we see, a quick review of some of the potential crises that might require the use of American military power turns up several that would demand the prolonged deployment of US forces as large as or larger than those currently in Iraq and Afghanistan, even on fairly optimistic assumptions. There are many other potential problems, including the challenges identified at the beginning of this section in Iran and North Korea. Iran, a country of nearly 70 million people, could well demand an American commitment of hundreds of thousands of soldiers in worst-case scenarios of regime collapse or regime change; force requirements of 200,000–300,000 are highly likely even in fairly optimistic scenarios for a war with Iran.

The point of this assessment is not to advocate any particular approach to any of these problems. The solution would have to be tailored to fit the precise circumstances of each crisis. But this survey highlights the potential challenges ahead. At a bare minimum, these scenarios point toward a lasting floor lower than the current level of American ground forces in the future; however, for present planning, together with the ongoing strains of Iraq and Afghanistan, they argue for a larger force.

In the past two decades, the majority of significant American combat operations have required the long-term deployment of US soldiers, marines, sailors, and airmen long past the end of major combat. US forces remained in Panama after the 1989 operation there; they were in and around Iraq for 12 years after Operation Desert Storm; deployments continued in Bosnia for a decade after the Dayton Accords; forces were stationed in Kosovo after the 1999 attack on Slobodan Milošević; and, of course, American troops have been in Afghanistan since 2001 and Iraq since 2003. The only two significant operations that did not see a prolonged post-conflict deployment were the debacle in Somalia in 1993 and the peaceful regime change in Haiti in 1994. Both were utter failures. Expanding the historical horizon only sharpens the point. Consider America's major deployments in Germany and Japan after World War II, in Korea after 1953, and even in the former Confederate States after the Civil War. Protracted post-war deployments are more common than not, and often absolutely essential to success, especially in regime-change operations. Any responsible US national security policy must provide forces adequate to this challenge.

The coauthors' long-term visions for the proper size of the American Army and Marine Corps, active duty and reserve elements, are not identical. In new circumstances, we might wind up disagreeing fairly sharply over how many ground forces the United States would require, as we have in the past. But at this moment in history, we agree completely about the immediate need—both the Army and Marine Corps must grow, as fast as is practically possible, for the foreseeable future. Indeed, the change is badly overdue and, as a result, increasingly hard to accomplish. But we must take every possible step in this direction, regardless of our belated start.

Manpower or Technology

Of course, the current national security debate is not simply over the appropriate size of the armed forces but also about how they are structured and equipped. Since the early 1990s, senior military and civilian leaders and outside analysts have argued that the armed forces must "transform" themselves to meet challenges of the future. The emphasis on transformation was for a long time technological: the military must invest in information technologies, including the means to identify, track, and destroy targets with precision-guided munitions from stand-off distances. As the decade progressed, the Army accepted this requirement for its own forces but began also to emphasize another aspect of transformation: the need for greater strategic mobility. An M-1 tank weighs 70 tons, and only one can be flown in a vast C-5 or C-17 airlifter at a time. Since many of the scenarios under consideration in the 1990s focused on the need to get large ground forces to distant theaters quickly and with no warning, this situation seemed unacceptable. Army transformation therefore began to include a reliance on long-range precision munitions to compensate for the vulnerability of the more lightly armored vehicles that were being built to be moved to distant conflicts more quickly. In the wake of September 11, 2001, transformation changed its meaning once again. Today, for many, it means the reliance on American Special Forces and air power to assist indigenous troops in their own struggle, avoiding the use of large numbers of American soldiers and marines. The epitome of this kind of war was the operation in Afghanistan in 2001–2002, which some held up as the model to be used in Iraq in 2003 and beyond.

All of these transformation initiatives are expensive, even when they emphasize modern electronics and automation technologies that are relatively affordable, or increases in American Special Forces involving relatively modest numbers of people. When vehicles are systematically replaced, as they inevitably must be, the bills can go through the roof. Reequipping the ground forces, purchasing advanced fighter-bomber aircraft for the Air Force and Navy, redesigning future Navy vessels to maximize their ability to hit distant targets precisely—all of this is extraordinarily expensive. The defense community owes the country vigorous debate over the latter, very costly types of proposed changes, since they may not always be worth the money. But many of the changes are necessary in order to outpace the capabilities of potential foes and deal with the dangerous world in which we find ourselves. The M-1 tank was designed in the early 1970s. It will not remain survivable on the battle-fields of the future, and its weight and fuel inefficiency are significant problems. The F-22, for all its flaws, replaces a generation of aircraft designed in the 1960s. The United States has not fielded a new design for a major surface combatant vessel since the AEGIS cruiser system in the 1970s. The "procurement holiday" of the 1990s, when the services largely avoided large-scale purchases or development of new weapons systems, compounded the problem. In addition, new technologies, of course, really do provide new opportunities, both for the United States and for our enemies. We must exploit them properly if we are to maintain the military predominance so essential to our security.

Some of these weapons programs may be less than crucial or excessively large and ambitious, to be sure, and nothing about our argument here precludes the idea of fully debating each and every one. If some are further curbed, the savings might pay for part of our recommended increases. But our central point here is that the needs for military personnel are so compelling and immediate that the issue of how to pay for them must not postpone a commitment to do so.

Moreover, if there was any doubt, Iraq proves technology will not let us cut back on people. Other recent operations in Afghanistan (as well as Bosnia, Kosovo, Panama, and so on) also revealed the ineffectiveness of attempting to replace people with machines on a large scale. In most of the post-conflict stabilization (or counter-insurgency) operations we have seen or can foresee, there can be no substitute for large numbers of trained and capable ground forces, deployed for a long time.

It is unacceptable, therefore, simply to demand a zero-sum soldiers-versus-systems trade-off in the defense budget. Prioritizing systems at the expense of soldiers has had dreadful consequences. If we overcompensate by now doing the reverse, it would store up enormous danger for the future. The truth is that the nation is at war now, the strategic horizon is very dark, and armed forces that were seized in the strategic pause of the 1990s are inadequate today. Transformation must proceed, possibly with a change in its intellectual basis and its precise course, and the ground forces must be expanded significantly. Meeting both requirements will demand increased defense expenditures for many years into the future, although there are some approaches we could pursue to mitigate that increase. But whatever the cost, a nation at war and in a dangerous world must maintain military forces adequate to protect its vital interests, or else face an intolerable degree of national insecurity.

Expanding the Ground Forces

The current military transformation program rests on a number of assumptions about the nature of war that have come increasingly into question in recent years. The priority placed on gathering and disseminating targeting data and striking the targets thereby identified has proven clearly inadequate in complex urban, post-conflict, counterinsurgent, and stabilization operations. New approaches focusing on the close interconnection between politics and military operations hold more promise, although the precise implications of these new approaches remain unclear. There will certainly be a vigorous debate over the coming years about the intellectual basis for further military transformation, on which we will not expand.

The urgent need to focus on the expansion of America's ground forces comes not merely from the mismatch between the force and real-world conditions. It also results from the fact that this problem has been played down in defense discussions and has not received the careful consideration it requires. Secretary of Defense Robert Gates has now wisely reversed Secretary Rumsfeld's adamant opposition to increases in the ground forces, proposing an overall increase of 92,000 relative to previous normal levels (although the increase totals only about 65,000 relative to actual levels today, which include some temporary wartime increases from emergency supplemental bills).

It is extremely difficult to estimate the precise number of additional ground forces required, since such estimates must rely on scenario-dependent calculations of the potential threats and challenges of various states around the world, as well as information not readily available to outside analysts. Really counting all the beans —in this case, all of the combat and support troops of all varieties necessary to have the capabilities outlined above—would require a cadre of analysts and is beyond the scope of an essay of this variety. There is nevertheless broad agreement in Washington policy circles about the need for a substantial increase in the ground forces, and we feel comfortable arguing that the United States now needs at least 100,000 additional active duty soldiers and marines, more than proposed by Secretary Gates. But even more important than such an overall goal is the need to start moving in the right direction, immediately, and as rapidly as recruiting constraints allow. The war in Iraq by itself demonstrates the need for an increase of this magnitude—even extensive (some might say excessive) reliance on National Guard and Reserve forces has required the Army to cycle troops through combat zones every other year, rather than being deployed every third year, with the traditional training cycle of two years back on the base in the US. That is to say nothing of the fact that the Army had almost immediately to change the rotational policy itself from the six-month tours standard in the 1990s to yearlong tours. Even with the additional 30,000 active duty troops temporarily authorized until now, the task of maintaining about 120,000 Army soldiers in Iraq for three years—a challenge on the low end of the many plausible scenarios we may face in the future—has been devastating to the force.

How Do We Get There?

Suggestions that the ground forces be enlarged are almost immediately countered by the assertion that they cannot be. Some senior retired officers point to demographic trends to show that there will simply not be enough healthy young men and women willing to serve. Others point to difficulties the services are already having in finding recruits of acceptable standards.

The conversation almost immediately drifts toward the need to reintroduce conscription. We argue that assertions about the impossibility of increasing the volunteer forces are unfounded, and that it would be catastrophic both militarily and politically to reintroduce conscription. We will consider this second, more emotionally charged issue first.

Should We Restore the Draft?

As casualty tolls have continued to mount in Iraq, active forces have been heavily deployed, and frequent call-ups of troops from the National Guard and Reserve have placed unusual strains on many of the nation's citizen soldiers. Some individuals have called for a return to military conscription. Congressman Charles Rangel of New York and former Senator Fritz Hollings of South Carolina even introduced a bill in Congress that would restore the draft. And one of Congress's most respected military veterans, Senator Chuck Hagel of Nebraska, has called for a serious national debate about the idea. Despite some allegations to the contrary by activist organizations during the last presidential campaign, there has certainly been no serious planning for the possibility of a draft within the Department of Defense in the modern era. Whatever the state of planning, the question remains—does a draft make sense? The short answer is no, given the outstanding quality of the all-volunteer force, which would surely be compromised by any plan to restore military conscription, and the impossibility of designing a fair system of military conscription. However, a more complete discussion of the pros and cons is warranted.

It is important to note that America is indeed making far greater demands on some individuals than others in the war on terror. Of course, at one level this is always true. Those who wind up being killed in war, and their families who are left behind, make the ultimate sacrifice, with those who are physically and psychologically wounded in combat and those who care for them also suffering enormous burdens. Current policies amplify this set of circumstances. In particular, the fact that the military is all-volunteer, combined with the fact that certain regions of the country and certain parts of society contribute disproportionately to that force, raise specific concerns. Among other anxieties, some now argue that policy elites, less likely than before to have themselves served in the armed forces or to have children who are presently serving, have become less sensitive to the human costs of the possible use of force.

These are indeed valid concerns. It is not a desirable thing for the country when an increasing share of total military personnel comes from certain geographic regions, ethnic groups, or economic sectors of society.[6] On the whole, a much smaller percent of today's population shows any interest in ever considering military service than has historically been the case.[7] And, of course, far fewer lawmakers today have military experience than during the Cold War.[8] In some ways the fact that only a modest fraction of the population wishes to serve is just as well. The modern American military is smaller than it has been in decades, even as population has continued to expand, so there is not room for everyone within the armed forces. But having large swaths of the country's population effectively elect out of military service cannot be good for the nation's cohesion. It is also troublesome that, even in the aftermath of the September 11 attacks, most Americans have made little or no sacrifice in financial terms—even having their taxes cut in the face of large war supplemental appropriations and mounting deficits.

That said, the draft is not the answer. For one thing, the fact that certain groups serve disproportionately in the military also means that the military offers opportunities to people who need them. The military, while not without its problems of discrimination and prejudice, is also now among the most progressive institutions in America providing many of the best opportunities for minorities and the economically disadvantaged.[9] Society indeed asks a great deal of its military personnel, especially in the context of an ongoing war in Afghanistan and another in Iraq. But it also compensates them better than ever before—with pay, health care, educational opportunities, retirement pay, and the chance to learn skills within the armed forces that are often highly marketable thereafter. These various forms of compensation are quite high by historical standards, and have eliminated any hint of a military-civilian pay gap except in certain relatively rare cases. Indeed, today's enlisted military personnel are now generally compensated considerably more generously than individuals of similar age and experience and educational background working in the private sector, once health and retirement benefits are factored in.[10]

A few facts and figures back up these assertions—and also underscore that today's military, while including some groups more than others, is not dramatically unrepresentative, racially or otherwise. Enlisted personnel in the current American military are about 62 percent white, 22 percent African American (reflecting a fairly steady level since the early 1980s), 10 percent Hispanic, and 6 percent other races. In addition, minorities do not make up a disproportionate share of the personnel in the most dangerous jobs. For example, of the Army's 45,600 enlisted infantrymen in early 2003, only 10.6 percent were black.[11]

The notion that conscription would somehow redress this mythical disproportion within the ground forces misses the central difficulty with conscription in the modern era: far too many young men (and women) come of military age every year than could possibly be accommodated within a military of reasonable size. In fact, about 2.1 million young men turn 18 every year. Conscripting even 20 percent of them for, say, 24 months at a time would generate ground forces of well over a million people, when the permanent professional officer corps and the percentage of women are factored in. The corollary is that only one in five young men would be *required* to serve, a fact that would generate an enormous sense of injustice. It was precisely that sense of draft "winners" and "losers" that helped destroy conscription so rapidly in the early 1970s. Attempting to reinstitute it in a similarly "unfair" way during another war would create a similar political backlash, as well as severely damaging the current military capabilities of the armed forces.

One must be careful not to break an institution in the process of purportedly fixing it. The US military is probably the most impressive in history—not only in terms of its technology but also the quality of its personnel, their basic soldiering abilities, and their other skills in fields ranging from piloting to computing to equipment maintenance to engineering to linguistics to civil affairs. Those who doubt this assertion need only review the decisiveness of recent American military victories in a range of combat scenarios, as well as the professionalism of US forces in post-conflict environments.[12]

With no disrespect intended to those who served in earlier generations, today's US military is far superior to the conscripted forces of the past. Today's soldier, marine, airman, airwoman, or sailor typically has a high school degree and some college experience, several years of experience in the military, and a sincere commitment to the profession he or she has chosen. Contrast that with the 10- to 24-month tours of duty that are inevitable in most draft systems, the small fraction of time that leaves for a trained soldier to be in an operationally deployable unit, and the resulting mediocre quality of militaries that are still dependent on the draft (as in a number of European countries).

Moreover, the frequently heard assertion that policymakers have become casualty insensitive is exaggerated. It was only a half decade ago when the nation was purported to have the opposite problem, an extreme oversensitivity to casualties that prevented the country from considering decisive military actions that its national security required—helping create a perception of American weakness that allegedly emboldened some adversaries.[13]

Some day, this assessment of the merits of a draft could change. The most likely cause would be an overuse of the all-volunteer force, particularly in the Army and Marine Corps, that led to an exodus of volunteers and a general perception among would-be recruits that service had become far less appealing. Clearly, a sustained period of high casualties in Iraq or another place would exacerbate any such problem as well. At that point, to maintain a viable military, the nation might have no option but to consider the draft—though in an era of high technology and highly skilled armed forces, such a policy would surely create as many problems as it solved.

Since the draft is not an option, or at least not a good one, we will have to be creative if we even wish to "grow the force" by 25,000 or more a year. The Army is already bending previous rules on age, aptitude, criminal record, and physical capabilities to meet current targets. More of this may be feasible, but we will need fresher approaches as well. A serious idea worthy of consideration, as proposed by author and analyst Max Boot, is to promise American citizenship to worthy foreigners who first agree to serve in the US armed forces.

Mitigating the Cost

While protecting the nation's security is perhaps the single weightiest responsibility of our political leaders, fiscal responsibility—ensuring the nation's prosperity, and maintaining good stewardship of the national budget—is not far behind. In fact, if handled irresponsibly, they could ultimately harm the nation's security by leaving it unable to defend its global interests. Moreover, for every dollar wasted, government deprives itself of the means to provide for the education, health care, day-to-day safety against crime, and other needs of the American citizenry, jeopardizing lives every bit as much as it would if it let down the national defense against foreign threats. To be sure, other actors within the United States share responsibility for the nation's domestic tranquility and economic well-being, whereas the federal government bears the exclusive burden of providing for the national defense. But defense policymakers, like anyone else, still have a responsibility to propose policy frameworks that do not misallocate or outright waste money.

In this spirit, we propose several categories of defense reforms that merit further attention. Given space constraints, they are only sketched out here. We take them seriously, and encourage policymakers to do so as well. But two caveats need to be borne in mind. First, the magnitude of the net savings we propose here—some $10 billion to $15 billion a year—will not begin to pay for all the parts of the defense budget that need to be increased. Continued real defense spending increases will still be needed in the future. Second, the case for our proposed increases is even more urgent than the case for savings. In particular, increasing the size of the nation's ground forces cannot be held hostage to achieving the savings we recommend. Ideally, reforms should be adopted promptly as well, but they should not be viewed as the literal sources of funding for the most critical new defense initiatives we discuss in these pages.

Emphasizing Advanced Electronics and
Computers in Defense Modernization

One reason the Pentagon budget is slated to grow so much in coming years has to do with buying weaponry. Some of the upward pressure comes from high-profile issues such as missile defense. Most, however, comes from the main combat systems of the military services, which are generally wearing out.

Despite President Bush's campaign promise in 1999/2000 to "skip a generation" of weaponry, his Pentagon has canceled only three major weapon systems—the Navy's lower-altitude missile defense program, the Army's Crusader howitzer (which was not even especially expensive), and more recently the Army's Comanche helicopter. Although procurement budgets must continue rising, the rapid increases envisioned in current plans are not essential. Economies can almost certainly be found through expanded applications of modestly priced technologies, such as the precision weapons, unmanned vehicles, and communications systems used so effectively in Afghanistan and Iraq.

A more discriminating and economy-minded modernization strategy would equip only part—not most or all—of the armed forces with extremely sophisticated and expensive weaponry. That high-end component would hedge against new possibilities, such as an unexpectedly rapid modernizing of the Chinese armed forces. The rest of the US military establishment would be equipped primarily with relatively inexpensive upgrades of existing weaponry, including better sensors, munitions, computers, and communications systems. This approach would also envision, over the longer term, greater use of unmanned platforms and other new concepts and capabilities, while being patient about when to deploy them. But even if adopted, this approach would not lead to cuts in procurement spending (which must continue to rise since we enjoyed a "procurement holiday" in the 1990s that must end as equipment ages and requires refurbishment or replacement). It will simply slow the rate of increase.

Privatization and Reform

All defense planners endeavor to save money in the relatively low-profile parts of the Pentagon budget known as operations and maintenance. These accounts, which pay for a wide range of activities such as training, overseas deployments, upkeep of equipment, military base operations, and health care costs—in short, for near-term military readiness—have been rising fast in recent years, and it will be hard to stop the upward trend.[14]

The base closure process, still playing out, has been a successful framework for avoiding waste and inefficiency in the nation's military base network. As bases continue to close in the years ahead, it will generate more savings—but not more than a few billion dollars in annual savings once complete: significant money certainly, but not huge by Pentagon standards. On the other hand, increases in the size of the ground forces, combined with the redeployment of US forces from Europe and Korea that is already under way, may end up requiring more base infrastructure than is currently foreseen. Selling it now and buying it later will generate much greater waste and inefficiency over the long term, so that this area of defense reform requires considerable care and more forward-thinking than it has so far received.

Overhauling military health care services by merging the independent health plans of each military service and introducing a small copayment for military personnel and their families could save $2 billion per year.[15] Other savings in operations and maintenance are possible. For example, encouraging local base commanders to economize by letting them keep some of the savings for their base activities could save a billion dollars a year or more within a decade.[16]

All that said, the activities funded by these accounts are crucial to national security and have proved tough to cap or contain. Privatization is no panacea; it takes time, sometimes raises various complicated issues about deploying civilians to wartime environments, and generally saves much less than its warmest advocates attest.[17] Often it leads to increases in the size of civilian personnel payrolls funded out of the defense budget without reducing uniformed strength—potentially thereby increasing, not reducing, total costs.

Many other possible savings can and should be found in a bureaucracy as large as the Pentagon, and they can help offset the high cost of repairing and transforming the nation's armed forces. But that repair and transformation are absolute priorities and cannot be put off without seriously endangering our national security now and into the future.

The United States is deeply unpopular in world public opinion, especially in Europe and much of the Islamic world, and Americans are understandably frustrated and saddened by a war in Iraq that is not going well, with a tragic human toll. For some, this frustration leads to discouragement over the US international role and desire to turn inward. But at such a time, Americans must remember two things. First, for all of our faults, and for all the controversies over recent American foreign policy, the United States still leads the greatest alliance system in human history, with some 60 nations and 75 percent of the planet's collective economic strength linked in some type of military partnership with the United States. This is a good thing, for it helps organize and stabilize the international order, making even countries such as China willing to accept American global leadership for the economic rewards and other benefits it brings. Second, there are threats to this global order, but they are threats we can generally do something about at affordable cost.

To be sure, defense planners and security specialists owe the country sound advice about how to do so economically, and about how to deploy force judiciously and carefully and effectively—though our past record is mixed. But we can afford to do what is needed to protect our security and global interests.

Notes

1 While Kagan advocates a return to the planning assumptions in the two-war framework as it stood previously, O'Hanlon supports the modifications made by the current administration.

2 See Sumit Ganguly, *Conflict Unending: India-Pakistan Tensions Since 1947* (New York: Columbia University Press, 2001); Stephen Philip Cohen, *The Idea of Pakistan* (Washington: Brookings, 2004), pp. 97–130; and International Crisis Group, *Unfulfilled Promises: Pakistan's Failure to Tackle Extremism* (Brussels, 2004).

3 On Indonesia, see Robert Karniol, "Country Briefing: Indonesia," *Jane's Defence Weekly*, April 7, 2004, pp. 47–52.

4 Andrew F. Krepinevich Jr., *The Conflict Environment of 2016: A Scenario-Based Approach* (Washington: Center for Strategic and Budgetary Assessment, 1996), pp. 23–27.

5 Thomas L. McNaugher, *Arms and Oil: U.S. Military Strategy and the Persian Gulf* (Washington: Brookings Institution, 1985), pp. 1–18, 160–206.

6 Ole R. Holsti, "A Widening Gap between the U.S. Military and Civilian Society? Some Evidence, 1976–1996," *International Security*, Vol. 23, No. 3, Winter 1998/99, p. 13.

7 David C. King and Zachary Karabell, *The Generation of Trust: How the U.S. Military Has Regained the Public's Confidence Since Vietnam* (Washington: American Enterprise Institute, 2003), p. 44.

8 Center for Strategic and International Studies, *American Military Culture in the Twenty-First Century* (Washington, 2000), pp. 32–33.

9 King and Karabell, *The Generation of Trust.*

10 Adebayo Adedeji, *Educational Attainment and Compensation of Enlisted Personnel* (Washington: Congressional Budget Office, 2004), p. 14.

11 On the latter figure, see Dave Moniz and Tom Squitieri, "Front-Line Troops Disproportionately White, Not Black," *USA TODAY*, January 21, 2003, p. 1. The officer corps is 8.3 percent African American and about 4 percent Hispanic, meaning that minority officer representation is far from proportional to the racial profile of the enlisted force, but much greater than for many other professions in the United States. The officer corps is also highly educated, with 91 percent holding at least a bachelor's degree and 11 percent of the total a higher degree as well. The enlisted force consists of 95 percent high school graduates and 5 percent GED equivalent degree holders. See Department of Defense, *Population Representation in the Military Services* (2001), available at *www.defenselink.mil/prhome/poprep2001/chapter3/chapter3_6.htm.*

12 For a good overview of how one US military service improved dramatically after Vietnam, see Robert H. Scales, Jr., *Certain Victory: The U.S. Army in the Gulf War* (Washington: Brassey's, 1994), pp. 1–38.

13 For a review of the debate of that time, see Steven Kull and I. M. Destler, *Misreading the Public: The Myth of a New Isolationism* (Washington: Brookings, 1999), pp. 81–112.

14 Gregory T. Kiley, *The Effects of Aging on the Costs of Operating and Maintaining Military Equipment* (Washington: Congressional Budget Office, 2001); Amy Belasco, *Paying for Military Readiness and Upkeep: Trends in Operation and Maintenance Spending* (Washington: Congressional Budget Office, 1997).

15 See Ellen Breslin-Davidson, *Restructuring Military Medical Care* (Washington: Congressional Budget Office, 1995); Russell Beland, *Accrual Budgeting for Military Retirees' Health Care* (Washington: Congressional Budget Office, 2002).

16 Robert F. Hale, *Promoting Efficiency in the Department of Defense: Keep Trying, But Be Realistic* (Washington: Center for Strategic and Budgetary Assessments, 2002).

17 P. W. Singer, *Corporate Warriors: The Rise of the Privatized Military Industry* (Ithaca, NY: Cornell University Press, 2003).

6

A Full-Court Press Against Nuclear Anarchy

Stephen E. Biegun and
Jon B. Wolfsthal

What Is the Nuclear Threat?

A small-yield nuclear weapon detonates near the White House. How often have we wondered whether this might happen or worried that it will happen? What have we done to prepare in case it should happen? And most critically, have we done all that we could do—and would do, with the benefit of hindsight—to make sure it does not happen? These are the questions we must address, as will many future generations of Americans, unless urgent action is taken now.

What is it about nuclear proliferation that really troubles us? Is it the challenge to American power that comes from a weaker adversary acquiring the ultimate asymmetric threat? Is it the degree to which the possession of "the bomb" makes a small state potentially impervious to our pressure, challenge, or threat? Is it the concern that the weapon will be used by another nation or a terrorist movement against our friends or allies—with devastating human consequences and the realignment of regional power structures? Or, is it the deep, chilling fear that it will be used against us, destroying in a single flash of fire and devastation our people, our homes, our industry, and our economy, shaking the fabric of our nation to its very core and perhaps permanently altering the fate of our nation? It is, of course, all of the above.

Concern about proliferation is not a phenomenon peculiar to the 20th century, nor is it limited to the spread of nuclear weapons. Civilizations across the millennia have been challenged by the spread of technologies and weapons that have altered the relative power of adversaries and even at times raised the specter of existential threats.

The long bow, gunpowder, the rifle, modern battleships, air power, over-the-horizon combat systems, and stealth technology, to name only a few, have revolutionized military capabilities and changed the course of history—for better and for worse. Today's proliferation threats—nuclear, biological, chemical and, to a lesser degree, missiles—may appear to us much more consequential than any in the past, but that is because our unprecedented power has blunted all other threats. We are so militarily strong at this moment that nothing besides weapons of mass destruction (WMD) threatens our existence.

While the proliferation of any WMD poses significant threats and challenges to the United States, it is the nuclear threat which today is the most grave and one that requires an urgent response. Chemical weapons are horrendous in their effect and, if deployed for maximum damage, can cause severe casualties whether used by terrorists or on a battlefield. Yet chemical weapons can also be defended against, remediation is within our capabilities, and ultimately their value as a weapon is limited to tactical or terrorist purposes.

Biological weapons are undoubtedly capable of causing far more damage than chemical weapons. It is even conceivable that the casualties from a biological weapon attack could exceed those of a nuclear blast. The human toll, the economic consequences, and the difficult remediation from a biological attack put these weapons in contention as potentially the most dangerous for the United States. But ultimately, people will be able to recover from any biological weapons attack. This is not to minimize the threat of biological weapons or deny the fact that, unlike chemical weapons, they can be used as a strategic weapon. Nonetheless, with biological weapons there is a prospect of recovery and remediation, a hope that after the attack itself has run its course, the consequences can be limited and, in some cases, even prevented or reversed.

The comparative permanence of a nuclear weapons attack's impact makes this, for us, the gravest threat we face as a nation. In a split second, the blast from a nuclear weapon could destroy every structure within its range. Every living creature within the blast would be incinerated. The immediate area of the blast would be so thoroughly irradiated that it would be uninhabitable for long periods of time. The secondary consequences from radioactive fallout, economic disruption, and perhaps even the decapitation of the US government would be incalculable. The devastation would carry across generations and the nation would be fundamentally altered.

Any assessment of this threat begins with the question of identifying the international actors that have the wherewithal to acquire a nuclear weapon. Today nine countries are known to have nuclear weapons: the United States, Russia, the United Kingdom, France, China, Israel, India, Pakistan, and North Korea. Iran is aggressively pursuing a nuclear weapon capability, and others in the Middle East, confronted by the regional implications of Iran's nuclear weapons program, are actively considering their nuclear options. This latter group includes Turkey, Egypt, Saudi Arabia, and other Gulf States. Add to this list the more than 40 states that possess either weapon-usable nuclear materials, the means to produce such materials, or the technical capability to produce nuclear weapons in weeks, months, or years.

In addition to the known and prospective nuclear powers, there are the nonstate actors. Terrorist movements, especially Al Qaeda, have long expressed a wish to acquire any kind of nuclear device. Rogue and criminal elements within the established nuclear powers have surely contemplated how they would acquire and profit from a nuclear weapon stolen from their nation's arsenal. It is entirely plausible that as North Korea—and perhaps Iran—acquire nuclear weapons, the difficulty of transferring them to terrorist movements will be eased substantially. And if a terrorist movement were to acquire a nuclear device, it is almost certain that the constraint on its use will be lowered even more.

Ultimately, there are many scenarios for how a nuclear weapon could be acquired for use against the United States. One possibility would be the transfer—intentional or otherwise—of a nuclear device from Iran, North Korea, or Pakistan to a terrorist organization. Also feasible is the theft and transfer of a weapon from Russia's nuclear arsenal. A terrorist movement might also acquire materials to build their own nuclear weapon from any of the aforementioned countries or some other source, though this would require additional equipment and know-how. At the less likely end of the spectrum would be the theft of a weapon from the other nuclear powers—the United States itself, China, France, the United Kingdom, or Israel. Finally, the threat of a nuclear exchange among the nuclear powers themselves cannot be dismissed, perhaps precipitated by some regional conflict or other unforeseeable sharp rise in tensions. It is ironic that, given the Cold War preoccupation with possible war between the major nuclear powers, this latter scenario seems to be the least alarming of all the potential threats.

Considering which governments have recently acquired or are actively seeking a nuclear weapon, and understanding the likelihood that a nuclear-armed terrorist movement might not be far behind, it is impossible to avoid the sense that we are losing control of nuclear weapons proliferation. Priorities for action must be identified right away. Policymakers must assess where the threats are greatest and where the proliferation chain is most vulnerable, and clarify what steps must be taken immediately and what can wait in order to formulate an effective response. At this juncture, no good idea should be put aside, and every element of policy must be vigorously reenergized—from multilateral diplomacy to military preemption. The consequences of failure are too catastrophic to approach the issue with anything less than the utmost urgency.

Why Do States and Terrorist Groups Want the Bomb?

Another key to understanding the proliferation challenge is to focus on why states seek nuclear weapon capabilities. For the most part, states seek to acquire nuclear weapons for security purposes. From the Manhattan Project to North Korea's nuclear efforts (and numerous cases in between), security motives have traditionally been at the core of nuclear development efforts. Some motives have been defensive, with states seeking to acquire nuclear weapons to deter an attack by an adversary, while others have sought to enhance their security by using nuclear weapons to demonstrate their power and wield influence. While some countries have sought nuclear weapons for their global security interests, others have focused on regional security problems or imbalances.

For states outside the international economic or legal mainstream, nuclear weapons acquisition is sometimes a means of achieving general political goals, helping to fend off any outside interference in their plans. Sometimes the aim of such "rogue states" is to alter the regional or global balance of power. Yet even in these cases, it is ultimately a quest for security (to shield a regime from any countering actions) that underlies the interest in nuclear weapons.

The acquisition of nuclear weapons by any new state poses a threat to the security of the United States, affecting our ability to protect the United States, our allies, or our national interests. In some cases, such as North Korea and Iran, this is a key part of their desire to acquire a nuclear capability: to affect US security calculations. While other potential proliferators may not present a direct or as immediate a challenge to US interests, all such cases threaten to complicate the international order by directly spurring subsequent proliferation, reinforcing the trend toward a more nuclear world, or increasing the chances of the loss of control over nuclear assets.

Security is not the sole driver for proliferation, however. Throughout the nuclear age, different states have acted out of a complex set of motives as they work to acquire nuclear capabilities. Nationalism and the desire for international prestige are growing as motivations for pursuing nuclear technology since, in many parts of the world, nuclear technology is still a potent symbol of development, advancement, and independence. Moreover, due in part to the behavior of the established nuclear weapon states, nuclear status continues to confer prestige on the international stage.

Some states seeking international respect have seen nuclear weapons as an effective means to that end. The fact that the five permanent members of the United Nations Security Council all have nuclear weapons is not lost on other countries. The connection between nuclear development and modernity is also a powerful symbol that leaders want to showcase for their own publics, most recently in Iran, but previously in India and Pakistan as well. As long as nuclear weapons and nuclear power are seen as landmarks of advancement, states will consider them important and worth pursuing. The domestic factor in proliferation is often critical, and often more difficult to address than straight security calculations.

The development of nuclear technology has a powerful domestic political effect in some countries, often after having been stoked by years of populist rhetoric. This is especially true in India and Pakistan, and apparently in Iran. Bureaucratic and institutional pressures within a government should not be discounted as a domestic factor in nuclear weapon programs. Once nascent nuclear development programs are initiated, they can be very difficult to restrain and reverse, and bureaucratic forces can be quite effective at exploiting domestic political or economic considerations for their own purposes.

In contrast, terrorist groups seek to acquire nuclear weapons for one reason: to use them (probably as quickly as possible). Those seeking such capabilities have likely done so with a particular target in mind. The acquisition and use of a nuclear device by a terrorist group would inflict massive damage and instill pervasive popular anxiety in the targeted country. This makes them the ultimate terror weapon. In the wake of a terrorist attack, there would be no way of knowing if the perpetrators had additional weapons in reserve. An attacker might therefore seek to blackmail countries with the threat of further nuclear attacks. With little hope of deterring future attacks, it is impossible to predict how a country's population or leadership would respond to such an ultimatum.

Key to any discussion of nuclear terrorism is the question of whether nuclear armed terrorist groups can be deterred. With all due respect to the academic debate on the issue, the risk that a subnational group would use a device in its possession is high, and the consequences are so great that no country or leader could take any comfort in the possibility that a terrorist organization might show restraint after having gone to the lengths required to build or acquire a nuclear device.

Aside from detonating a weapon to terrorize the target population and leadership, are there other motives for terror groups to go nuclear? One could imagine a competitive drive to inflict more damage than the 9/11 attack or mount a challenge to Al Qaeda as the top global terror group. But these are merely secondary motives when compared to the desire to inflict ultimate terror with the ultimate weapon.

While states and substate groups might have distinct motives for acquiring nuclear weapons, the link between state and substate proliferation is a direct one. Terrorists cannot produce their own nuclear materials, and thus must seek to acquire them from the peaceful or military stocks of state programs. Therefore, the distinction often drawn between a nuclear terror threat from a state versus nonstate terrorism is false, and the two types of threats should always be considered in connection with one another. This is clearly the case in Iran, where concerns are high that Tehran might pass nuclear capabilities to terrorist groups, but this link has been often overlooked in other cases of potential proliferation.

Where Do We Go From Here?

For the past 15 years, the debate over how best to address the proliferation of nuclear weapons and other WMD has been viewed as a choice between response and prevention. For the pro-"regime" camp, which emphasized the arms control norms and laws as a bulwark against proliferation dating back to the 1960s, any policy options treating proliferators as a new or emerging reality detracts from the "primary" effort. At the same time, the counterproliferation and preemption camps pushed for aggressive action to counter the inevitable spread of such weapons, even at the expense of diplomacy and support of the traditional nonproliferation regime, with its tools of inspection and collective response. These different points of emphasis obscure the fact that many nonproliferation professionals believed in the importance of both efforts, but the public and political debates have tended to sharpen the image that the two approaches are mutually exclusive. Those who thought proliferation could be stopped were portrayed as naïve, and those who thought it inevitable were cast as warmongers.

Likewise, the inaccurate picture of an either/or between a focus on state or substate proliferation has severely hampered efforts over the past decade and a half. The link between the two, critically in the realm of nuclear proliferation, was often overlooked as those more focused on states questioned the ability of terror groups to acquire or utilize nuclear weapons, and those focused on subnational threats often downplayed the dangers posed by the spread of nuclear weapons to states. In fact, both present a threat to US security interests and should be the focus of the highest priority in US policies. Moreover, many policies needed to address state proliferation would have the added benefit of reducing the risks of substate proliferation as well.

The debates over prevent vs. respond and state vs. substate that have consumed so much attention in the recent past have missed the point—unnecessarily pitting against one another parties and officials who actually share the common goal of protecting the nation by preventing additional states and terrorists from acquiring, possessing, or using (politically and militarily) nuclear weapons and other WMD. If one could introduce a fresh and constructive discussion of nonproliferation policy in the United States, the tools preferred by political figures, policy experts, and military planners across the spectrum are complementary and can be combined into a comprehensive strategy to prevent the spread of nuclear weapons. Moreover, many of the elements are either in place, are being pursued, or have been supported by both political parties and could generate broad support if pursued in a bipartisan manner. While the issues of terrorism, homeland defense, and the stewardship of US security tend to be highly politicized, the effort to prevent the spread of nuclear weapons should be kept above the partisan or ideological divide.

Experts and political leaders of all stripes should seek to strengthen all the tools at our disposal to prevent states from acquiring nuclear weapons, to prevent states that have nuclear capabilities from using them against US interests, and to ensure that states with nuclear assets—friend or otherwise—protect them so that no subnational group can gain access (intentional or otherwise) to nuclear weapons. Success in these efforts will require a new national and international consensus both within and outside of the narrow traditional province of nonproliferation policy specialists—including areas such as nuclear weapons policy, broader political alliances, military spending and planning, intelligence, and law enforcement.

What Is to Be Done?

The world now stands at a nuclear precipice. There is broad and growing concern that if current trends continue, the United States will be forced to live in a more nuclear world, where multiple nuclear states and even nuclear-armed terrorist groups exist to the detriment of stability, security, and overarching US interests. The increased salience of nuclear weapons as instruments of power, prestige, and security, unless checked, threaten to undermine the basis for global stability and American power.

There is a growing sense that the United States should do all it can to avoid a more proliferated world. Preventing the spread of nuclear weapons and nuclear production capabilities to new states and especially to terrorist groups is a common goal of all political stripes. Skepticism about whether such a world can be avoided also exists on all sides, but this skepticism should not be allowed to prevent the aggressive pursuit of policies that have the potential to reduce the nuclear threat—*provided these do not undermine the ability of the United States to deal with such a world should it come to pass.* While the value and relative importance of some of the tactics used to pursue nonproliferation goals have been in dispute, the underlying goal is the same: prevent, and when prevention is not possible, deter and prepare to defeat as needed.

Just as it has in the past, the United States must be at the forefront of international efforts to reduce the supply and demand for nuclear weapons through a comprehensive effort. If the United States fails to provide such leadership, then the world is sure to be a more proliferated one. And even if the best US-led international efforts do falter or fail, then we must be in a position to protect our vital national interests in a more nuclear world.

A Turning Point?

A remarkable political and policy convergence occurred in January 2007 when a bipartisan group of senior statesmen issued a collective warning: "Unless urgent new actions are taken, the United States soon will be compelled to enter a new nuclear era that will be more precarious, psychologically disorienting, and economically even more costly than was Cold War deterrence."[1] The combined heft of a group that included George Shultz, William Perry, Henry Kissinger, and San Nunn could help open up the political space for a new president to seek a new consensus in American politics regarding how to address the growing nuclear dangers. Indeed, it was just such a collective realization in the 1960s that led the major powers to cooperate in reducing the demand for nuclear weapons and largely kept their spread in check. A new commitment to ambitious, international action is absolutely critical in order to avert the impending threat of widespread proliferation.

The United States' ability to build global consensus on a new nonproliferation agenda will no doubt be complicated by the war in Iraq and concern over the United States' more active use of the military in the post-9/11 period. For the United States to lead a new international effort on the nuclear front successfully, a concerted effort to restore its international image and influence will be essential. This will require action on multiple fronts beyond the nuclear agenda itself, including the more effective use of multilateral diplomacy and bolstering the United States' conventional forces—both to give it better military options to deal with proliferation and to reduce Washington's reliance on nuclear weapons as a nonproliferation tool.[2] Despite these challenges, a US policy of active diplomacy, support for international norms and institutions, and leading by example will attract international support and significantly boost the chances of success.

In implementing such an agenda, the highest levels of government must pursue all elements with equal vigor. The cooperative measures are just as important as the more aggressive counterproliferation steps: potential deep reductions in nuclear weapons, support for a broad set of negotiated agreements, engagement with states friendly and otherwise to achieve stated goals, and an effort to undercut the basic assumptions of why states acquire nuclear weapons and the lengths to which the United States should go to prevent their proliferation. In practical terms, this will involve exploring anew the means through which agreements are verified; helping to rebuild and reinforce the nonproliferation norms as codified in international legal agreements; supporting deep, verifiable, and irreversible nuclear reductions in the United States, Russia, and other nuclear arsenals; and enlisting broad support to enforce international norms and legal obligations. It will be necessary to reexamine traditionally sacrosanct issues such as the contours of the Non-Proliferation Treaty (NPT) regime, cooperation and engagement with non-NPT members, and a healing of the ideological breach that has characterized traditional nonproliferation debates. Neither more of the same nor more of the past has any chance of succeeding.

At the same time, all sides must recognize the possibility that trends and developments may have already gone too far to prevent the wider spread of nuclear weapons. Such an ambitious new agenda will take time, and the timeline of nuclear programs in Iran, North Korea, and elsewhere may have lent nuclear proliferation an irreversible momentum. Given the difficulty of nuclear rollback, the United States must also prepare itself to operate in a world of greater proliferation. This includes maintaining a large and robust conventional military force with improved mobility; global strike and intelligence capabilities; as well as a safe, reliable, and robust nuclear deterrent.

Moreover, in a world where many more countries have nuclear weapons, there is a greatly increased risk of both nuclear terrorism through theft and diversion of nuclear materials and of accidental or unintended nuclear use through miscalculation. The United States must ensure that it can protect itself, its friends, and its allies as well as its global interest in such a world; this includes pursing the most effective defense against potential attack, and preparing itself to rewrite longstanding legal and political norms to adjust to a more nuclearized world. At some point, such a reassessment will have to consider a revision of US nonproliferation laws and restrictions as well as deeper engagement and cooperation with friendly states that possess nuclear capabilities outside of the NPT.

In their statement, Shultz et al. list key points that should be included in a new initiative with broad international support. It is worth reviewing this agenda to take stock of the issues and what action will be needed.

- *Reduce the alert status and deployment of Cold War-era nuclear arsenals (de-alerting).*
  Whatever the threats facing the United States, they do not require the maintenance of thousands of nuclear weapons on alert, ready to launch in minutes. The United States should, in conjunction with other nuclear states, reduce the risk of a nuclear accident by removing a large proportion of its weapons from their delivery platforms to secure storage sites, thereby lengthening the nuclear fuse and reducing the number of targets for terrorist theft or attack. A major diplomatic push should be made to convince Russia, China, and other nuclear powers to do the same.

- *Make substantial reductions in the nuclear arsenals of all states.*
  The number of nuclear weapons in the world remains too high and undercuts the credibility of commitments by the nuclear powers to a nuclear-free world.

Seeking continued, real, and verifiable reductions in global nuclear arsenals should be a central pillar of international efforts to prevent proliferation, and the United States should remove any doubts about its compliance with its international obligations, including the NPT.

- *Eliminate tactical nuclear weapons designed for forward deployment.*
  The United States has done this with many, but not all of its weapons. Russia has reversed previous moves to reduce its reliance on battlefield nuclear weapons. Efforts to secure and eliminate tactical nuclear weapons dating back to the early 1990s should be revived, accompanied by a new multilateral push to verifiably rid the world of these weapons, which are especially prone to theft and terrorist use.

- *Initiate a new process within the US Senate to boost confidence in and to achieve the ratification of the Comprehensive Test Ban Treaty (CTBT), as well as push for ratification by other states.*
  The Senate rejection of the CTBT was based in part on concern over the reliability of the United States' nuclear deterrent under a test ban and also regarding the verifiability of the agreement itself. An effective, global legal prohibition against nuclear testing would help impede the progress of nations developing nuclear weapons. There should be strong bipartisan support for an agreement that could be effectively verified. A new, blank-slate assessment of verification and modeling technology will be essential for the reconsideration of an effective CTBT.

- *Ensure the highest level of security for all nuclear weapon-usable materials worldwide.*
  The vulnerability of nuclear materials around the world remains an acute security threat and must be the focus of renewed efforts by the US government, the G-8, and all governments that seek an end to proliferation and the threat of nuclear terrorism. The political, technical, and economic means to achieve this goal must be marshaled.

- *Achieve international control of the nuclear fuel cycle through multilateral efforts, including the International Atomic Energy Agency (IAEA), nuclear suppliers group, and other efforts.*
  This complex issue has been the subject of serious proposals by the United States, Russia, and the IAEA. Bureaucratic efforts at the working level to develop new ideas are ongoing. However, the complexity and costs associated

with such efforts cannot be solved by technical experts and will require sustained involvement by the top political levels. Control over the production of nuclear fuel is critical to ensure that the spread of technical know-how does not undermine the goals of nonproliferation.

The authors differ over the future role of the NPT, but agree on the underlying need for international political consensus over nonproliferation norms. The NPT played an important role in stemming the proliferation of nuclear weapons through the Cold War period, although it is difficult to distinguish how much of that effectiveness was due to the influence of two superpowers that both sought to limit the spread of nuclear weapons, rather than the treaty itself. Nonetheless, the Cold War-era experience does point toward the importance of consensus among the established nuclear weapons states as a sine qua non for effective multilateral action against proliferation. Thus the United States should also seek to bring together leaders from key states—including, but not restricted to, the P-5 members of the UN Security Council—to forge a new nonproliferation consensus. The 1991 meeting of the heads of state of the UN Security Council that declared the proliferation of WMD was a "threat to international peace and security" is an important precedent, but new political efforts will require much greater high-level attention as well as a more detailed set of goals. It would be surprising if such a new consensus did not include a reaffirmation of the NPT itself but, in the end, it is the consensus and the effectiveness of its results that are most important and should be the primary focus.

- *End the production of fissile materials for weapons worldwide and end the use of weapons-grade uranium in civil applications.*
  The United States stopped production of all such materials in 1988, and has endorsed a negotiated ban in the Conference on Disarmament. However, the United States has opposed verification measures for such an agreement, believing it inherently unverifiable. The goal of US policy should be to engage in comprehensive negotiations, including consideration of verification, and ideological preconditions should not stand in the way of pursuing the benefits of an agreement. A fissile fuels agreement with adequate verification terms and sufficient scope should receive US support and Senate consent.

- *Redouble efforts to resolve regional tensions that give rise to new nuclear powers.*
  Festering regional disputes and instability feed the proliferation threat in multiple ways. They can spark further demand for nuclear weapons, lay the seeds for regional nuclear wars, and threaten to drag the United States into

conflicts and potential confrontation with other nuclear powers. Nightmare scenarios are easy to imagine. The United States thus must lead in resolving such disputes.

• *Continue to develop effective measures to impede or counter nuclear-related conduct that threatens the security of any state or peoples.*
  Any comprehensive nonproliferation effort must include the means to detect and respond to violators, particularly those who illegally traffic in nuclear technologies. Extending global detection and interdiction efforts and bolstering the United States' own political and military capacity to counter the spread of nuclear weapons and technology is fully consistent with the goals outlined above. American policymakers should build both unilateral capacity and international cooperation as urgently and energetically as possible.

To be successful, the ambitious agenda outlined here will require a tremendous investment in political and other resources. If pursued diligently, this agenda offers hope that the current trends toward a more nuclear proliferated world can be stopped, and even reversed. Yet while these steps constitute a bold policy agenda, they must be considered merely a part of a wider ongoing effort. Traditional tools designed to reduce the availability and incentive to acquire nuclear weapons have been a critical part of past efforts to prevent the spread of nuclear weapons, and will remain a valuable set of tools in the years to come. This intricate and interlocking set of activities includes:

• Export controls to block the transfer of sensitive technologies and thereby increase the barriers facing states in their efforts to develop weapons.

• Unilateral and multilateral economic and diplomatic sanctions against states seeking or trading in illicit technologies.

• Homeland security and national defense programs, including detection and interdiction.

• Development of missile defense technology to reduce the odds that a would-be attacker could succeed in striking the United States.

These efforts, taken together, form the backbone of current nonproliferation efforts and must be continued and continually reinvigorated.

The Case of Iran

Iran is the single most pressing case confronting US nuclear nonproliferation strategy today. Unlike North Korea, Iran does not currently possess a workable nuclear device and may be several years away from producing one. Thus it is still possible to envision an outcome where Iran remains a nonnuclear power, either as a result of diplomacy or due to a combination of cooperative and coercive means.

Iran's pursuit of nuclear capabilities is of serious concern in and of itself, but especially because of its ties to and support of extremist terrorist organizations. There is a very plausible threat that Iran might transfer nuclear capabilities to nonstate actors who are far more difficult to deter or contain than Iran itself. Iran's pursuit of a weapon will also have a direct impact on regional neighbors, forcing them to consider developing their own nuclear weapons as a countermeasure or to take preemptive military action to prevent Iran from going nuclear. There is yet another danger that Iran's open hostility toward the United States and Israel could lead them to launch an unprovoked nuclear attack.

Even if the United States were to develop new robust nonproliferation measures, there is not sufficient time for such instruments to make a major contribution toward ending Iran's nuclear ambitions. Thus this challenge must be addressed with the tools already at the disposal of policymakers. The diplomatic partnership of the United States with key European powers is a critical initiative, and the maximum use of multilateral institutions such as the IAEA and the UN Security Council will remain important instruments in seeking to convince Iran to change its nuclear direction. Iran has consistently deflected such efforts and it is conceivable that nations with competing interests can block action—particularly in the UN Security Council. Moreover, Iran's leadership is clearly working to exploit the frustration or suspicion in the Middle East and elsewhere in the developing world toward US policy of the past decade. The United States must therefore pursue a full-court diplomatic press using all available and conceivable tools to reinforce its nonproliferation goals in Iran.

The first level of action is political and economic pressure, including the most restrictive sanctions possible if Iran refuses to halt its nuclear enrichment program in particular, and its pursuit of a nuclear weapon more generally. The position of Iran's leadership is not as strong economically or politically as it might appear at first glance. The internal political and economic impact of sanctions may be greater than many expect. This pressure can then be used to create a greater incentive for Iran's leaders to compromise on key issues. To this end, direct, bilateral diplomacy between the United States and Iran should be pursued if there is any reasonable prospect of halting Iran's nuclear weapons program. Notwithstanding the other broader and serious concerns regarding the Iranian regime, preventing the acquisition of nuclear weapons by Iran must remain a top policy goal. Other objectives—including regime change—should be secondary as long as a chance remains to end Tehran's nuclear ambitions through peaceful means. This does not mean that the United States should discontinue its efforts to detect and deter Iranian support for terrorism and to push Iran to permit its people to enjoy the full liberties of a free society—including the right to choose their leaders. It means only that ending Iran's nuclear weapons program should be the highest priority.

Given the existing US military commitments in Iraq, Afghanistan, and elsewhere, Iran and other countries in the Middle East believe the United States is either incapable of or unlikely to consider military actions against Iran. Most regional players oppose the use of military force to stop Iran's nuclear program. Yet stopping the development of an Iranian nuclear weapon remains a US national security imperative of such enormity that the use of military force must remain a real option for American decision makers. The United States should continue planning for such an operation and preparing for the potential consequences of such an action—especially the likely increase in terrorist attacks worldwide and the potential disruption of energy supply lines from the region. Such contingency preparation, pursued within reason, would increase the sense of vulnerability in Iran and could make it more willing to seek a compromise on the nuclear issue.

While the United States does not currently have sufficient military resources to invade and occupy the nation of Iran, it does have the ability to use force to disrupt those nuclear capabilities that it can identify. While even this, in the end, may not prevent Iran from going nuclear, it must remain a possible option if for no other reason than to reassure US allies in the region that Washington is committed to their defense and protection as well as to maintaining pressure on Iranian decision making on nuclear and other issues.

The crisis over Iran's nuclear ambitions is likely to continue for many more months. Developing and implementing a comprehensive new nonproliferation agenda will take much longer. But commencing the work toward such an agenda could have immediate benefits for the effort to slow or end Iran's nuclear efforts. Demonstrating in an international context that the United States and the world's major powers understand and recognize the risk of unchecked nuclear proliferation and the responsibility to include themselves within a new broader system of controls may prove critical in the intensifying diplomacy surrounding Iran's nuclear program. Coming on the heels of renewed efforts to develop diplomatic solutions to the North Korean nuclear crisis, any progress on the Iran front—even a suspension of Iran's enrichment program and the start of a real dialogue between Iran and the outside world on security issues—could go a long way in laying the foundation and building global political momentum for the new nonproliferation agenda laid out in this chapter.

Nuclear Weapons and US Policy

In pursuing such a multifaceted agenda, the United States must also engage in a long-needed public discussion about what role nuclear weapons do, should, and will play in US policy. Fundamental questions should be raised and debated, including why we have nuclear weapons; how many we need; what role can they play, if any, outside of the nuclear deterrent calculation; and whether and how the United States can work toward complete nuclear disarmament. The continued direction of US nuclear policy must not be driven by the mere inertia of the Cold War momentum. General James Cartwright, commander of Strategic Command, has endorsed the need for a new national dialogue on the role of nuclear weapons in US policy: "The challenging security and threat environment of the 21st century signals the need for an informed national level discussion to hear the voices of government leaders, military, academia, and the public if we are to effectively establish a long-term nuclear investment plan."[3]

There are serious decisions to be made in this process. Key among them will include the United States' strategy for maintaining its current nuclear arsenal, possible efforts to develop new weapons, how to ensure reliable and robust delivery capabilities as long as the United States retains a nuclear arsenal, and how to balance US nonproliferation and nuclear deterrent requirements.

If the spread of nuclear weapons is indeed the principal threat of our time, then every means at the government's disposal must be focused and integrated to prevent these threats from harming US security. Therefore, US nuclear weapon and conventional military capabilities must be configured and geared toward supporting overarching US efforts to prevent the spread of nuclear weapons. For some, this argues for the development of new, smaller, battlefield nuclear weapons to put adversaries' underground targets at risk, while others invoke nonproliferation objectives to advocate a ban on nuclear testing, a reduction in the number of nuclear weapons, and a declaration that US nuclear weapons will only be used for nuclear deterrence.

For a new international nonproliferation consensus to have any chance of success, the United States must throw its full political weight behind such an effort. This will require a delicate balance between political and military aims. For instance, the first priority in any effort to develop a reliable replacement warhead must be to develop technologies to ensure reliability while avoiding the need to test nuclear weapons. The current efforts within the nuclear establishment have been prudent and sound—aiming to design a reliable replacement warhead without testing that could be put into service if weapons in the existing US nuclear stockpile were to prove defective. Ultimately, if pursued within the context of a broader, more robust nonproliferation agenda, this capability would also build the basis for reconsideration of the CTBT.

Also, the United States, together with the other nuclear powers, should provide assurances that nonnuclear states will not be the subject of *nuclear* threats. The proposed development of new nuclear weapons by the United States for possible use in essentially a conventional capacity—to reach deep underground targets—is based on a premise that does not seem credible. The United States could not develop and deploy, much less use, such weapons without shredding any global consensus that remains regarding the taboo on the use of nuclear weapons. Any US use of a nuclear weapon of any type against a nonnuclear state would cross a line that simply would not be understood or accepted by the rest of the world. There is no meaningful distinction between a large and a small nuclear weapon when used against a nonnuclear state.

Brave New World

For more than 50 years, the United States relied upon a robust nuclear arsenal as a deterrent to any party that may attack our nation with a nuclear weapon. As successful as that strategy has been, the world in which it worked is largely gone. The threat of state-to-state nuclear conflict involving the United States now rates among the least likely of contingencies we may face. As the challenge of nuclear proliferation has evolved, so must our strategy.

None of the many types of action suggested in this paper to meet the challenge of nuclear proliferation are new. To some degree, many of them are either current policy or have been in recent administrations. The real evolution needed in the United States' strategy is in the architecture of the solutions. The policy must include both multilateral diplomacy and robust unilateral action. It must balance cooperative initiatives on arms control and the maintenance of a safe and effective US nuclear arsenal. It must involve diplomacy and the willingness to use force. In short, it will contain combinations that appear inherently contradictory. It must be a total effort.

This task will require a genuine commitment at the highest levels of government to build a united international front. Allies must be recruited, including among the new nuclear powers such as India and even Pakistan. With the broadest possible international support, the United States and its partners must launch a layered approach to meet the challenge of nuclear proliferation.

The full set of international regimes and norms, of treaties and laws should be invigorated and further refined to close off any trade in nuclear weapons technologies with states that do not abide by the NPT—whether they are a party or not. A comprehensive, global effort must be launched to catalog, secure and, where possible, recover and destroy nuclear materials. The existing nuclear powers should cooperate in reducing their own nuclear arsenals in concert—down to the minimum level necessary for a deterrent against each other. The remaining warheads should then be stored in the most secure manner possible. Every effort must be made to disrupt and interdict the trade of nuclear materials, especially fissile material. Stopping nations and individuals who participate in this illicit trade should be a priority for intelligence services and the military.

Underneath the ambitious strategy laid out by Shultz et al., the United States will need to maintain safe, reliable, and robust nuclear forces—in the most strategically stabilizing manner possible—to remain capable of deterring the use of nuclear weapons by other states against the United States and its friends and interests abroad.

Finally, in order to lessen the need for nuclear weapons as well as respond more effectively against any incipient nuclear threat, the United States must maintain large and well-equipped conventional military forces to defeat any potential adversary. The United States must also, as aggressively as possible, locate and defeat terror plots, disrupt terrorist networks, deny substate groups safe havens, and preempt such groups anywhere in the world. Beyond the detailed policy agenda outlined here, protecting the United States from all serious threats will remain the primary constitutional duty for any president.

In the end, we may not succeed. At the current pace of proliferation, it seems likely that new nuclear powers will yet emerge in this decade. With the large number of nuclear weapons in various arsenals around the world—under what may be described as, at best, suspect security—the theft of a device at some point is a distinct possibility. With the growth of terrorist organizations of global reach, the delivery of a nuclear weapon to America's shores is by no means far-fetched. The explosion of such a device on US territory would then be only a matter of time. If we are to succeed in meeting the challenge of proliferation, we must act—now—as if our lives depend upon it. Someday, they actually might.

Notes

1 *The Wall Street Journal*, January 7, 2007.
2 The actions needed in a number of other policy areas are covered in other chapters of this volume.
3 April 4, 2005, testimony before the Senate Armed Services Committee.

7

Keeping Tabs on China's Rise

Michael Schiffer and Gary Schmitt

China Rising

With almost clockwork precision, every 50 years for the past two centuries China has appeared to be at a "hinge" moment in its history. Once again that is the case, as China stands poised at the verge of a return to great power status. By all appearances it is already, or soon will be, a dominant player in East Asia—whether on economic, political, or security issues—and is playing an increasing global role. And, in decades ahead, China could even present a challenge to US primacy.

Indeed, the rise of China is the principal strategic fact of the 21st century. Where China goes—and how fast—will have a significant, if not defining, impact on the shape of the international system and will exert considerable influence on the future of US security and prosperity. The rise of China presents challenges to the United States across several dimensions of power (military, diplomatic, political, economic, even cultural), and there is virtually no issue critical to America's future—global economic growth, nonproliferation, controlling potential pandemics, climate change, energy security—that is not affected by the US-China relationship.

Despite several encouraging trends in bilateral relations, America's relationship with China faces significant challenges: economic and trade practices contribute to a troubling trade deficit; China's adherence to its international commitments and norms (such as human rights) is mixed at best; China's military buildup has made the already difficult-to-manage Taiwan question that much harder, and has greatly complicated relations with Japan, and with the US-Japan Alliance.

A conclusive answer to the question of whether China will continue to rise is beyond the scope of this chapter. China faces immense problems, including pollution, disease, poverty, inequality, corruption, abuses of power, an aging population, and shrinking labor force that make an answer to this question far from a foregone conclusion. Nonetheless we assume that China will continue to rise, and we will address the implications of China's growing power—for China, for the United States, and for the rest of the world.

Although all too often the debate about China's rising power tends to focus on the military dimension, it is critical to understand that the challenge the United States faces is not necessarily only or even primarily a military one (although that element can't be ignored). The challenges posed by China's rise cut across all dimensions of power. Indeed, in many ways Chinese capabilities do not represent a unique challenge; we face other major powers that are authoritarian and don't respect human rights, that import energy and employ mercantilist energy strategies, that have savings surpluses that affect global and bilateral trade balances. What makes the rise of China so important to the United States, however, is that China, alone among other nations, has the potential to be competitive across several dimensions of power. In recent memory, the United States' experience in great power competition has been with one-dimensional challengers, such as the Soviet military threat during the Cold War or Japanese economic power in the 1980s. China, however, has the potential to be a true peer competitor—a regional hegemon with global aspirations—which makes the question of how to best manage the US-China relationship critically important.

The rise of China is one of the most remarkable transformations the world has ever seen. Following a "hundred years of humiliation," it is a testimony to the power of Chinese history, Chinese culture, and the Chinese people.

A few statistics give a sense of the magnitude of China's rise thus far, and of its potential. China, Japan, and the United States are the world's three most productive economies, but China is by far the fastest-growing, at an average rate of 9.5 percent per annum for more than two decades. Even the 8 percent slowed-down target set by Premier Wen Jiabao is blazing fast by any standards. China is today the world's sixth largest economy by conventional measures (the United States and Japan being first and second), and the United States' third largest trading partner after Canada and Mexico. However, according to CIA statistics, China is already the second-largest economy on earth, measured on a purchasing power parity basis—that is, in terms of what China actually produces rather than prices and exchange rates.

The CIA's National Intelligence Council forecasts that China's gross domestic product (GDP) will equal Great Britain's in 2007, Germany's in 2009, Japan's in 2017, and the United States' in 2042. Shahid Javed Burki, former vice president of the World Bank's China department predicts that by 2025 China will have a GDP of $25 trillion in terms of purchasing power parity and will surpass the United States as the world's largest economy.

China's trade volume for 2004 was $1.2 trillion, third in the world after the United States and Germany. China's trade with the United States grew 34 percent in 2004 and has turned Los Angeles, Long Beach, and Oakland into the three busiest seaports in America.

Chinese domestic economic growth is expected to continue for decades, reflecting the pent-up demand of its huge population, relatively low levels of personal debt, and a dynamic underground economy. Most important, China's external debt is relatively small and easily covered by its reserves. (The United States, by contrast, is approximately $700 trillion in the red.)

Along with this economic growth, China's military has made a quantum leap in recent years. Chinese military spending will be up 17.8 percent this year, according to recent announcements, following a decade-plus of double-digit growth. The official military budget of some $45 billion (with more in unofficial spending) represents a significant increase in efforts to enhance military capability.

There is little doubt that China's current military modernization efforts and defense spending have been increasing, and increasingly focused. Beginning in the early 1990s, modernization of the People's Liberation Army (PLA) was elevated from a low priority to a central one for national policy. China's ambitions as a rising power —combined with PLA threat perceptions that are driven by displays of US military dominance in the Gulf War, Kosovo, Afghanistan, and Iraq and the US 2002 national security strategy document—have all prompted a rich debate in China over the need to upgrade Chinese military capabilities and refine its military doctrine.

According to China's own 2006 White Paper on national defenses, the Chinese Navy is moving to extend its offshore capabilities and increase its strategic maritime depth. In addition to building out its amphibious assault capabilities, it has assembled a fleet of 29 modern submarines, including 13 Kilo-class submarines purchased from Russia, along with ten additional submarines under construction in Chinese shipyards. China has also added seven new destroyers, including two Sovremennyy-class destroyers purchased from Russia since 2000. Chinese naval doctrine has begun to emphasize the ability to operate in the South and East China Seas. China may view these moves as purely defensive, intended to safeguard China's territorial waters and the sea lanes that carry critical natural resources, but any objective assessment would have to note their offensive capabilities as well.

When one adds the purchase of advanced fighters from Russia; a continued missile buildup across the Taiwan Straits; and the December 2004 Defense White Paper's emphasis on extending China's ability to project power, develop strike capabilities, and conduct regionwide operations, serious questions about the portent of these changes emerge. It is just these sorts of changes that led then-CIA Director Porter Goss to comment in 2005 that China may soon "tilt the balance of power in the Taiwan Strait."

Likewise, although China has for several decades calibrated its nuclear forces to a doctrine of minimum deterrence (with 24 ballistic missiles capable of hitting the United States), there are new signs, highlighted recently in congressional testimony by Admiral Lowell Jacoby, that China might be in the midst of preparations for a "nuclear breakout," involving a seven-fold increase in warheads by 2015.

By these measures, China's growth in the past few decades has been tremendous. Looking at China though the prism of these statistics one would conclude that China is rising, and fast; that the Pentagon's 2006 Quadrennial Defense Review conclusion that "China has the greatest potential to compete militarily with the United States" is somewhat understated; and that the advice of analysts such as John Mearsheimer that the United States should do all it can to "slow the rise of China" now as decades from now it will be too late, seems prudent counsel.[1]

China's Military Power in Context

But this now-familiar litany of the rise of China and the potential military and economic challenges that it presents to the United States is only part of the story.

To begin with, as William Perry and Ashton Carter comment in a recent article, no one, including perhaps the Chinese themselves, knows where they are going.[2] China could be a friend, foe, or something in between. The rise of China could disrupt the international system or add a strong new pillar for upholding international norms. What the future holds is as much a mystery to the Chinese as it is to anyone else.

Second, in the effort to "right-size" US policy, the rise of China presents what one analyst has termed the *baseline versus trend-line* problem: While there is no doubt that certain trends in the growth of Chinese power appear deeply troubling, when placed in context of a broader baseline of measure, the implications are ambiguous. And, while it is clear that we must take seriously the trend in China's growing military power, including its growing desire to project that power, context suggests we need not panic.

For example, while China might want some day to exercise military power in a region outside its own, its ability to do so will be very limited for quite some time. China has no operational aircraft carriers (let alone the fleet of destroyers necessary to sail with one); no long-range bombers or long-range airborne capabilities and very limited strategic reconnaissance capabilities. China is in no position today to challenge American military might outside of a perhaps very limited scenario in the Taiwan

Strait. Despite the Chinese modernization efforts, a vast gulf still exists between the United States and China across a range of measures of military power, including research and development, hardware, training, information warfare, command and control, and lift. This gulf will not be bridged for years to come; assuming that the United States does not stand still, it may never be bridged.

In fact, the United States is not standing still. More submarines have been added to the Pacific fleet, advanced fighters and bombers and an additional carrier group are being moved into the region, new basing arrangements have been made with Asian and Pacific countries, and Washington has expanded and consolidated regional security partnerships.

In short, whatever else China's accelerating defense spending and military modernization efforts may suggest, the facts don't support a simple argument that China is today a major military threat to the United States—or that it will be any time soon. China remains far short of a peer competitor, and actually presents complications for only a limited handful of military scenarios.

China's Economic Power on the World Stage

Moving beyond the military dimension of power, the growing impact of China's economy is a second area of both concern and ambiguity. The metrics of an economically rising China support, at best, muddy and unclear conclusions about what it all means for the United States and the rest of the globe.

Since 1978, China's economy has grown at an average annual rate of more than 9 percent. And while it does not appear that China's economic growth will slow significantly any time soon, its ability to keep growing at this blistering pace, or grow at all, depends on myriad factors, including whether China's leadership continues to implement economic reforms, the strains on political and social stability as economic growth causes societal shifts, constraints associated with lingering weaknesses in infrastructure, a huge burden of nonperforming loans, and chronic water shortages. Indeed, while it is easy to offer scenarios in which China's economy continues to boom, it is just as easy to offer others in which it starts to falter.

To keep this in perspective, while China's GDP is at $7 trillion on a purchasing power parity basis (60 percent of our own), on a straight dollar-for-dollar basis China's economy is just the size of California's, and per capita GDP stands at $1,300 as compared to nearly $40,000 for the United States.

Even so, China's emergence in the world economy presents the United States with both a great economic challenge as well as a great opportunity. In 2005, China exported $243 billion in goods to the United States while importing only $42 billion, leaving the United States with a $201 billion trade deficit—nearly 30 percent of America's overall trade deficit and 40 percent of its non-oil deficit.

For example, China's unfair restrictions on US market access demand redress, but this is somewhat mitigated by the near tripling of US exports to China since China received permanent normal trade relations and joined the World Trade Organization (WTO), exceeding initial expectations. While our exports to China are lower than we may want, they have risen about ten times faster than American exports to the rest of the world, and include everything from soybeans to aircraft. On the import side of the balance sheet, a Morgan Stanley study estimates that China alone has saved US consumers $600 billion over ten years: $521 in disposable income for every American household each year for ten years. Moreover, although other variables such as China's low labor cost are significant, the single biggest factor in the US trade deficit with China may well be the very low US savings rate rather than the value of the Chinese currency.

While it is true that China's control of the world's second largest reserve of foreign currency—and its current status as the world's largest recipient of foreign direct investment (FDI)—gives it a potentially powerful tool to use to deter or punish the United States, the reality is that China is as trapped by the situation as we are. If China were to take steps to drive down the dollar, for example, the impact on China's own economy would be at least as damaging as its impact on ours—but with political ramifications likely much graver and more destabilizing for China and the party leadership than for the United States.

China's Soft Power

A third element of the challenge posed by China's future trajectory is the rise of China's "soft power." Here again the record is unclear, although China's ability to compete with the United States in "soft power" is highly significant in and of itself, which again underscores the need for a multidimensional US policy to deal with and engage China in world affairs.

China has embarked on a "charm offensive" in Asia, courting US allies, settling disputes with neighbors, supporting multilateral forums, forging free trade agreements, signing contracts for imports, and conducting a staggering level of sophisticated diplomacy. All of which has led to a notable increase in Chinese soft power—a broad concept that, as Harry Harding has noted, includes the new excitement about China as a place to live and work, now viewed as a land of opportunity for many young Americans, Japanese, and Europeans. This has also been manifest in China's creation of "Confucius Institutes" to promote its culture and meet the rising international demand for the study of Chinese language, as well as expanding educational opportunities and training programs for foreigners inside China.[3]

There is also a growing international interest in the Chinese model of development—and the increasingly explicit (although still indirect) Chinese presentations of that model as a preferable alternative to the "Washington Consensus" or the "American model." It is, however, troubling to see that the exercise of Chinese diplomatic efforts in this context often appears tightly tied to competition over scarce energy resources in Africa and Latin America.

Thus the Chinese model of poverty alleviation, presented as an appealing alternative development model—the so-called "Beijing Consensus"—presents a direct and formidable ideological challenge to the United States. This is not the China of the "permanent revolution," actively proselytizing Mao's brand of agrarian-based communism, but rather a benign China, building hospitals and schools and providing loans and aid, all with no questions asked about the nature of local political structures and elites, and accompanied by pledges of noninterference.

A recent BBC poll of global public opinion shows that in all but 12 countries China's influence is seen as more positive than America's. China polls better than the United States even with traditional American allies like Canada, the United Kingdom, France, Germany, Saudi Arabia, and Australia. In India, the two countries are tied.

Yet many around the globe still have their doubts about China, and China has not done the ideological spadework to transform opportunistic rhetoric into a global ideological battle. Despite the damage to America's image over the past several years, most of the globe still appreciates the United States' role as security guarantor and economic partner. As in baseball—a team is never as good as it is when it is winning, or as bad as it is when it is losing—US influence in Asia has not declined, per se, but we can no longer take our friends in the region (or elsewhere) for granted.

Lastly, any attempt to understand the nature of China's rise must take into account the fact that China's economic development—and social stability—remains extremely vulnerable, largely because of unevenness of development, income inequality, education bottlenecks, ethnic strife, and underdeveloped capital markets. For many who watch China, there is both a sense of awe at what China has accomplished as well as a sense that it could all unravel overnight.

Indeed, the priority that the Chinese leadership has given to the maintenance of harmony and social stability is a strong indication of the stress that China is under, and how close to the breaking point China may be—or at least how close China's leaders believe it to be.

Internal Economic Stresses

Examined more closely, China's economic boom has also created tremendous stress that threatens to rip China apart. Twenty-six of China's east coast cities account for 82 percent of China's import-export and trade-led growth, meaning that the rest of China—some 900 million to one billion people—have received just 18 percent of the benefits of this economic boom. In fact, while eastern China booms, recent statistics suggest that middle and western China may actually be in economic decline, with living standards moving backward not just relative to China's east coast, but in absolute terms.

The explosive and highly uneven economic growth over the past decade has led to a great deal of labor unrest, with an attendant series of mine disasters, a record number of strikes, and a migrant workers' crisis surpassing an earlier such crisis in the 1980s. Recent years have seen a sharp increase in spontaneous riots across China, over issues as diverse as access to food, perceived police abuses, and environmental problems. In fact, there has been a steady pattern in which Chinese cities (some as large as 50,000) are "taken over" by protestors for a matter of hours, and sometimes days, before police and the military restore order.

There has been a marked increase in citizens' petitions to local as well as central government for redress of judicial, political, economic, or other wrongs. Estimates are that more than 10 million petitions are ongoing in China at any given time. As a result, Beijing's southern bus terminal has become the site of what amounts to a migrant village of thousands of people who camp out, sometimes for months at a time, while they wait to present their petitions to central authorities.

China's government has also become more concerned about the combination of economic and social stress, the inability of local governments to function, and the rise and widespread dissemination of online communication. The ability of disaffected individuals and groups to organize and share information via e-mail, cell phones, and other modern technology—and in real time—creates a real challenge for central government control.

Rising Nationalism

Similarly, the increasingly visible role of nationalism as a political force in China represents a double-edged sword for the central government. On the one hand, it has become a, if not the, key source of legitimacy for the post-Communist Chinese Communist Party. On the other hand, many international observers, and many Chinese, see nationalist protests ostensibly directed outward as, in actuality, a thin cover for those whose real grievances are with their own government. It is far from clear whether the government can control these nationalist impulses given the other stresses Chinese society is under, or whether, once unleashed, nationalism may take on a life of its own. If "performance legitimacy" (the requirement for the party and its leadership to deliver economic performance to retain their legitimacy) has now replaced revolutionary ideology as the key legitimizing function for the party, then the party's legitimacy is at serious risk if the economy falters.

As such, China may be a rising global power, but it also may be a colossus with clay feet, unable to reach its potential due to the cross-pressures that threaten to rip it apart. No one, least of all the Chinese themselves, knows what kind of China to expect in the future, or how China will use its new capabilities on the global stage. Policymakers, however, do not have the luxury of simply throwing up their arms and shrugging over known unknowns and unknown unknowns. Assessments and best guesses—even if they are only guesses—are a necessary part of policy development.

Problems and Prospects for Reform

Ever since Mao's death and the demise of the Gang of Four, China watchers have been divided into optimists and pessimists. Certainly, no one would deny the progress that China has made in the past 30 years. By almost all measures, Chinese citizens today are better off than their parents were a generation ago. Life expectancy in China is the third highest in East Asia, behind only Japan and South Korea. Since 1979, China's GDP has been growing at a near double-digit rate. As a result, urban and rural per capita income have each shot up more than tenfold, and a once virtually nonexistent middle class now numbers some 40 million households, with an increasing number owning their homes. And, of course, for the average Chinese citizen, the sphere of personal autonomy he or she enjoys has expanded significantly, just as the political chaos associated with the old order becomes a distant memory.

And there are good reasons to believe that such progress will continue. Key fundamentals, such as a high savings rate, a prevailing work ethic, and a huge labor pool give China a solid base on which to build. It is not difficult to be bullish on China and, indeed, most analysts have consistently underestimated China's economic growth.

Yet there is another view of China. Despite its progress, China has not lived up to the expectations built up by propagators of the Marco Polo myth. Shanghai is a case in point for this more wary and worried view of China. Looking at Shanghai's skyline is like looking at the futuristic skyline from the classic American television cartoon, *The Jetsons*. The city only needs flying cars jetting from the top of one ultra-modern skyscraper to another to complete the picture. At the same time, these skyscrapers have an occupancy rate that would drive any normal real estate market into a recession. Impressive as Shanghai is, one walks the streets as if on a razor's edge, with a keen sense that it could all collapse as quickly as it has risen.

Similarly, China's economic performance, while impressive, is by no means record-shattering. Between the late 1970s and today, China's per capita GDP grew at a compound rate of little over 6 percent. This was lower than the growth rates of Japan, South Korea, and Taiwan during comparable periods of economic development. In terms of return on investment, American firms consistently report lower profit margins in China than in their other global operations.

A large part of the problem is that China has only partially opened up its economy. The government still controls a significant segment of the Chinese economy through state-owned enterprises (SOEs). By some accounts, less than a third of China's economy is in private hands. In fact, more than half of its fixed industrial assets are owned by the government—including many by the PLA—and the government continues to hold a dominant position in key economic sectors such as banking, energy, heavy industry, steel, and transportation. Reflective of the control the state retains over the economy, of the 1,500 Chinese companies listed on domestic or foreign stock exchanges, less than 4 percent are private corporations.

This level of government control over the economy might be tolerable if the SOEs were profitable, except that they aren't. More than a third lose money; the ones that do make money do so at an extraordinarily low rate of return on assets (1.5 percent in 2003). Almost 20 percent of the SOEs would have long ago filed for bankruptcy had standard accounting rules been followed.

What keeps these companies afloat is the giant piggy bank controlled by the state-owned banks. Drawing on the capital resulting from the extraordinarily high personal savings rate of Chinese citizens, nearly half of the banks' loans go to SOEs. The result is a staggering level of nonperforming loans (NPLs), estimated at $480 billion in 2002 but probably much higher after a major expansion of credit by these same banks between 2002 and 2004.

All of which leaves nagging but serious questions about China's economic liberalization thus far, and its future prospects. Even after more than a quarter-century of economic reform, many of the leading industrial and technology companies in China remain SOEs. Lacking access to financing and at the mercy of arbitrarily enforced laws and state regulations, private industrial firms have had a tough time. (This is one reason that most of China's new crop of billionaires are real estate speculators.) Moreover, neither SOEs nor private firms have incentives for the kind of long-term investment in technological capabilities that marked Japan's and Taiwan's development.

Fearing the social unrest that the closure of SOEs might spur, and faced with a massive influx of rural Chinese into urban areas, China's leadership has used the banks, billions of dollars of FDI, and an undervalued currency to keep its industrial base running and its export manufacturing capacity growing. So far, the strategy has worked, as reflected in the growth in China's GDP. Nonetheless, huge questions and uncertainties remain. Can such a strategy continue to work and maintain a glide path for the transition toward a genuine market economy? Are problematic bubbles building within China's economy?

Perhaps more problematic is that this nexus of local party officials, government-controlled capital, and corporate life is an open invitation to engage in self-dealing and corrupt practices. Even today, the party picks the vast majority of SOE CEOs—with party secretaries dominating corporate boards more often than not. And while this form of crony capitalism had resulted in misguided investments, it has also, if Minxin Pei's analysis is correct,[4] created a dynamic in which China's elite are co-opted and political liberalization deemphasized.

So far, however, the hope that broad and deep political reforms would follow economic reforms has not fully materialized. In fact, party and elite interest in democratization is far lower today than it was in the late 1980s. Officially, China's recent White Paper on democracy makes clear that the Communist Party has no intention of giving up its primacy: "Democratic government is the Chinese Communist Party governing on behalf of the people." Chinese democracy is one with "vivid Chinese characteristics," meaning the West's notion of democracy appears to be of no or little interest as a model for Beijing. And despite the recent National People's Congress decisions on private property and the laogai system, these signs of potential progress are more than offset by the stalled innovation of village committee elections, the failure to create a real system of checks and balances by empowering the National People's Congress, the lack of independent, nationwide civic associations, or by the level of censorship, which, in aggregate, create trend lines that are not particularly encouraging.

One critical factor in the direction these trends take will be China's still relatively small and underdeveloped middle class. Experience elsewhere suggests that without a significant demand-led and middle class-based drive for political liberalization, it is highly unlikely that it will occur; and it will certainly not transpire as a result of a top-down process—given from above, rather than mandated and shaped from below.

Regardless of whether one views China's leadership as fundamentally and implacably antidemocratic or merely as trying to control a process of tremendous economic, social, and political change without everything flying apart, the upshot is that the only reforms the current leadership will pursue are those that seek to make the party's own governance more efficient and less corrupt. Such reforms, however well-intentioned, are bound to run into the fact that the Chinese patronage system itself lies at the root of elite privilege and loyalty to the party's rule in the absence of any ideological attachment to Marxist-style socialism. To all appearances, many of China's high-profile corruption cases seem mainly to be a battleground on which one faction in the leadership uses corruption charges to undermine another and consolidate power rather than an effort to actually wring corruption out of the system. Hence, as the Chinese themselves admit, serious corruption remains a pervasive problem and may well be getting worse.

Ultimately, this system can continue to work as long as the economy continues to grow at its current pace. However, it would be unprecedented for an economy to keep chugging along at this rate year after year. Assuming that the above analysis is largely correct, there are some serious structural flaws in China's economy that cannot be fixed without some short-term dislocations and slowed growth.

The real question is what happens when China finally hits a jarring bump in the road. Does it possess the social cohesion and civic institutions necessary to keep the bump from leading to a crash? In fact, many Chinese, including those in senior leadership positions, make precisely this argument for why China cannot move too quickly toward democracy: given all the cross-stresses at work within China and the uncertainties about China's current situation, the risk of total and catastrophic failure is simply too great. Yet there is an equal risk that without the shock absorbers of pluralism and democracy, resentments about rising inequality, workplace safety, public health, the environment, and government corruption could spill into the streets, leaving China's leaders with little option but police crackdowns. Mechanisms of democratic governance such as an independent judiciary or a duly elected representative body are the only sure ways to manage such pressures.

China's leaders today are, thus, holding a tiger by the tail. They have built the legitimacy of their continued rule largely on meeting the rising expectations of a billion-plus people, but to meet those expectations they eventually have to release the reins of economic and political power that they are clutching so tightly.

International Expectations

China's rising expectations are not limited, of course, to domestic prosperity. As it has for every rising power predecessor, China's new national wealth has created both the incentives and resources for the country to become a far more formidable player on the regional and world stage.

The domestic and foreign dimensions of rising expectations are not necessarily in tension as long as China's rise does not duplicate the violent history of previous rising powers. A truly peaceful rise will rest on the recognition that China's future success depends on its supporting and benefiting from the globalization of economic markets and the institutions of a liberal international order. If China adopts this approach, its ascent will be, as some in China have suggested, a post-modern one—freed from the traditional concerns with hard power and competition among states.

Yet, as a recent *Economist* editorial asked: "Why are there so few takers outside of China for its self-proclaimed doctrine of 'peaceful rise'?"[5] In part, of course, China's closed decision-making circle, combined with its military buildup, is bound to make neighbors nervous. But it also stems from the fact that despite the unprecedented level of trade between China and Japan and China and Taiwan, relations between Beijing and Tokyo and Beijing and Taipei remain tense. In addition, Beijing's decidedly mercantilist approach to locking up as much energy supply as it can is seen by some as belying its supposed faith in markets.

Perhaps most troubling, China's rise has also given rise to an increased level of old-fashioned Chinese nationalism. This is hardly surprising; following what Chinese refer to as a "century of humiliation," the Chinese naturally take pride in what their nation has become. But for a party whose legitimacy is no longer assured by Marxism, this nationalism can be both a bulwark of its rule and a standard by which its policies can be judged. As former Clinton State Department official Susan Shirk argues in her new book, *China: Fragile Superpower*, Chinese nationalism is a product of state propaganda organs but is also the inevitable result of popular satisfaction with the country's growing strength. Assuaging that nationalism—by righting the wrongs of the past "century of humiliation"—without disrupting the peaceful and stable international climate they need for continued economic growth, is perhaps the Chinese leadership's most daunting task.

Has China's foreign policy fundamentally shifted
in the past two decades?

For more than 20 years and under both Democratic and Republican administrations, US policy toward China can best be described as a modified hedge. In judging the continued wisdom and relevance of a hedging approach to China—or whether an alternative might be preferable—it is critical to assess China's foreign policy and national security orientation.

There can be little question that Chinese foreign policy has undergone a significant change since the mid-1990s, reflecting a more nuanced approach to both regional and global affairs. This change is reflected in China's increased engagement with the United States, and with international institutions and norms. For example, numerous Chinese analysts have suggested that China, as a rising great power, needs to act in a way that is commensurate with the responsibilities of a great power in upholding the international system.

Although these trends in foreign policy orientation are likely to continue in the near and medium terms, it is essentially unknowable, whatever China's intentions today, whether China's intentions will change over time with the growth of its capabilities and interests. There is also considerable debate over whether China's evolving foreign policy orientation represents a tactical or strategic shift.

Since the end of the Cold War, and especially since 9/11, China has adopted what can best be seen as a pragmatic approach to international relations, believing that a stable world order is necessary for China to be able to solve its internal problems. Playing the long game, many in China are also convinced that its rising power status will inevitably lead to Taiwan falling into its lap and allow China to take its rightful place as the preeminent power in East Asia and the Western Pacific.

As Francis Fukuyama, among others, has argued, China's diplomacy is no longer governed by a vision of China as merely the victim of the global order.[6] Instead, Beijing increasingly sees itself as a power that can shape that order. But, again, the particular shape it seeks is determined by a mix of interests and ambitions that are not always in harmony with one another.

For example, China has sought membership in several multilateral political and security regimes. On nonproliferation, China recently joined the Nuclear Suppliers Group and, after some foot-dragging, published its first export control laws. Similarly, China's quest to join or play a role in Asia's emerging architecture (such as the East Asia Summit, APEC, and ASEAN), as well as heightened bilateral diplomacy (such as the Free Trade Agreement reached with Chile, and those under consideration with Korea and Australia) all seem to point to a China that has developed a keen sense of its interests in such forums and arrangements. Some, of course, help stabilize political and economic relations. Others, such as the East Asia Summit and the Shanghai Cooperation Organization, have their origins in Beijing's desire to counter what it perceives to be hegemonic policies and strategies on the part of Washington.

China clearly values its new status on the world stage, but with that status comes increasing scrutiny of whether or not it acts in a manner befitting (to use former Deputy Secretary of State Robert Zoelleck's now famous phrase) a "responsible stakeholder" in the international system. And, here again, the record is mixed. Beijing garners praise for its role in the six-party talks on North Korea's nuclear program, but it has been, more often than not, an obstacle rather than a help with regard to Europe's effort to rein in the Iranian nuclear program. Similarly, Beijing has become an active contributor to UN peacekeeping efforts, yet continues to provide political support to a global roll call of dictatorships for what appears to be a very narrow set of self-interests.

So while one can reasonably conclude that China has made significant progress in normalizing its foreign policy and today appears as a defender of the liberal international order, China's behavior still at times has something of a "supermarket" approach—picking off the shelves what it wants and ignoring what it doesn't. Most significantly, even given that China's orientation today is fundamentally changed from what it once was, there is no guarantee that an ascendant China, like other rising powers before it, will not seek to rewrite the rules of international politics and economics in the years and decades ahead.

Interests and Ambitions

For the United States, developing the right approach toward China is complicated by the fact that the China of 2007 is a country with unfamiliar characteristics. China is a rising, nondemocratic power, with no overriding totalitarian vision for the world. The last time the United States faced anything remotely similar was Japan of the late 19th and early 20th centuries. More recently, of course, US habits of strategic thinking were primarily shaped by the superpower competition between the United States and the former Soviet Union. Today the world's other great powers are either democratic or, like Russia, not rising. In this respect, US-China policy will inevitably be *sui generis*.

The fact that China, for the moment at least, does not have an overriding vision of a new world order, suggests that its policies will be tied to what its leaders believe will promote either their own, or their nation's, interests. As such, we should expect fewer decisions designed to score ideological points on the world stage. Yet the image of a China that sets policy on the basis of its best interests is complicated by the possible divergence between the interests of the nation and the interest of the party's leaders in retaining power. While liberal democratic states do not always choose policies that are truly in the best interests of their citizens, simple political survival compels democratically responsible leadership to be in sync with the public interest or risk losing its position of leadership. Over time there is little question that democratic states do a better job of capturing and reflecting national interest than do nondemocratic states.

Mutual Interests

That said, the United States and China have a number of shared interests that can provide the basis for productive relations. First and foremost, of course, is China's need to continue to expand its economy and improve its citizens' quality of life. This is the sine qua non for the leadership's legitimacy, now that communism has hit the dustbin of history. However, China's economic expansion will only continue if the global economic order on which China depends is properly sustained and cared for. (Addressing climate change, in this context, may provide a unique challenge to China's continued economic growth, and for US-China relations.)

As two of the world's leading economies, the United States and China have compatible interests in many areas. Given Chinese leaders' desire for broad-based growth to create the so-called "harmonious society," US trade and investment in China's rural hinterland can help with this objective. As a rapidly aging society, China could benefit if the US private sector helped to develop health care and pension systems in China. China's first banking and financial reforms should, if fully implemented, provide business opportunities for US companies and lay the ground for the opening of China's capital markets and freeing its currency—both of which are priorities for the United States. Finally, China's desire to construct a "knowledge economy" creates a mutual interest in protecting intellectual property and preventing counterfeiting.

Broadly speaking, the United States and China have a common interest in global economic and financial stability. China's low-cost exports to the United States keep our own inflation low, while its investment of earned dollars in US government financial instruments helps keep our interest rates low. This, in turn, helps keep America's economy growing, with a capacity to continue buying China's exports. Although in the long term this may create some real problems for the US economy, it is, at least in the near term, a "win-win" situation.

To the extent that this system functions effectively, it is in the interest of both countries to fend off any steep fall in the value of the dollar, increase in oil and gas prices, or rise of US protectionist policies. Of course, the United States and China also share an interest in curtailing pollution, global warming, and the spread of infectious diseases.

China's economic growth creates opportunities for the United States to benefit from its rising prosperity, but it also raises expectations in America that China will be a responsible international economic actor. But it is not clear that China's leaders have fully embraced a win-win approach to economic affairs. As noted earlier, China retains the vestiges of a mercantilist approach when it comes to monetary affairs, banking, and energy supplies. And although there are encouraging trends indicating that China will shed those vestiges as it further integrates into the world economy and adheres to the norms of conduct of the WTO, it is by no means a given that this happy outcome will, indeed, come to pass. And as long as China remains a one-party state, there will always be tension between maximizing economic gains and sustaining the party's rule through preferential treatment of China's governing and business elite.

The Taiwan Question

Underlying this tension, of course, is the fact that economic interest is not Beijing's only interest. Other concerns continue to make US-China relations more than simply a matter of baking and carving up the world's economic pie. On the security and diplomatic front, there is first and foremost the question of Taiwan. While the Taiwan Strait has been kept from flaring up for decades now, the numerous Taiwan crises of the past 15 years reveal that stability is tenuous. The United States' view has been that there is only "one China" and the matter of how the Taiwan question is resolved can remain open—as long as it is resolved peacefully. Yet, after a decade of double-digit increases in Chinese military expenditures, there are indications that some in the Chinese military increasingly believe that China is on the verge of being able to coerce Taiwan into unification with the mainland—and on the mainland's terms. At the same time, as the process of democratic consolidation moves forward in Taiwan, the Taiwanese are less and less interested in simply becoming part of "one China." Polls show that although most Taiwanese prefer the status quo, fewer than 5 percent think of themselves as simply Chinese. Not surprisingly, as Taiwan has moved away from being governed by one party and toward democratic self-rule, many in Taiwan have come to think of themselves as an independent nation.

The risk is that democratic consolidation and national identity in Taiwan may be on a collision course with the expanding sense of nationalism among China's citizens, compounded by the fact that China's leaders have staked some of their own legitimacy on not allowing Taiwan to remain permanently separate from the mainland. This form of nationalism, and resentment over what is perceived to be "lost" territory, is of course nothing new when it comes to rising powers. What it does suggest, however, is that while China certainly has an interest in working with the United States and others to maintain a calm international political climate and ensure its own economic growth, China's interests will not be static. It is a rising power whose ambition to play a larger role in the region and on the world stage will grow as its power grows—which, in turn, will generate new "interests" on China's part.

From this, China appears to have concluded that its own strategic interest is best served to the degree that the world is less unipolar—that is, less dominated by the United States. To this end, China has tried to create new security, economic, and diplomatic structures in Central and East Asia that exclude Washington and allow Beijing to play the part of "first among equals." In addition, China has apparently decided that it can gain international leverage by cultivating ties to states that either the United States or Europe have tried to isolate, be they Iran, Burma, Sudan, Zimbabwe, or Venezuela. China's leaders seem careful never to push these relations to a point where they cause a major rift with the United States, but neither do they accept the idea that real pressure should be brought to bear on those states in a manner that might lead them to change. Beyond creating new institutions through which it might seek to balance US power, China has also come to recognize that one advantage of playing the role of a status quo power in already existing international institutions is that it may also serve to effectively bind US power and freedom of movement by simply challenging the United States to live up to its own standards and values.

Conflict with China is not inevitable. And while it is sensible to argue that China's interest lies with a peaceful and stable regional and international order, nevertheless, China's ambitions may well keep it from following those interests in what the United States would think is the most coherent and reasonable fashion.

"Managing" China's Rise

"Managing" China's rise is largely out of US hands. With China in the WTO, the United States has relinquished one potentially powerful tool to shape Chinese behavior—the withholding of trade and economic ties. Of course, the underlying hope was that bringing China into the WTO, and engagement itself, would be a significant shaper of Chinese behavior, and the WTO's "rules of the road" would gradually lead China into a pattern of behavior that is in step with the world's other great powers. It is still perhaps too early to tell if this bet turns out to be a good one.

It is still unclear, for example, whether China's growing buy-in and adherence to international institutions and norms is tactical or strategic in nature. Without additional decisive action to irreversibly "lock" China in as an upholder of the current system, China's current rhetorical efforts to portray itself as a nonthreatening status quo power may not suffice.

Perhaps tellingly, Zoellick's call for China to become a responsible "stakeholder" in the international order has had something of a contradictory impact in China. On the one hand, China's leaders were quite pleased with the idea that the speech signified, to their minds, Washington's public acceptance of China as a power to be respected. It was a speech, they believed, that signaled they were to be taken seriously. On the other hand—and probably not the intention of the speech's author—the term *stakeholder* is now used as a standard for judging China's each and every action on the world stage. What China does or does not do at the United Nations on Sudan, Iran, et al., is routinely held up against the question of whether that behavior is consonant with the world's expectation of what it means to be a responsible "stakeholder." This may prevent China from ignoring the opinions of the other great powers altogether but not to the degree that it fundamentally changes its international behavior.

For many Chinese, reflecting on the historical experience of "one hundred years of humiliation," the wish to become strong in order to protect China against exploitation by other powers is understandable. And many Chinese are undoubtedly sincere in this belief. But the fact remains that as China's power grows, so will its range of options. While the "economy first, military second" approach may look reasonable and non-threatening from the Chinese perspective, to the United States and to others in the region and around the globe it nonetheless raises questions. If the purpose of a peaceful rise is economic development to build China's strength, at some point won't China want to start flexing its military muscle as well? It's hardly reassuring that this is a pattern followed not just by imperial Japan and Germany but also by the United States.

For the foreseeable future, the United States will be dealing with a nondemocratic China whose ambitions will probably grow alongside its economic and military power. In the best of all scenarios, the United States and its democratic allies will insist on political liberalization within China as a quid pro quo for good relations. But such a policy has two problems. First, China is now part of the world economy. No one in the West, the United States included, has the stomach for putting at risk prospects for greater access to the Chinese market. Second, for China's leaders, staying in power is very likely worth whatever difficulties that come with being seen as autocrats. Indeed, if China's leaders learned one thing from watching the West's reaction to the massacre at Tiananmen Square, it is that such behavior may bear a minimal long-term cost internationally.

Unless there is a change domestically, however, unless China begins to undertake political reforms, the United States and its allies will be left with policy options that work on the margins—cooperating where we can, yet probably unable to head off the competition for regional hegemony. China's vision of its national security will not change unless it changes internally and, arguably, a liberalized China may well move in a populist nationalist direction, at least in the short run, bringing another set of problems.

Current US policy is a mix of engagement and hedging, as it was in the previous administration. In theory, this is a perfectly reasonable response to the complexity of Chinese interests and ambitions we have described. But getting the right mix of engagement and hedging in practice is no easy thing. The challenge is complicated by the fact that China's lack of strategic transparency keeps us from ever being quite sure about the impact of our policies in China, either now or over the long run.

For example, does hedging against China's ambitions require less or more deterrence on our part? On the one hand, it could be argued that pragmatically strengthening our military and strategic posture will help prevent China from misjudging either US strategic interests or our will. On the other hand, if our hedge is viewed not as prudence, but rather as a bid for supremacy or an effort to block China from assuming its rightful place in the region, it might fuel further resentments and incite precisely the reaction we don't seek, a redoubling of countervailing military, economic, and diplomatic strategies. Moreover, ratcheting up our deterrent posture with respect to China will be doubly hard since—unlike with the Soviet Union—the United States is engaged with China on numerous fronts, such as trade, and hedging against China's larger ambitions will complicate efforts to cooperate with China on issues of mutual interest.

There is no less a conundrum for a policy of engagement. Both Presidents Clinton and George W. Bush have articulated a similar rationale for that approach. Engagement, combined with China's economic growth, will eventually foster a dynamic within China that will lead to political liberalization. But there is no agreement about the time horizon in which significant progress could be expected on that front or, for that matter, the character of the progress made to date. For policymakers, this uncertainty matters a great deal. If China's "turn" were to be relatively soon, one could expect policymakers to overlook problems in Chinese behavior on the sensible ground that there is no reason to complicate a relationship that in time will work itself out to our benefit. On the other hand, if China's "turn" is a distant thing, policymakers will be forced to make choices based on the realities of today. Moreover, while it may well be the case that economic modernization generally does lead to political liberalization, is it as inevitable as is sometimes suggested? If not, could a policy of relatively unconditional engagement with China actually be counterproductive, leading, as some have argued, to a stalled reform process in China?

In sum, designing a US policy toward China will take far more sophistication than US policymakers from either political party have previously shown. In the best of all worlds, China's desire to take care of its internal development would lead it to be a rational actor, in which economic reasoning would control its policies. While there would certainly be disagreements and competition between the United States and China even on this front, they would be the sorts of disagreements and competition that trade negotiators and economists routinely hash out to the ultimate advantage of both countries. The skilled handling of China's rise will require a smart, forward-leaning, and concerted effort by the United States. Policymakers will have to craft an approach that will lock in the gains thus far from China's political and economic development, and also encourage China to make positive future choices. Without such a well-balanced and calibrated policy, the Communist Party's ambitions to remain in power and the rise of Chinese nationalism may well make a more straightforward relationship with China more a hope than a reality.

Notes

1 John J. Mearsheimer, *The Tragedy of Great Power Politics* (New York: W. W. Norton & Co., 2003).

2 Ashton B. Carter and William J. Perry, "China on the March," *The National Interest*, March–April, 2007.

3 Harry Harding, presentation to Stanley Foundation conference on "Leveraging US Strength in an Uncertain World," Washington, DC, December 2006.

4 Minxin Pei, *China's Trapped Transition: The Limits of Developmental Autocracy* (Harvard University Press, 2006), Chap. 3, "Rent Protection and Dissipation: The Dark Side of Gradualism," and Chap. 4, "Transforming the State: From Developmental to Predatory."

5 "China's Great Game in Asia," *The Economist*, March 29, 2007.

6 Francis Fukuyama, "Re-Envisioning Asia," *Foreign Affairs*, January–February, 2005.

8

Are We All Nation-Builders Now?

Andrew Erdmann and Suzanne Nossel

The national debate over post-conflict stabilization and reconstruction policy—so-called "nation-building"—has shifted dramatically since 9/11. In the 1990s, progressives championed efforts to help vulnerable countries recover from conflicts and stand on their own. They felt compelled to forestall humanitarian disasters and promote democracy and human rights. On the other side of the political aisle, in his 2000 campaign, candidate George W. Bush promised a more "humble" foreign policy than his predecessor's, famously declaring "I don't think our troops ought to be used for what's called nation-building."

Despite this promise to avoid prolonged post-conflict entanglements, the Bush administration is deeply enmeshed in Afghanistan and Iraq, two of the most challenging and costly experiments in nation-building ever undertaken. As it undertook these missions, the administration argued that in order to be secure at home, the United States must use its power to promote democratic transformations in other societies, most notably in the Middle East. During the same period, influenced especially by the debacle in Iraq, some liberal supporters of nation-building have turned into critics who now see such missions as neo-colonial intrusions that can do more harm than good.

Today, whatever else divides them, advocates and skeptics of nation-building all agree that US efforts to stabilize and rebuild Iraq and Afghanistan have stumbled badly, putting US national interests at risk both in those countries and beyond. Across the political spectrum, many Americans increasingly wonder whether the challenge of nation-building exceeds the United States' skills, competence, resources, and sensitivity.

The next administration will face important questions about potential US involvement in nation-building: when the United States should get involved; how it should participate and with whom; and what capabilities, resources, and preparation are required. Under the shadow of Iraq and Afghanistan, these questions will breed controversy, potentially realigning the poles of the nation-building debate yet again. To the extent that bipartisan consensus can be built in advance, it may help prevent future nation-building efforts from becoming a political football.

Progressives and conservatives should unite in a hardheaded, pragmatic approach to nation-building. If history is any guide, the United States will continue to commit military and civilian resources to nation-building missions. Such missions will have high stakes in both political and human terms. The United States will need to face squarely the profound challenges of nation-building—namely, that these missions are difficult, costly, long, and oftentimes only partly successful. Sound policies must take into account the reality of the United States' unique place in the world, both as a standard-bearer of liberal ideals and as a superpower whose strength is both respected and resented. New missions will prompt new debates over costs, benefits, and US strategic priorities. One lesson from Afghanistan is that US national security interests can render pointless the many philosophical or academic arguments against nation-building.

In response to the events of the past decade, practitioners and scholars have probed the practical challenges of post-conflict reconstruction, producing important studies of its political and operational dimensions.[1] These independent reports thoroughly analyze the gaps in current US post-conflict capabilities, and make many sound recommendations for the structures and policies that could remedy them. While these studies comprise an invaluable resource for any future US efforts, this chapter will identify new common ground on points of policy where progressives and conservatives have at times disagreed.

To define our term, *nation-building* is the use of all the tools of statecraft—military and civilian—to help stabilize and reconstruct a country emerging from an armed conflict. Such missions include security; governance and rule of law; humanitarian relief and recovery, if necessary; restoration of essential services, such as electricity, water, and education; immediate economic rejuvenation; and, ultimately, the transition to long-term development. Such missions often involve strengthening or even building from scratch the state's capacity to govern. As Iraq and Afghanistan highlight, nation-building is not a linear process; it may involve renewed or new conflicts after an initial "conventional" battle is "over." Stabilization and reconstruction missions have distinct challenges, differing from the lifesaving mission of strictly humanitarian relief and recovery operations, as well as from long-term foreign aid and development programs.

After reviewing the debates surrounding US engagement in post-conflict operations since the end of the Cold War, the chapter will describe the proper expectations
for US involvement and the outcome of such operations, the relative merits of
unilateral and multilateral post-conflict operations, steps to better equip both the US
government and international partners for stabilization missions, and how to build
domestic political support for an effective post-conflict policy.

Nation-Building Debates Since the End
of the Cold War

In the 1990s the most important foreign policy initiatives of the Clinton administration were its efforts to end deadly conflicts and promote stability and democracy
in their aftermaths. The administration's experience was mixed. Early abortive
missions in Somalia and Haiti demonstrated the difficulty of trying to solidify a fragile
peace when guns were still blazing. The tendency toward so-called "mission creep" and
the elusiveness of quick and bloodless "exit strategies" meant that operations became
more complex, costly, and protracted than the administration or the American public
had bargained for. But the relative successes eventually achieved in Bosnia and Kosovo
helped convince policymakers that nation-building missions were both politically
and practically tenable. The administration also began to learn from its mistakes. In
approaching the reconstruction of Kosovo in 1999, the administration was determined
to draw on the experience of Bosnia to mount a more international approach with
tighter coordination between civilian and military components, and between the
United States and key international organizations.

The Clinton administration's nation-building campaigns were not without their
critics. Some derided these efforts as "social work" that took time, resources, and
energy away from other pressing national security challenges.[2] Inside and outside the
military, voices complained that nation-building missions in the Balkans and elsewhere distracted the US armed forces from their conventional mission, namely,
"fighting and winning wars." For many conservatives, their critique of the efficacy
of nation-building abroad was an extension of their skepticism of "social engineering"
at home. Suspicion of nation-building became a central element in the Republican
critique of the Clinton administration's foreign policy during the 2000 presidential
campaign. Future National Security Advisor and Secretary of State Condoleezza
Rice criticized the Clinton administration's Balkans efforts in vivid terms: the 82nd
Airborne should not be used to escort children to kindergarten.

The Bush administration entered office in 2001 committed to avoiding nation-
building as a distraction from high priorities such as missile defense, abandoning the

Anti-Ballistic Missile Treaty, and redefining relations with China. In the early months of the Bush administration, Clinton-era post-conflict initiatives were largely abandoned. President Clinton's Presidential Decision Directive 56 "Managing Complex Contingency Operations" was scrapped and efforts to draft a successor directive to guide interagency planning and operations stalled.

The Al Qaeda terrorist attacks of 9/11 stimulated a fundamental rethinking by the Bush administration of the place of nation-building in US national security strategy. Al Qaeda's exploitation of Taliban-controlled Afghanistan brought home the threat posed by failed states that could serve as terrorist staging grounds. After toppling the Taliban regime, the administration accepted the obvious: unless Afghanistan was stabilized and a new, more robust government established, the terrorists could simply return. The Bush administration's seminal 2002 *National Security Strategy* reflected this shift in thinking. The United States, the document declared, "is now more threatened by weak and failing states than we are by conquering ones." By the end of 2002 the National Security Council quietly began considering ways to improve US post-conflict capabilities, potentially as part of the broader international effort to augment peacekeeping and civilian police forces.

The Bush administration's nascent commitment to nation-building was tested in Iraq. That conflict demonstrated that the United States could use its unsurpassed military power to accomplish "regime elimination." However, true "regime change" —i.e., replacing the old regime with something, new and better—was far more challenging than "regime elimination." The initial planning assumptions for a rapid stabilization mission were wildly optimistic. Military planning and preparation for the aftermath of overthrowing Saddam Hussein's regime (so-called "Phase IV" operations) proved woefully inadequate. The entire civilian side of the operation was bedeviled by a lack of qualified experts in areas ranging from policing and budget programming to electricity and education. A host of seemingly mundane details such as contracting processes proved ill-suited to fostering Iraq's rapid recovery. The main features of this tragic story continue to be documented elsewhere.

Since 2003, Iraq and, to a lesser extent, Afghanistan have made nation-building a subject of daily headlines and a matter of the utmost political and public concern. As the human, material, and strategic costs of Iraq and Afghanistan mounted, so too did criticism from both the right and the left. Conservative opinion split. Epitomized by then Deputy Secretary of Defense Paul Wolfowitz, many so-called "neo-conservatives" backed the Bush administration's ambitious vision of a stable and democratic Iraq that would supposedly open the way toward further democratic transformations in the region. Others broke ranks, however. Francis Fukuyama, for instance, eloquently rebuked fellow neo-conservatives for forgetting their traditional "distrust of ambitious social engineering projects" when they turned their eyes abroad and advocated democracy promotion as a defining element in US foreign policy.[3] Meanwhile, traditional "realists" chided President Bush on his latter-day conversion to nation-building, pointed to the visible cracks in the Iraq project, and questioned the wisdom of prioritizing the promotion of democracy over other national security objectives.

At the same time, progressives' traditional support for nation-building took a heavy beating. When post-war inspectors failed to find evidence of a current nuclear weapons program or stockpiles of chemical and biological weapons in Iraq, the Bush administration increasingly invoked the promotion of democracy as the main justification for the Iraq war. From a progressive vantage, this reformulation tainted a once-proud commitment to expanding liberal freedoms with a war that was becoming widely unpopular. During the occupation phase, for example, the high-handedness and insularity of the US-led Coalition Provincial Authority only reinforced a perception of neo-colonialism. The anti-Iraq war movement attacked not just the conduct of the war, but the very idea of the United States occupying foreign territory. While some confined their criticism to the Bush administration's tactics and mismanagement—including its eschewal of a new United Nations Security Council resolution to authorize the invasion and its disregard for previous post-conflict experience—others questioned the broader premise of US stabilization efforts.

At the same time, many progressive policymakers were determined that the baby of stabilization assistance and democracy promotion—including the progress made in these areas during the Clinton years—not be cast out with the fouled bathwater of Iraq. They assert the importance of stabilizing failed states and fostering the spread of democracy for long-term US interests, and are determined that a pledge to avoid the mistakes of Iraq not become a promise to forswear nation-building altogether. On the contrary, they hope to strengthen and recast US post-conflict efforts through improved structures, additional resources, and better planning.

The policy debate over US policy and capabilities for nation-building is thus at a turning point. Experience in Iraq and Afghanistan—when added to those in Somalia, Haiti, the Balkans, and elsewhere—has dispelled any illusion that nation-building can be quick or easy. On both the conservative and the progressive side, some would avoid another Iraq by staying out of the nation-building business completely, while others favor the opposite solution: investing significantly in stronger nation-building capabilities so that the United States can be more effective. On the one hand, as Stewart Patrick has wryly observed: "We may be seeing the emergence of a strange alliance on the Hill: liberals who don't want any more Iraqs, conservatives who don't want any more Bosnias."[4] On the other hand, there are bipartisan efforts on Capitol Hill (led by Senators Richard Lugar and Joseph Biden) to increase funding for post-conflict capabilities, including the creation of a long-promised Civilian Reserve Corps. In its most ambitious form, this is described as a commitment to augment US capabilities for post-conflict missions up to a level commensurate with the US military's capabilities for traditional warfighting.

The Nature of the Post-Conflict Stabilization and Reconstruction Policy Challenge

Looking beyond Iraq and Afghanistan, conservatives and progressives alike should accept nation-building as a necessary mission, but a difficult one that we should share with others as much as possible.

A Necessary Mission

Forswearing nation-building is not a realistic policy option for three reasons.

First, the United States has a series of often overlapping interests in stabilizing post-conflict situations. While maintaining peace among the great powers and other "traditional" challenges of statecraft will remain central to US foreign policy, the Bush administration's 2002 *National Security Strategy* and its successor of 2006 correctly highlight that a host of transnational threats—including terrorism, international crime, trafficking in drugs and persons—are equally important. These threats can destabilize regions as well as directly affect US national security. They often originate in, or exploit, failed states and the "ungoverned space" that can emerge after conflict. Al Qaeda's use of pre-9/11 Afghanistan as a training and operational hub is the exemplar. Effective nation-building helps check the spread of such "negative externalities." Evidence also suggests that countries receiving effective post-conflict assistance are less likely to slide back into violence than those that do not. This carries humanitarian implications (e.g., preventing genocide, ethnic cleansing, etc.), as well as geostrategic ones (e.g., eliminating a vacuum that regional actors may try to exploit).[5]

The United States also has an interest in the character of states emerging from conflict. Ideally, from Washington's perspective, such states would align with Western interests and values. In some cases, US interest in a post-conflict mission may be to check another country in the region from expanding its power and influence over an unstable neighbor. In other cases, international credibility and ethical imperative may be at stake. Former Secretary of State Colin Powell's "Pottery Barn rule" is alive and well as a moral obligation. Where the United States has a hand in disrupting a society, it will be called upon to help put that country back together again. In the face of such interests, sitting on the sidelines—or leaving the work entirely to others—carries unpalatable risks to US security and its international stature.

Second, the challenge of nation-building will not disappear from the international scene any time soon. There are many "fragile" states around the world. Consider possible contingencies in the Caribbean, the Horn of Africa, and Central Asia. As one indicator of this harsh reality, since the end of the Cold War, the United Nations has launched a new peacekeeping operation roughly every six months, while the United States has undertaken a major nation-building operation every two years.[6] Although it is doubtful that the United States will choose to hazard another nation-building experiment on the scale of Iraq, smaller scale operations somewhere in the world are highly likely.

Third, the United States cannot realistically rely upon others to do all the heavy lifting. Although cliché, it bears repeating that the United States is—and will be for the foreseeable future—the most powerful country in the world, economically, politically, and militarily. It is highly unlikely that other nations will respond to these challenges so that American interests in preventing state failure and its consequences will be adequately protected. With few exceptions (perhaps Great Britain, France, and Australia), other countries lack the resources and motivation to intervene independently in situations if we do not.

Taken together, these premises lead to the conclusion that the United States should prepare for nation-building, even if we'd prefer to avoid it.

In light of the difficulties of nation-building in Iraq, two arguments against boosting US capabilities are heard most often. First, some claim that improving preparations for post-conflict reconstruction and stabilization may only embolden future leaders to embark upon unnecessary military interventions abroad. Second, others contend that the solution to the challenge of nation-building is to avoid the mission altogether: It is too hard, so "just say no."

These arguments are unconvincing. The first argument—that being prepared for nation-building missions heightens the likelihood of ill-advised post-conflict interventions—doesn't square with the US position in the world. Today the United States cannot forswear to develop its capabilities—as Germany and Japan did after World War II—because no other power would fill the gap as we did in both Europe and Asia after 1945. In the case of the United States and post-conflict missions, today there is oftentimes no other international actor ready and able to intervene when the United States opts out. Furthermore, history provides no example of where too much preparation for effective post-conflict stabilization tipped the balance in favor of intervening. A refusal to prepare is irresponsible and would deprive the US government and people of a strategic tool that they may badly need. Recent experience has taught the harsh consequences of failing to train, equip, and prepare adequately for post-conflict missions. Quite simply, do we want to repeat the past when the next crisis emerges, cobbling together an ad hoc response, with the burden falling primarily upon the US military? To do so would only compound the problem of foisting upon the US armed services manifold missions for which they have neither the training nor the resources. The second point—that even when nation-building is strategically important, it's simply too hard—ignores successful historical precedents. Since the end of the Cold War, we have seen relatively successful nation-building in El Salvador, Bosnia, and Kosovo, to name a few. Moreover, we should never underestimate the United States' ability to innovate in the face of new threats and challenges.

A Difficult Mission

While the United States must prepare better for the nation-building mission, there should be no illusions about the ease or inevitability of success. Recent experience has reaffirmed the conservative skepticism of externally directed "social engineering." Indigenous actors and dynamics guide difficult social and political transitions much more than external forces do. Outsiders can assist and enable, but are not in a position to deliver lasting results. In post-conflict societies, existing institutions are often fragile, and their reach limited. Yet it is precisely by working through such institutions as much as possible that their legitimacy and capacities can be strengthened. Such state-building consumes time, resources, and patience. Moreover, "spoilers" often enjoy the advantages of popular support, and the local knowledge and know-how to wreak havoc. Success thus demands a truly integrated political, economic, and military effort—in strategy as well as actual implementation. This, in turn, requires strategic vision, administrative competence, adequate resources, time, and no small amount of luck. In sum, nation-building missions are fraught by their very nature.

We counsel strongly against any grandiose visions of simple, rapid transformations when debating future stability operations. Although modest ambitions go against the usual grain for making the case publicly or inside government, the reality is that such missions often require years of significant investments to achieve even modest results. Containing a problem, not curing it, will often constitute a major success. Even when backed by the best intelligence, resources, and policy judgment, an initial plan and commitment may prove inadequate to the challenge. Stakes—as well as the strategies of key actors—evolve with the situation. The mission may change through time, and perhaps even expand or deepen. However, our concern should not be with "mission creep" per se, but rather with the possibility that policymakers will not consciously calibrate means to ends as the situation evolves. (Somalia in 1993 inevitably comes to mind.) Policymakers, therefore, must find the delicate balance between commitment to action and an ability to reassess, recognize "sunk costs" as truly sunk, and adjust course accordingly.

Approaching post-conflict missions with realistic expectations requires careful consideration of US objectives and a finely tuned definition of success. Historically, the United States has had a host of different objectives for nation-building operations, on a spectrum from modest and narrowly self-interested to visionary. These include preventing war from resurging; averting a failed state or power vacuum; preventing large-scale refugee flows to US shores; forestalling the emergence of a rogue regime that is not integrated into international systems and norms, and/or hostile to the United States; stopping large-scale human rights and humanitarian violations; fostering a friendly state (i.e., a political and economic partner); and promoting democracy. In any given case, the criteria of "success" will depend upon the context, the interests at stake, and trade-offs with competing policy considerations.

Rarely, if ever, will success be a simple matter of handing off a stable, economically prosperous and maturely democratic state over to a responsible and friendly government capable of ruling without outside assistance. More often the timing of the United States' exit will be driven by a pragmatic calculus involving domestic political support, an assessment of the marginal return on further investment of resources, and the prospect that the country in question may backslide and again threaten US strategic interests. Before an operation even begins, therefore, it is misguided to seek a precise "exit strategy" or commit to a date certain for withdrawal. As Gideon Rose has argued, "the focus should not be on developing exit strategies, but on articulating precise American interests and coming up with ways to advance them."[7]

The ambitious goal of promoting stable, democratic regimes in the aftermath of conflict merits special attention, in light of recent experience. Consistent with American values, conservatives and progressives can agree that promoting democratic governance abroad should be a long-term policy objective. However, the specific tactics and timeline to reach this strategic goal must be tailored to each unique situation. Holding elections alone does not a democracy make. In post-conflict environments, as we have seen in Iraq, early elections can harden politics along polarized sectarian or ethnic lines. Nor does democracy, even when it is achieved, guarantee that regimes will be friendly or share our values, particularly in places where the local cultural, religious, and political environments differ sharply from our own. In many situations, moreover, achieving basic levels of security and state capacity will be preconditions for a successful democratic transition. The Iraq experience should remind us that the United States cannot control political outcomes within other societies, and that attempting to do so can backfire. We risk undermining the ideal of democracy, if we reinforce a perception that it is a made-in-America formula that is forced upon vulnerable societies. This is not to deny that Washington has an interest in seeing open democracies rise in former conflict zones, but rather to accept that successful political transitions are complex, organic processes that may stretch beyond a post-conflict stabilization and reconstruction phase.

A paradox lies at the heart of the nation-building challenge, when we weigh these issues domestically in our own democratic system. When policymakers and the public appreciate the challenge's full magnitude, it could lead us to avoid these missions altogether—not because they lack strategic import, but because the requisite political will to bear the costs and burdens is tenuous. If we had known in 2003 what the Iraq war would eventually entail, would the administration or the Congress have decided to begin it? Will—or should—the United States ever again undertake a mission of such magnitude and complexity? For that matter, would the public have accepted the deployment of US forces to the Balkans in 1995 if they had been told the commitment would stretch out over a decade?

On the one hand, some argue that policymakers must both squarely face nation-building's inherent difficulties in their policy deliberations and then, having decided, clearly convey the implications to the public so that they, too, understand the interests and risks. On the other hand are those who question whether such clarity is feasible, given the unknowns inherent in stabilization operations. We can easily imagine situations where overemphasis of the risks may make us too cautious for our own good.

While such questions will inevitably engender impassioned debates, a few clear conclusions are possible. Policymakers and the public alike will need to look before they leap when embarking on such missions. Mustering and sustaining the political will to see nation-building efforts through to satisfactory conclusions presents its own set of challenges. Ultimately, this task will be much easier if it is built upon a firm bipartisan foundation.

A Shared Mission

That the United States will be involved regularly in nation-building does not imply that it must tackle every challenge alone. Just the opposite: wherever possible, the United States should try to share the work of nation-building with others.

The United States would quickly exhaust its resources and political will if it attempts to single-handedly stabilize all failed states and conflict-ridden societies. Moreover, the Iraq situation illustrates an inherent problem that may arise with post-conflict missions the United States might lead outside a multilateral umbrella: such missions run the risk of being perceived as self-interested, and imposed upon the affected population. In Iraq, these perceptions helped fuel a violent backlash against US presence. Furthermore, nation-building operations dominated by the United States can generate additional negative externalities abroad and at home. The perceived unilateralism of US actions in Iraq, for instance, has prompted a series of reverberating ill-effects. Because the United States was undeniably the main foreign force in the original occupation in Iraq and remains the primary external force supporting the government of Iraq, anti-occupation sentiment has fed anti-Americanism in Iraq and the broader Middle East. This has played into the hands of Al Qaeda and others who seek to foment anger toward the United States. Iraqi violence against US forces has, in turn, triggered a backlash at home. Many Americans now wonder why their soldiers protect a population whose majority reportedly believes that attacks against these same forces are legitimate.

Ad hoc "coalitions of the willing" may, in certain cases, be the best option for nation-building missions. Historical experience suggests, however, that operating under some multilateral aegis is usually preferable. Conservatives fear that operations under such an umbrella may diminish US forces' operational effectiveness and overall freedom of maneuver. To be sure, coalition operations are complex and carry some unique risks. Nonetheless, if we accept that nation-building operations are typically lengthy and resource-intensive, the benefits of spreading the burden will often outweigh these costs. Quick action does not always require prior UN approval, but forging a consensus within another multilateral organization such as NATO can provide a highly useful alternative, as we saw in Kosovo in 1999. Practically speaking, operating within a multilateral framework helps legitimize nation-building operations in the eyes of our allies' publics, thereby enabling them to sustain their commitment to difficult missions. Great Britain's announcement in early 2007 of its plan to shift its military's operational focus from Iraq to Afghanistan reflects this sort of domestic political reality: the British public increasingly views Iraq as illegitimate while Afghanistan remains a "good war." Conservatives may therefore eventually recognize that multilateral nation-building may be the worst form of nation-building, except all the others.

Even if the United States consistently seeks partners in nation-building, we must also address the reality that other countries may often lack the skill or operational capabilities, even if they possess the will. Many partners, for instance, lack the lift and logistics to deploy rapidly and sustain their forces. Looking forward, therefore, the United States must continue to encourage our partners to augment their capabilities strategically and maintain their readiness for multinational operations even in times of relative peace.

Taken together, the lessons of Afghanistan and Iraq for future post-conflict missions are thus twofold: the United States needs to augment its capabilities to conduct nation-building missions more effectively and also work to ensure that, insofar as possible, it does not undertake such missions on its own.

A Policy Planning and Monitoring Matrix

There is no cookie-cutter formula for effective post-conflict stabilization and reconstruction. Each mission is unique. Yet there are essential tasks common to all such operations.[8] As they assess possible future operations, US policymakers should survey not only the capabilities and resources the United States has within its own means but also the potential contributions other nations might realistically offer and what steps the United States could take to elicit that help.

For simplicity's sake, a matrix can be devised that appraises the value and availability of partner contributions across three main factors: "skill," "will," and "US influence" (Figure 1). "Skill" encompasses potential contributors' available capabilities and resources that could be realistically employed in a specific operation. These range from providing financial support or critical enablers (such as logistical assistance) to specific post-conflict stabilization and reconstruction capabilities across the primary mission areas. "Will" includes an assessment of the potential contributors' level of commitment to the mission, including national interest and level of internal organizational or domestic political support. Finally, "US influence" measures the United States' ability to favorably influence a potential contributor's "will"—and also takes stock of how best to exercise this influence. For instance, during the Iraq war, the administration tried to keep coalition partners "on side" by meeting specific requests for equipment or diplomatic support in other areas.

In a planning phase, such a framework would help highlight critical gaps in capabilities and resources, thereby enabling planners to focus their efforts most effectively. Once an operation is under way, this framework could serve as a performance management "dashboard" to monitor whether an operation continues to have all the commitments to perform all of the core tasks needed to succeed.

Steps to Improve US Capabilities for Post-Conflict Reconstruction and Stabilization

The attention of policymakers and the public is understandably focused upon the ongoing missions in Iraq and Afghanistan. As the continued difficulties in staffing provincial reconstruction teams in Iraq make clear, there are still basic problems of interagency coordination and shortfalls in capacity after more than four years of operations.

Potential Contributors	"Skill": Available capabilities and resources suited to specific operation							"Will": Interests, level of internal/domestic support	"US Influence": Ability to affect potential contributor's "will"
	Money	Enablers (e.g., logistics, C4ISR)	Security	Governance and Participation	Humanitarian Assistance and Social Well-Being	Economic Stabilization and Infrastructure	Justice and Reconciliation		
United States									
United Nations									
Regional Org. (e.g., NATO in Kosovo)									
Regional power (e.g., Australia in East Timor)									
Other major country contributors									
Major NGOs									

Figure 1: *Skill, Will, US Influence post-conflict stabilization and reconstruction matrix*

Nevertheless, behind the headlines, and starting in earnest in 2003, the Bush administration began to look beyond the current crises to build new US capabilities to strengthen response in the future. As President Bush explained at the International Republican Institute in May 2005, the United States "must improve the responsiveness of our government to help nations emerging from tyranny and war. . . . [It] must be able to move quickly to provide needed assistance." Similar policy statements and strategic assessments such as the Quadrennial Defense Review reiterated the importance of preparing for future stability or nation-building operations.

Three major initiatives lay at the center of the Bush administration's new approach: first, the July 2004 establishment of the State Department's Office for Reconstruction and Stabilization (S/CRS) to coordinate interagency planning, preparation, and execution of post-conflict operations; second, designation of "stability operations" as a "core US military mission . . . given priority comparable to combat operations" in Department of Defense Directive 3000.05 in November 2005; and, third, the grant of broad responsibility by President Bush to the secretary of state to "coordinate and lead integrated United States government efforts, involving all US departments and agencies with relevant capabilities to prepare, plan for, and conduct stabilization and reconstruction activities," in the December 2005 National Security Presidential Decision Directive-44 (NSPD-44, entitled "Management of Interagency Efforts Concerning Reconstruction and Stabilization").[9]

It is time to take stock of these initiatives to assess progress in the preparations for future post-conflict stabilization and reconstruction missions. To be fair, any organizational change in the US government is notoriously difficult. We are, after all, still trying to "unify" the operations of the military services 60 years after the National Security Act of 1947. Transforming the way that agencies combine to plan, prepare, and operate in nation-building is a decades-long endeavor, and it is too soon to tell whether the Bush administration's reforms will lead to a dead end or blaze a new trail. That said, the early results are mixed at best. Bureaucratic and organizational factors— along with the classic constitutional "invitation to struggle" between the executive and legislative branches—have been much more influential than any substantive debate over the importance of nation-building missions.

One problem is the lack of a natural bureaucratic home for these matters. Both inside and outside the Department of Defense, all bureaucratic and policy players initially agreed that responsibility should *not* rest solely with the Pentagon. The military services are eager for increased civilian participation and have consistently been the strongest backers of a new office for post-conflict policy outside of the Pentagon. For others, the concern is to avoid further "militarization" of US foreign policy. One potential bureaucratic home, the United States Agency for International Development (USAID) has long-term economic development as its core mission and it lacks the bureaucratic clout to coordinate the activities of Cabinet-level departments. The National Security Council (NSC) at the White House is formally positioned to coordinate interagency policy, but lacks the permanent staff or resources to oversee large, complex operations. In the end, responsibility fell almost by default to the Department of State and its newly created Office of Coordinator for Reconstruction and Stabilization.

From the moment it was established, S/CRS was an uncomfortable fit within the Department of State. First, the S/CRS mission, which emphasizes advance interagency contingency planning and preparation, is directly at odds with the department's prevailing culture. Diplomats tend to prefer flexibility, not plans, and view the tools of their trade as the memorandum, cable, conversation, and briefing. Second, S/CRS is not viewed within the Department of State as a high-prestige office. The regional bureaus remain the most influential within the department, putting the so-called functional offices at a bureaucratic disadvantage in everything from recruiting staff to claiming the attention of the secretary. They have not welcomed S/CRS' efforts to coordinate conflict prevention activities, which they see as trespassing on their turf. Likewise, the bureaus of Political-Military Affairs and International Narcotics and Law Enforcement have vigorously defended their perceived prerogatives as well. Compounding matters, the post of coordinator of S/CRS was not given "ambassador-at-large" status as the coordinator for Counterterrorism or the co-ordinator for War Crimes Issues were. This further weakens its image in relation to the assistant secretaries of state (and other similarly ranked officials), a critical bureaucratic constituency. S/CRS' location in an annex physically separate from "Main State" reinforced the perception that it is distant from the core mission of the department. Finally, in March 2007, the coordinator of S/CRS became the deputy to the director of Foreign Assistance, who is himself dual-hatted as the administrator of USAID. This was widely viewed inside the Department of State as a demotion of S/CRS.

In its first three years, furthermore, the S/CRS did not receive the resources to command respect within the interagency or represent a significant augmentation of the government's nation-building capabilities. On Capitol Hill, a desire to protect the legislative branch's prerogatives vis-à-vis the funding and structure of the executive played a further role. Even beyond S/CRS, the Department of State, moreover, lacks a natural constituency on Capitol Hill comparable to the Pentagon's, which is tied to its much more visible presence in the domestic political and economic scene.[10] Within the Bush administration, support never matched the exceedingly broad mission given to S/CRS in NSPD-44, one which spans from identifying lessons learned and developing doctrine to providing decision makers with "detailed options" in response to specific crises. In early 2007, for example, the administration once more showed its inconsistent support, by advocating (again) the establishment of the Civilian Reserve Corps, but failing to include it in the administration's fiscal year 2008 budget request. Then during the spring 2007, Secretary of State Rice pushed for and received a provision in the Iraq supplemental appropriations law for up to $50 million to jumpstart the Civilian Reserve Corps.

In sum, S/CRS has suffered from a bit of a Catch-22 problem: it has not convinced skeptics of its potential so it has not been given the opportunity to prove itself, but it will not be given such an opportunity until it can convince the skeptics. S/CRS has not played a major role in either Afghanistan or Iraq policy, based on the logic that these missions were too large and complex for a new office to handle. Progress on other fronts lagged. For instance, nearly three years after S/CRS' creation, the Active Reserve Corps of trained and deployable US government employees for post-conflict environments stood at approximately ten. As of early 2007, no comprehensive "inventory" of the US government's civilian nation-building assets even existed. S/CRS' initiative to harmonize interagency plans for the implementation of NSPD-44 has taken over 18 months to reach a conclusion.

Meanwhile, across the Potomac, the Pentagon's Directive 3000.05 marks a significant change—subsequently reaffirmed in the Quadrennial Defense Review—in the department's perspective toward stability operations. So far, however, the Department of Defense and uniformed services have only begun to embrace this fundamental change in mission and, indeed, in their identity. Changes in doctrine and educational curricula are under way. But some traditional warfighters still resist the notion that stability operations should be their business. Officials working to implement the new directive admit that they face resistance in an organization that continues to believe that it will return to "traditional" warfare after Afghanistan and Iraq and that the civilian departments and agencies will soon have the "surge" capabilities to undertake stability operations without significant military support. Nothing less than a transformation of organizational culture is needed—away from a technological and weapons systems focus to new missions and new ways of thinking.

At the same time, skepticism within the Department of Defense that the civilian departments (especially the Department of State and S/CRS) will ever step up to the plate is growing. If the civilian departments and agencies cannot fill the mission gap, the argument runs, then the Department of Defense will be forced to, out of necessity. The Department of Defense has recently obtained what is known as "Section 1206" authority to help train and equip other countries' armies separate from the traditional Department of State channels for these missions. In May 2007, moreover, the Department of Defense proposed legislation (the Building Global Partnerships Act) that would expand its authority to train other nations' internal security forces as well as their regular national military forces (with the concurrence of the Secretary of State). Informally, some Defense officials have hinted that they may even have to develop their own "civilian reserve" capabilities.

So, while the Bush administration has taken initial steps toward improved US capabilities for post-conflict reconstruction, much more is needed to spur a quantum leap in post-conflict capacity. Senior-level engagement in these issues is absolutely critical to build and sustain momentum. We offer three concrete recommendations for improving civilian capabilities. While early results of the S/CRS experiment are disappointing, we believe it should be given the opportunity to prove its worth. This would require, first of all, pressing Congress for a regularly budgeted conflict response fund, administered by S/CRS, at least on the order of the $100 million originally suggested by Senators Lugar and Biden. Such a fund should have "notwithstanding authority" to enable rapid, flexible targeting of funds during a crisis. Even before the first penny is spent, such funding would give S/CRS the bureaucratic clout that it lacks. Second, S/CRS should be given lead responsibility not merely for planning, but coordinating an actual small-scale operation. (The US relief operation during the Lebanon war of 2006 provided such an opportunity.) Third, S/CRS needs to draw up a coherent strategic vision and detailed roadmap for the establishment of a civilian reserve capability—and then translate these into operational reality. This will require not only a robust plan to harness all existing US government capabilities but also a clear vision of what the reserve itself will look like once it is "stood up" (including size, specific capabilities, and missions, etc.). The May 2007 Iraq appropriations supplemental's provision of up to $50 million for a Civilian Reserve Corps is a positive signal. The true test for S/CRS, however, will be whether or not the administration and Congress can be convinced to commit real resources over the long haul to empower it and support its mission, including a Civilian Reserve Corps. If the S/CRS experiment does not prove itself in these tests, then it will be time to consider more drastic organizational remedies, including perhaps establishing a new office within the National Security Council to drive interagency planning and implementation of policy for post-conflict contingencies.

The executive branch will not be able to transform the nation's approach to these challenges on its own. Congress must recognize the importance and the unique requirements of post-conflict stabilization and reconstruction missions. In recent years, we have often heard voices on Capitol Hill declare that the post-conflict mission cannot be the military's alone. True enough. But Congress must allocate the funds needed to turn rhetoric into reality. It must overcome its traditional aversion to providing flexible funding. With proper design and oversight, a rapidly deployable conflict response fund will enable more efficient and effective action during the critical early weeks and months of future nation-building operations.

A fundamental shift in the politics surrounding these issues is required. What is needed is a sustained, bipartisan commitment to the mission of post-conflict stabilization and reconstruction across future administrations. Without that, any reforms will be short-lived.

The Multilateral Dimension: The United Nations and
Regional Capabilities

The need to keep the United States from having to undertake post-conflict stabilization missions single-handedly requires steps to build up capability and political
will within other nations and institutions.

As we take stock of both the shortfalls and existing capabilities, the unique
contributions of the United Nations should not be overlooked. Conservatives fairly
fault the United Nations on many counts for its lack of efficiency and the difficulty
of mustering political consensus among the world's largest powers. Nonetheless,
the UN has over the last 15 years distinguished itself by assisting dozens of countries
to overcome chaos. In Namibia, El Salvador, Cambodia, East Timor, Kosovo, and
Afghanistan—to name some of the more successful examples—the UN has facilitated
political reconciliation, demilitarization, the holding of elections, and the building of
civil society institutions. The UN is currently administering some 15 peacekeeping
missions involving 98,000 personnel. While not always popular, none of these multilateral interventions has evoked anything close to the resentment triggered by the
US occupation of Iraq. By contrast, the United Nations' most egregious peacekeeping
failures—in Bosnia, Rwanda, and Somalia—resulted from missions being mounted
where there was "no peace to keep." Where active hostilities have ceased, the UN has
generally done well.[11]

Despite the organization's manifest political limitations and management inefficiencies, the United Nations' near-universal membership is a major advantage when
it comes to stabilization operations. Inherent in most stabilization missions is at
least a partial ceding of certain sovereign prerogatives of the territory in question. The
traditional indicia of sovereignty—including state monopoly on the use of force,
control of borders, freedom to make foreign policy, and freedom from outside intervention—are often absent in failed and recovering states that depend on outside
assistance to administer themselves. When a failed or toppled state is incapable of
exercising full sovereignty, the power vacuum is filled somehow, whether fragmented
among warring militias or concentrated in a single occupying power.

The United Nations and, to a lesser extent, other multinational organizations have
an advantage when it comes to filling governance or administrative gaps in transitional
societies. Unlike global or regional superpowers, the United Nations' presence usually
does not stir fears that intervention will be permanent, nor that foreign powers will
dominate at the expense of the affected society. At the extreme, UN trusteeship, or
its modern equivalent, is viewed as considerably more palatable and less sinister than
foreign occupation. As illustrated in Iraq, when such suspicions are aroused by a single
powerful country, the effectiveness of the entire operation can be undermined. Given

the slow pace of stabilization processes, the availability of a disinterested multinational organization to oversee transition processes without being seen as an interloper can be a decided advantage. In Bosnia, for example, an ad hoc international coalition has held responsibility for civilian administration for more than 11 years, without generating high levels of local resistance.

The evolution of the international debate on sovereignty suggests that the advantage held by multinational bodies in post-conflict situations will only become more pronounced over time. The recognition by the United Nations of an international responsibility to protect (RTP) warranting humanitarian intervention encompasses acknowledgment that countries failing to protect their populations from genocide and like crimes may temporarily forfeit their sovereignty. There remains considerable debate over the circumstances in which RTP and the surrender of sovereignty apply. The willingness of powers like China and Russia to accede to the abrogation of sovereignty in places like Darfur may depend heavily on what sovereignty is temporarily replaced with. If the only substitute is occupation by a Western power, they may be more resistant than if the United Nations is ready and able to step in.

The deficiency in what the UN participation can offer lies not only in the limitations of the organization's in-house capabilities but also the time and difficulty associated with passing the hat to member states for contributions of capable troops and appropriate equipment. The current method for authorizing and deploying UN stabilization operations requires that such contributions be solicited and offered anew for every mission. As former UN Secretary-General Kofi Annan has described it, the United Nations is the only fire department in the world that begins to muster personnel and equipment after the fire has already broken out. Augmenting the United Nations' ability to reliably coordinate and participate in post-conflict stabilization missions requires a new look at the possibility of expanding the organization's standing peacekeeping capabilities. The expansion of UN rapid reaction capabilities has been debated actively for more than a decade, but only half-measures have been taken at best. With more trained, equipped, and prepared troops at the ready within the national militaries of member states, conflict zones could be stabilized more quickly and countries voting for missions could do so with greater confidence that the needed troop contributions are available.

The traditional reasons for resisting the establishment of standing UN capabilities are overtaken by 21st-century realities. First off, the very term "UN military capabilities" is a misnomer. UN peacekeeping troops do not and should not report to the secretary-general. The United Nations' only troops are those donated for specific missions by individual member states. These troops remain under their national government's control, except when that control is voluntarily ceded. Earlier fears of a UN run amok, acting without US authorization, are thus unfounded. As noted by the

2006 report of the Princeton Project on National Security, the bigger problem for the United States now is the inability to muster Security Council action due to vetoes and threatened vetoes by individual member states. The United States' own veto power ensures that UN forces would not be deployed without American approval. A larger number of troops dedicated as on-call for UN peacekeeping troops would be no more able to act autonomously than are blue-helmeted forces today. The size and structure of a UN stabilization force dispersed among the national militaries of UN troop contributors requires careful consideration, and should be determined with significant input from US military leadership who can help ensure that such a force is efficiently designed and can work effectively with the American military and other partners. By refusing to entertain the creation of readily available peacekeeping troops, the United States perpetuates an ad hoc and suboptimal approach to post-conflict missions.

While recognizing that the United Nations has played a constructive role in some post-conflict situations, conservatives remain skeptical of its ability to manage and coordinate a more elaborate system of standing stabilization forces. The United Nations' administrative and management failings are well documented. Moreover, conservatives question whether improved rapid deployment capabilities, even if feasible, would do anything to cure the UN Security Council's inability to summon the collective will to act in the most difficult circumstances. If there were such ready forces, would China have been any more willing to accept UN operations aimed at preventing genocide in the Balkans or Africa? In a world of finite resources, would not investments in capabilities that might be more readily activated be wiser—such as within NATO framework? From this perspective, we might encourage the United Nations to improve its rapid deployment capabilities where it already contributes to post-conflict environments—for example, helping with humanitarian and refugee issues—before asking it to press for expanding standby peacekeeping forces that key member states may be unwilling to deploy.

While ad hoc coalitions of the willing can play an important role in post-conflict missions, they suffer from some potentially important limitations. The first is timing: cobbling together a political coalition and convincing members to muster troops necessarily takes time. In post-conflict situations, there is a premium on speedily deploying troops to help consolidate a cease-fire and prevent resurgent violence. A standing institution that can convene quickly and has a secretariat capable of planning as well as actually deploying personnel can have a decided advantage when it comes to speed. Ad hoc coalitions also have limitations in their perceived legitimacy. If such groupings are seen as mere cover for a meddling power, or as overstepping their regional ambit, the intervention may not be accepted. For example, while NATO has shown itself in Kosovo, Afghanistan, and elsewhere to be capable of effectively running post-conflict stabilization operations, the idea that it might intervene in the

Middle East or Africa is widely rejected in those regions. But where there is a group of countries that can quickly and credibly intervene—as, for example, the Australian-led force in East Timor—this can help distribute burdens efficiently across the international system.

Both progressives and conservatives have expressed support for building the capacity of regional bodies like the African Union to deal with post-conflict needs in their own "neighborhoods." While this is an important long-term effort, the failure of the African Union Darfur peacekeeping mission to build peace demonstrates that in the near term, capacity-building efforts are not a substitute for the intervention of more capable parties.

Beyond the UN context, US policy will need to adapt its approach to operational cooperation in order to encourage increased commitments by other nations. By approaching stabilization operations as true partnerships, the United States will elicit higher levels of international participation. Willingness to share information and decision-making authority will be essential to gaining the confidence of potential contributors that they are partners rather than subordinates. As the Iraq mission illustrated, failure to enlist broad participation within a multilateral framework at the outset of a mission may preclude international help later when the need becomes urgent.

The Next Time

Recent frustrations in Afghanistan and Iraq will inevitably cast a long shadow over debate on possible future missions. The task of maintaining domestic political support for such operations—which are by their nature lengthy, difficult, and costly—has never been easy, and will only get more difficult. But the mission is not impossible. The American public will be most receptive to a new operation when their leaders can demonstrate that it meets the following criteria:

- **Clearly defined US strategic interests.** Americans need to understand why a post-conflict mission is being undertaken: To avert terrorism that might emanate from a failed state? To prevent wider instability in a strategically important region? To stop a genocide that is under way? Where the rationale is unclear or shifting, the public will become skeptical. If the strategic interests cannot be defined concisely, that is probably a sign that the mission should not be undertaken.

- **A realistic plan.** After defining the stakes, policymakers must develop a convincing plan to advance US strategic interests. The resources committed political reform in societies under authoritarian rule . . . the percentage of countries designated Free has failed to increase for nearly a decade. . . ."[1] In sum, then, Bush's new attention to democracy promotion has not resulted in more people living in freedom.

Not surprisingly, many in Washington on both the left and right are pressing for a change in US foreign policy objectives. Only those at the extremes on both ends of the political spectrum advocate the complete abandonment of democracy promotion as a US foreign policy objective. Instead, skepticism is largely couched as "realism," and a "return" to a greater focus on "traditional" US national security objectives. From this perspective, democracy promotion should take a back seat to strategic aims such as securing US access to energy resources, building military alliances to fight terrorist organizations, and fostering "stability" within states. A partisan gap has also emerged on this issue. In a German Marshall Fund survey released in June 2006, 64 percent of Republicans agreed that the United States should "help establish democracy in other countries," but only 35 percent of Democrats concurred.

We do not reject the importance of focusing on the more traditional goals of national security. However, we do reject the simple assumption that there is a zero-sum trade-off between these traditional security objectives and democracy promotion. We also share the negative assessments of the Bush administration's efforts to promote democracy in the past few years. However, our response to this mixed, if not disappointing, record of achievement is not to downgrade or remove democracy promotion from US foreign policy priorities. Rather, after presenting the case for why the United States should promote democracy, we suggest new strategies and better modalities for pursuing this objective.

Our chapter proceeds in three parts. Part One outlines the positive case for including democracy promotion as an important component of US foreign policy. Part Two then presents the counterarguments, followed by our reasons for viewing them as ultimately unpersuasive. Part Three outlines some new modalities for promoting democracy—including a return to several established practices—that can make US and international efforts to promote democracy more effective.

The Case for Democracy Promotion

American Interests

No country in the world has benefited more from the worldwide advance of democracy than the United States. Not all autocracies are or have been enemies of the United States, but every American enemy has been an autocracy. Because of geography and

should be proportionate to the original objectives. If not, either the objectives need to be scaled back or the commitment increased. Otherwise, when too wide a gap exists between the ambitions and means, public disenchantment will grow as the stated grand objectives are not achieved, or not achieved at a reasonable cost. The American people have demonstrated the will to bear heavy burdens in the past, but that support can only be sustained when the public sees a realistic plan forward.

- **International support.** The American public is more likely to accept missions with broad international endorsement and participation. Where the United States is doing its part as one among many, missions will be less closely scrutinized than if Washington goes it alone. And if the United States does decide to act unilaterally, then the strategic case must be absolutely compelling to the American people—with a palpable threat to their own security.

- **Resources used wisely.** The corruption, cronyism, and massive expense overruns witnessed in Iraq fueled public skepticism about the management of the operation. Transparency, effective controls, and administrative vigilance are necessary to build public confidence that post-conflict resources are being used for their intended purposes.

- **Demonstrated progress.** The American public will be patient with prolonged missions as long as they do not appear exorbitantly costly, especially in terms of lives. Casualties make news, bad news. In any operation, tackling security issues early and decisively is the best way to minimize the risks to the operation itself as well as to its support back home. In a way, a good indicator of progress is when the operation moves off the front pages of daily newspapers. Thereafter, progress can proceed at a pace more attuned to local rhythms, not those of the 24-hour news cycle.

The post-conflict stabilization and reconstruction mission is important and inevitable. Despite the frustrations with the Afghanistan and Iraq missions, we should recognize that the United States now has an unprecedented pool of talent—military and civilian, inside and outside government—with vast, hard-earned experience in post-conflict environments. Whether this talent and experience will be harnessed in ways that will improve future nation-building efforts will be a major question in US foreign policy in the coming years. Whichever party occupies the White House or controls Congress, both progressives and conservatives should seize this opportunity and find common, credible approaches to nation-building. Together, we need to demonstrate success in order to convince skeptics that the United States is not forever condemned to repeat the mistakes of the past.

Notes

1 See, for example, Hans Binnendijk and Stuart Johnson, eds., *Transforming for Stability and Reconstruction Operations* (Washington: National Defense University Press, 2004); Simon Chesterman, *You, The People: The United Nations, Transitional Administration, and State-Building* (New York: Oxford University Press, 2004); Chester Crocker, Fen Olser Hampson, and Pamela Aall, eds., *Leashing the Dogs of War: Conflict Management in a Divided World* (Washington: USIP, 2007); James Dobbins, et al., *America's Role in Nation-Building: From Germany to Iraq* (Santa Monica: RAND, 2003); James Dobbins, et al., *The UN's Role in Nation-Building: From the Congo to Iraq* (Santa Monica: RAND, 2005); James Dobbins, et al., *The Beginner's Guide to Nation-Building* (Santa Monica: RAND, 2007); Francis Fukuyama, *State-Building: Governance and World Order in the 21st Century* (Ithaca: Cornell University Press, 2004); Francis Fukuyama, ed., *Nation-Building: Beyond Afghanistan and Iraq* (Baltimore: The Johns Hopkins University Press, 2006); John J. Hamre and Gordon R. Sullivan, "Toward Postconflict Reconstruction," *The Washington Quarterly* (Autumn 2002); Robert C. Orr, ed., *Winning the Peace: An American Strategy for Post-Conflict Reconstruction* (Washington: CSIS, 2004); Robert M. Perito, *Where is the Lone Ranger When We Need Him? America's Search of a Postconflict Stability Force* (Washington: USIP, 2004); Jane Stromseth, David Wippman, and Rosa Brooks, *Can Might Make Right: Building the Rule of Law After Military Intervention* (New York: Cambridge University Press, 2006). The United States Institute of Peace's Center for Post-Conflict Peace and Stability Operations has an ongoing "Filling the Gaps" initiative to develop specific, actionable recommendations for key nation-building topics. Its Stabilization and Reconstruction series of special reports is available at *http://www.usip.org/peaceops/filling_gaps.html*.

2 Michael Mandelbaum, "Foreign Policy as Social Work," *Foreign Affairs*, January–February 1996.

3 Francis Fukuyama, *America at the Crossroads: Democracy, Power, and the Neoconservative Legacy* (New Haven: Yale University Press, 2006), p. 49.

4 Stewart Patrick, "An Integrated U.S. Approach to Preventing and Responding to State Failure: Recent Progress and Remaining Challenges," Remarks to the Eisenhower National Security Series Conference on Stability Operations, April 19, 2006.

5 Stewart Patrick, "Weak States and Global Threats: Fact or Fiction?" *The Washington Quarterly*, Spring 2006.

6 Dobbins, et al., *The Beginner's Guide to Nation-Building*, p. xvii.

7 Gideon Rose, "The Exit Strategy Delusion," *Foreign Affairs*, January–February 1998.

8 See, for example, US Department of State, Office of the Coordinator for Reconstruction and Stabilization, "Post-Conflict Reconstruction Essential Tasks," April 2005.

9 For useful overviews of recent congressional and administration efforts to reform the interagency for post-conflict operations, see Bernard Carreau, "Transforming the Interagency System for Complex Operations," Case Study No. 6, *Case Studies in Defense Transformation* (Washington: NDU Center for Technology and National Security Policy, 2007); Corine Hegland, "Pentagon, State Struggle to Define Nation-Building Roles," *National Journal*, April 30, 2007. Stewart Patrick offers a thoughtful overview of the recent US policy in context of the broader challenge posed by "precarious states," in "The U.S. Response to Precarious States: Tentative Progress and Remaining Obstacles to Coherence," forthcoming.

10 See Gordon Adams, *The Politics of National Security Budgets*, Policy Analysis Brief (Muscatine, IA: The Stanley Foundation, February 2007).

11 Dobbins, et al., *The UN's Role in Nation-Building*.

9

Should Democracy Be Promoted or Demoted?

Francis Fukuyama and Michael McFaul

In his second inaugural address on January 20, 2005, President George W. Bush used the word *freedom* 25 times, *liberty* 12 times, and *democracy* or *democratic* 3 times. Bush did not enter the White House with a mission to promote freedom around the world. Rather, as a presidential candidate, he put forward a modest foreign policy agenda that eschewed nation-building. The events of September 11, 2001, however, radically jarred his thinking on the nature of international threats and triggered a fundamental reevaluation of his administration's national security policy that elevated democracy promotion as a central objective of his foreign policy agenda.

In the years since September 11, though, the rhetorical attention devoted to the advance of freedom, liberty, and democracy has greatly outpaced any actual progress in expanding democracy. To date, democracy has failed to take hold in the two countries where Bush ordered the forcible ouster of autocratic regimes: Afghanistan and Iraq. In its 2006 survey of freedom around the world, Freedom House labeled Iraq as "not free" with a 6 rating on a 1–7 scale (with 1 being most free and 7 being least free). Afghanistan barely earned the designation "partially free" with a 5 ranking. Nor did the toppling of these dictatorships send liberty rippling through the greater Middle East as some Bush officials and supporters had hoped. Instead, autocratic regimes in the region have used the excuse of terrorism (Egypt, Pakistan) or the alleged threat of US invasion (Iran) to tighten autocracy. Outside this region, some countries have made some progress toward developing democracy (Georgia, Ukraine) but just as many have moved toward greater autocracy. Freedom House concluded, "The year 2006 saw the emergence of a series of worrisome trends that together present a potentially serious threat to the stability of new democracies as well as obstacles to

US military power, most autocracies over the last 200 years have lacked the capacity to attack US territory. But the exceptional autocracies that became sufficiently powerful either did attack the United States (Japan, Al Qaeda) or threatened to attack (Germany under Hitler, the Soviet Union, North Korea). Conversely, Great Britain and France do have, at least theoretically, the military capacities to threaten the United States, but the thought of French or British attack is inconceivable simply because both are democracies.

The transformation of powerful autocracies into democracies has likewise served US national security interests. Most obviously, the end of dictatorship and the consolidation of democracy in Germany, Italy, and Japan after World War II made the United States safer. Beyond keeping imperial and autocratic leaders out of power, democratic consolidation in these countries served as the basis of US military alliances in Europe and Asia. At the end of the 20th century, regime change in the Soviet Union ended the Cold War and greatly reduced this once-menacing threat to the United States and its allies. Russia today lacks the military strength of the Soviet Red Army from 20 years ago. Yet Russia today remains the only country in the world capable of launching a massive military attack against American people on American soil. The threat of such an attack has significantly diminished because of regime change in the Soviet Union. And it is not a coincidence that Russia has become more antagonistic toward the United States and the West at the same time that the current regime there has become increasingly authoritarian.[2]

During the Cold War, some viewed the Soviet threat as so paramount that all enemies of communism, including dictators, had to be embraced. They predicted that any political change to the status quo in autocratic societies would not produce democratic regimes and US allies, but communist regimes and American enemies. There were enough examples of this trajectory—Cuba, Angola, and Nicaragua—to warrant worry. But these are the failed cases of democratic transition, and US involvement in the internal changes of these countries can hardly be called democracy promotion. In contrast, *successful* democratic transitions did not undermine US security interests. Transitions in Portugal, Spain, Taiwan, the Philippines, South Korea, Chile, and South Africa helped deepen American ties with these countries.[3]

The parallels to today are obvious. Once again facing a new worldwide ideological threat in the form of radical Islamism, American strategic thinkers both in and outside of government worry that political change in autocratic US allies will produce theocratic regimes hostile to American interests. The concern is valid, but is often overplayed by the very same autocrats as they seek to retain power. So far, successful democratization has never brought to power a government that then directly threatened the national security interests of the United States or its allies. In the Palestinian Authority (which is not a country), we are witnessing the first case of such a potential outcome. Hamas seems to be capitalizing on its new status and resources to threaten America and its allies. In the long run, however, participation in democratic institutions and the assumption of responsibility for governance might moderate Hamas or undermine its popularity. It is still too early to assess the results of this transition (see the discussion of Hamas below).

The advance of democracy in Europe and Asia over the last century has made the United States safer—giving reason to hope that democracy's advance in other regions of the world will also strengthen US national security. But this is a hypothesis about the future based on analogy, and not a certainty. In the long run, we expect consolidation of democratic regimes in the greater Middle East would increase the legitimacy of the governments and thereby reduce the appeal of anti-systemic movements like Al Qaeda. In the shorter term, democratic government throughout the region would increase internal stability within states since democracies have longer life spans than autocracies. If democratic regimes ruled all countries in the region, conflicts between states would be less likely, and consequently demand for weapons, including weapons of mass destruction, would decrease. Finally, a more secure and stable region would reduce the need for a US military presence, just as a Europe whole and free dramatically reduced the need for American deployments in that region. And for major powers such as Russia and China, democratic development also should reduce the possibility that they would pursue balancing policies against the United States.

In the short run, however, there are potential risks for US security associated with democratic development in the greater Middle East. Without question, the toppling of the Taliban regime in Afghanistan deprived Al Qaeda of a base of operations that had more assets than its current base in Pakistan. Yet this advantage for US strategic interests is not a result of democratization. In fact, the difficult process of developing democratic institutions in Afghanistan has failed to produce stable government or a growing economy to date—a situation that has created an opening for the Taliban's resurgence. In Iraq, neither democratic government nor an effective state has taken root. To date, the American people are not safer as a result of regime change in Iraq. In both countries, US-led invasions brought about regime change. But because these operations were neither launched to bring democracy nor followed through toward that end, the resulting new or resurgent threats to US national security emanating from Afghanistan and Iraq cannot be blamed on democratization in general or US democracy promotion in particular.

Elsewhere in the region, the limited progress toward democratization in recent years is also tenuously tied to US security. The Cedar Revolution and subsequent 2005 pullout of Syrian troops from Lebanon raised hopes for stability there. Yet the Hezbollah-Israeli war in the summer of 2006 underscored how premature these hopes were. Soon after President's Bush second inaugural speech, Egypt's President Mubarak seemed to react by implementing incremental political reforms. A year later, he rolled them back almost entirely, a development that has heightened tensions within Egypt and strained US-Egyptian relations. We have yet to see whether partial reforms in Bahrain, Kuwait, Saudi Arabia, and Morocco will lead to further incremental political liberalization or serve instead as camouflage for continued autocratic rule. The net effect of these reforms on US security is still entirely unclear.

We admit that we do not know whether the analogy between democratization in the wider Middle East and democratization in other regions will hold and yield the same benefits. The destruction of fascist and communist regimes and the emergence of more democratic regimes, first in Europe and Asia after World War II and more recently in Eastern Europe and the former Soviet Union, significantly enhanced US national security. It is reasonable to expect a similar outcome in the wider Middle East; that is, the emergence of more democratic regimes in the most autocratic region of the world should also make the United States more secure. As we say, it is still an untested hypothesis.

American Values

Debates about democracy promotion cannot be couched solely as a balance sheet of material benefits and liabilities for the United States. American values must also enter the discussion. Since the beginning of the American republic, US presidents have to varying degrees invoked America's unique, moral role in international affairs. The loss of this identity, both at home and abroad, would weaken domestic support for US involvement in world affairs and undermine American ability to persuade other countries to support our foreign policies. Apart from serving US strategic interests, democracy promotion is also the right thing to do.

First and foremost, democracy is the best system of government. Winston Churchill was right: democracy is a terrible system of government, but still better than all of the others that have been tried. Democracy provides the best institutional form for holding rulers accountable to their people. If leaders must compete for popular support to obtain and retain power, then they will be more responsive to the preferences of the people, in contrast to rulers who do not govern on the basis of popular support. The institutions of democracy also prevent abusive rule, constrain bad rule, and provide a mechanism for removing corrupt or ineffective rule. Furthermore, democracy provides the setting for political competition, which in turn is a driver for better governance. Like markets, political competition between contending leaders, ideas, and organizations produces better leaders, ideas, and organizations (which is the premise of the Bridging the Foreign Policy Divide project). At a minimum, democracy provides a mechanism for removing bad rulers in a way that autocracy does not. The absence of political competition in autocracies produces complacency, corruption, and has no mechanism for producing new leaders.

Second, democracies provide more, and more stable, welfare for their people than do autocracies. Democracies avoid the worst threats to personal well-being, such as genocide and famine. Over the last several decades, democracies around the world have not produced higher economic growth rates than autocracies: "the net effect of more political freedom on growth is theoretically ambiguous."[4] Instead, compared to democracies, autocracies produce both much higher and much lower rates of growth. For every China there is an Angola. Democracies tend to produce slower rates of growth than the best autocratic performers, but also steadier rates of economic development. The old conventional wisdom that dictators are better at economic modernization than the democratic counterparts is not supported by data.

Third, the demand for and appeal of democracy as a system of government are widespread, if not universal. Public opinion surveys of people throughout the world, including the wider Middle East, show that majorities in most countries support democracy.[5] Ideological challengers remain, such as the modernizing autocrat or Osama bin Ladenism. But compared to earlier historical periods, these opponents of democracy have never been weaker.

The United States, therefore, has a moral interest in promoting democracy. If democracy is the best system of government, demanded by the majority of people around the world, then the United States should help promote its advance. Conversely, any US involvement in sustaining autocracy is immoral. Obviously, American leaders constantly face situations in which immediate security interests require cooperation with autocratic regimes. But such policies should not be defended on moral or ethical grounds.

Engaging the Case Against Democracy Promotion

Three broad categories of reasons are offered for why the United States should not pursue democracy promotion. The first is normative, based on the view that democracy is culturally rooted and not a universal good; the second prudential, concerning the principle of respect for sovereignty as the basis for international order; and the third also prudential, concerning the need for sequencing in the introduction of democratic reforms.

The first argument—that democracy is not a universally valid or desirable goal— has a number of proponents. Postmodernism and other relativist philosophies argue that there are no universally valid political or institutional orders because it is impossible to arrive at philosophical certainty per se. A more common assertion is that democracy is culturally rooted, and that societies with other cultural backgrounds may choose other forms of government as they wish. Samuel Huntington, while preferring liberal democracy for the United States, makes this kind of case.[6] According to him, liberal democracy is rooted in Western Christianity, which proclaimed the universal dignity of man made in God's image; thinkers from Tocqueville to Nietzsche have argued that modern democracy is simply a secularization of Western values. There is no particular reason why other civilizations based on other cultural premises should prefer democratic government. Lee Kwan Yew and other proponents of "Asian values" have argued that, given the poor performance of many democratic regimes in non-Western settings, this form of government is distinctly less desirable than a growth-oriented authoritarian regime.

Full consideration of this argument is beyond the scope of this chapter. There are certainly serious philosophical and political cases to be made against the universality of liberal democratic values on a number of grounds. While acceptance of democratic norms and basic human rights has spread far and wide since the onset of the Third Wave of democratization, there are still parts of the world where they are openly rejected on cultural grounds. The Chinese government, various East Asian leaders and thinkers, Islamists of assorted stripes, and many Russian nationalists are among those arguing that their cultures are inherently inimical to one or another aspect of liberal democracy.

We offer the following observations in contention. In the first place, democracy promotion never implied the "imposition" of either liberalism or democracy on a society that did not want it. By definition this is impossible: democracy requires popular consensus, and works only if the vast majority of a society's citizens believe that it is legitimate. Democracy promotion is intended only to help reveal public preferences in the society itself. Dictatorships often resort to violence, coercion, or fraud to prevent those preferences from carrying political weight; democracy promoters simply try to level the playing field by eliminating the authoritarians' unfair advantages.

A second counterargument that is somewhat more difficult to make is that human rights and the democratic institutions that spring from them are immanently universal. In keeping with the case made by Tocqueville in *Democracy in America*, the historical arc toward universal human equality has been spreading providentially for the past 800 years. It has now encompassed not just the Western, culturally Christian world, but has spread and taken root in many other parts of the world as well—India, Japan, Korea, and South Africa. This suggests that democracy has spread not as a manifestation of a particular civilization's cultural preferences, but because it serves universal needs or performs functions that are universally necessary, particularly at higher levels of economic development. One can argue, for example, that the procedural rules of liberal democracy guarantee that governments behave in a transparent, law-governed way and remain accountable to the people they serve. Even if a culture does not put a value on individual rights per se, liberal democracy is ultimately required for good governance and economic growth.

The second argument against democracy promotion is made by international relations "realists," namely, that world order depends on states accepting the Westphalian consensus to respect each other's sovereignty and mutual agreement not to meddle in the internal character of each other's regimes. The Westphalian consensus arose out of Europe's wars of religion following the Reformation, when European princes fought over the confessional allegiances of their neighbors. Peace was obtained only when all agreed to a principle of *cuius regio, cuius religio*, and noninterference in each other's internal politics.

Among contemporary writers, Henry Kissinger has been one of the most articulate and consistent proponents of this view. Since his earliest writings,[7] he has argued that idealistic concern with the internal character of other regimes leads to messianic crusades that in the long run provoke resistance and undermine world order. The idealistic Tsar Alexander I prolonged the destabilization of Europe begun by the French Revolution. International peace and stability reigned from 1815 to 1848 only due to the efforts of the arch-conservative Metternich to forge a balance of power in Europe, heedless of ideological concerns.

There are countless variants of realist theory today, united primarily in their opposition to democracy promotion as a component of foreign policy. Some argue not from a world-order point of view, but from the perspective of narrower American interests: the United States needs oil, security, trade, and other goods that are compromised by an emphasis on human rights or democracy. These views have acquired particular resonance since the Iraq war, which was seen as being driven by a neo-conservative agenda of democracy promotion and political transformation in the Middle East. These critics would argue that US pressure for liberalization of political space and calls for elections empower groups like Hamas in Palestine, Hezbollah in Lebanon, and the Muslim Brotherhood in Egypt, all of which are illiberal and hostile to US interests. There has been criticism especially of the Bush administration's use of coercive regime change as a means to spur the political transformation of the Middle East.

We make several arguments in response to the realists. The first has to do with prudence in means. To say that the United States should promote democracy in its foreign policy does not mean that it should put idealistic goals ahead of other types of national interests at all times and places—or that it should use military force in pursuit of these goals. Indeed, the United States has never made democracy promotion the overriding goal of its foreign policy. The Bush administration invaded Iraq primarily out of concern over weapons of mass destruction and terrorism; democracy promotion was a tertiary goal that received heavier emphasis only ex post, when the other justifications for the war proved hollow. The United States has promoted democracy in places like Germany and Japan after World War II, but only when in concert with its security goals. In these cases, transformation of two former enemies into democratic countries did indeed align with US strategic interests, and few realists would argue that the United States would have been better served by an alternative policy.

The real trade-offs come in regions like the Middle East, where the United States' closest strategic allies are autocracies like Saudi Arabia, Jordan, Morocco, or Egypt. The Bush administration has made the general argument that the deep root cause of terrorism and Islamist radicalism is the region's lack of democracy, and that promoting democracy is therefore one route to eradicating the terrorist threat. Natan Sharansky has argued that the Oslo peace process was fatally flawed because the United States and Israel relied on Yasser Arafat's authoritarian Fatah as an interlocutor, instead of pressing for democracy in Palestine prior to peace negotiations.[8] Prior to the invasion of Iraq, some observers similarly hoped that a democratic Iraq would be a strategic partner of the United States and recognize Israel. By this view, democracy, security, and peace with Israel all went hand in hand.

It is quite clear in retrospect that this reading of the sources of Arab radicalism was too simplistic. The deep sources of terrorism are much more complex than just the Middle East's democratic deficit. One can argue in fact that it is precisely the modernization process that produces terrorism and that more democracy is likely to exacerbate the terrorism problem, at least in the short run.[9] Many of the Iraqis who went to the polls in the various elections of 2005 were Shiites who wanted not liberal democracy but Shiite power, and who have subsequently worked to establish an Iranian-style Islamic republic in areas under their control. The winners of democratic elections elsewhere in the region tend to be profoundly illiberal Islamist groups, who are also more hostile to America's ally Israel than to the authoritarian governments they would like to displace. The political tide in the Middle East is not running in favor of pro-Western liberal opposition groups. In addition, the United States' authoritarian allies like Hosni Mubarak of Egypt and Pervez Musharraf of Pakistan have been quite clever at sidelining liberal opponents to accentuate the threat from the Islamist opposition. The assertion of President Bush's second inaugural address that there is no necessary trade-off between US security interests and its idealistic goals would thus seem to be false.

In our view, the appropriate policy in response to this political landscape needs to be a calibrated one that takes account of particular circumstances. There are some countries like Saudi Arabia where there is no realistic democratic alternative to the current authoritarian leadership, or where likely alternatives would clearly be worse from a strategic perspective. In these cases, authoritarian allies indeed represent the lesser of two evils. While quiet pressure on Egypt to liberalize might be appropriate, provoking a major showdown to strong-arm Cairo into permitting free and fair elections is not likely to work. On the other hand, there is a democratic alternative to General Pervez Musharraf in Pakistan—in the form of the newly created alliance between the Pakistan People's Party's Benazir Bhutto and former Prime Minister Nawaz Sharif. While this group had an uneven record when they were in power, they have pledged to crack down on the Taliban in the Northwest Frontier Province and may indeed prove to be more reliable allies than Musharraf. An open election in Pakistan would risk further gains by Islamist parties, but the country has a sizable middle-class electorate and significant public sentiment that is wary of an anti-Western course.

Hamas in Gaza represents a more difficult case, since it is not only illiberal but also committed to the destruction of America's ally Israel. The strategic problem here is whether it is better to have this group on the inside of a long-term peace and Palestinian state-building process or outside as obstructionists. Hamas represents a significant part of the Palestinian electorate, and the party will continue to play an influential role in Palestinian politics regardless of whether the United States and Israel accept it. A strong argument can be made that it is better to relent to Hamas' participation in a government in hopes that their goals will moderate over time. It is, in any event, difficult to see how reliance on a corrupt Fatah government as in the past will help bring peace or even a legitimate interlocutor in the Palestinian Authority.

The final argument against the current agenda of democracy promotion concerns the sequencing of democratic reforms, especially elections. State-building, creation of a liberal rule of law, and democracy are conceptually different phases of political development, which in most European countries occurred in a sequence that was separated by decades if not centuries. State-building and creation of a rule of law are more critical for economic development than democracy is. Jack Snyder and Edward Mansfield have argued that democratization's early phases pose special dangers of promoting nationalism and illiberal politics.[10] Authors from Samuel Huntington[11] to Fareed Zakaria[12] have consequently argued that US policy ought to focus on a broad governance agenda and delay pushing for democracy until a higher level of economic development has been achieved. This so-called "authoritarian transition" has been followed by a number of countries like South Korea, Taiwan, and Chile, and is often recommended as a model for US policy in regions like the Middle East.

There is no question that such liberal authoritarianism has worked quite successfully in places like Singapore, and even less liberal variants, as in China, can boast impressive economic growth rates. If these countries eventually follow the Korean and Taiwanese paths toward a broadening of political participation, it is not obvious that an accelerated democratic transition would bring about a better long-term result. In addition, there are specific instances (primarily in post-conflict/failed state settings) where outside pressure for early elections arguably resulted not in the emergence of democratic political parties, but rather the locking in place of the same groups responsible for the original conflict.

As Thomas Carothers has recently pointed out, however, there are a number of problems with the sequencing strategy.[13] First, in most parts of the world it is very difficult to find liberal, developmentally minded authoritarians on whom such a strategy can be built. The more typical cases in Africa, the Middle East, and Latin America have been characterized by authoritarian governments that are corrupt, incompetent, or self-serving. The vast majority of liberal or developmentally minded authoritarian regimes or leaders are clustered in East Asia, for reasons that probably have roots in the region's Confucian culture. This means, in practice, that in most of the world, exactly the same groups want both liberal rule of law *and* democracy; it is simply not an option for the United States to promote the former and delay the latter.

A further problem with the sequencing strategy is that it presumes that the United States and other foreign powers can somehow control democratic transitions, holding back pressure for democratic elections while pushing for rule of law and good governance. This vastly overestimates the degree of control outsiders have over democratic transitions. The toolbox for democracy promotion is more modest, a subject that we will consider next.

Modalities of Democracy Promotion

To argue that the United States has strategic and moral interests in the spread of democracy does not mean that the United States *can* spread democracy. Domestic factors, not external forces, have driven the process of democratization in most countries. Consequently, and especially in light of the tragedy in Iraq, some have argued that Americans can best promote democracy abroad by simply watching it develop "naturally."

We disagree. While we recognize the limits of America's ability to promote democracy abroad—limits that have become more severe in the past few years—we also know that US policies can be very important in helping nurture democratic development. The war in Iraq has fostered the false impression that military force is the only instrument of regime change in the US arsenal, when in fact it is the rarest used and least effective way to promote democratic change abroad. A wiser, more effective, and more sustainable strategy must emphasize nonmilitary tools aimed at changing the balance of power between democratic forces and autocratic rulers and, only after there has been progress toward democracy, building liberal institutions.

Restoring the American Example

Inspiration for democrats struggling against autocracy and a model for leaders in new democracies are two US exports now in short supply. Since the beginning of the republic, the American experiment with democracy provided hope, ideas, and technologies for others working to build democratic institutions. Foreign visitors to the United States have been impressed by what they've seen, and American diplomats, religious missionaries, and business people who traveled abroad inspired others by telling the story of America's democracy. In the second half of the 20th century, when the United States developed more intentional means for promoting democracy abroad, the preservation and advertisement of the American democratic model remained a core instrument.

Today this instrument needs repair. The American model has been severely undermined by the methods that the Bush administration has used to fight the so-called global war on terrorism. Irrespective of the legal particulars that may or may not justify the indefinite detention of combatants/terrorists at Guantanamo Bay in Cuba, opinion polls demonstrate overwhelmingly that most of the world views US detention policies as illegitimate and undemocratic. Thankfully, senior American officials did not try to defend the inhumane treatment of prisoners at Abu Ghraib in 2004. The news media's exposure of the abuses committed at Abu Ghraib and adherence to the rule of law through the prosecution of guilty soldiers was a first step in correcting the problem. But the failure to hold higher-level officials accountable for the breakdown in authority raised questions about how seriously the United States took the issue, and the images of torture greatly damaged America's international reputation. Furthermore, the debate surrounding the unauthorized wiretappings of American citizens helped create an impression (false) abroad that the US government will sacrifice the civil liberties of individuals in the name of fighting terrorism—the very argument that autocrats across the world use to justify their repressive policies. Finally, the Bush administration's propensity for unilateralism, most centrally in its decision to invade Iraq, coupled with its general suspicion of international law and international institutions, has encouraged the perception that Americans do not believe in the rule of law. Again, the merits of these claims about American behavior are debatable. But it is indisputable that America's image abroad as a model for democracy has been tarnished.

Therefore, the first step toward becoming a more effective promoter of democracy abroad is to get our own house in order. To begin with, the political costs to America's credibility as a champion of democratic values and human rights outweigh the value of holding prisoners at Guantanamo indefinitely. The facility should be closed, and the law passed last year on enemy combatant detentions should be repealed or amended. In place of legalistic attempts to pretend that the United States does not engage in torture, a broader range of prohibited techniques should be explicitly defined and ruled out. More generally, the next president of the United States must demonstrate a clear commitment to restoring and perfecting the US democratic system of government.

In parallel, our efforts at public diplomacy have to improve.

The United States cannot hope to recruit people to its side, or to the side of democratic values, if it does not pay attention to what non-Americans say *they* want, rather than what we think they should want. In the Middle East, many Arabs have argued that America is disliked not for its basic values, but for its one-sidedness in the Palestinian-Israeli conflict and its lack of sympathy for Palestinian aspirations. In Latin America, populist leaders like Hugo Chavez and Evo Morales have gained enormous support by promoting social policies aimed at the poor, an issue that America's democratic friends in the region have largely ignored. The starting point for a better public diplomacy therefore is to stop talking so much about ourselves and to start listening to other people, to compare the product we're offering to the actual aspirations of democratic publics around the world.

Indeed, in light of the Bush administration's widespread unpopularity, it may be better for the United States to dramatically tone down its public rhetoric about democracy promotion. The loudly proclaimed instrumentalization of democracy promotion in pursuit of US national interests (like the war on terrorism) taints democracy promotion and makes the United States seem hypocritical when security, economic, or other concerns trump our interests in democracy (as they inevitably will). Acting in concrete ways to support human rights and democratic groups around the world, while speaking more modestly about American goals, might serve both our interests and ideals better.

The idealistic component of US foreign policy has always been critical to maintaining a domestic American consensus in favor of a strongly internationalist stance, so we do not recommend permanently abandoning this rhetorical stance. We have to recognize, however, that the Iraq war and other events related to the war on terrorism have for the moment tainted valid and important concepts like democracy promotion and democratic regime change. This is the case not only for foreign audiences but for many Americans as well. Until this perception changes, administrations will have to "sell" foreign policy to domestic audiences on different grounds.

Revitalizing Dual Track Diplomacy

It is naive to believe that the United States should only deal with other democracies. After all, in our own history, the creation of the United States as an independent country required military assistance from France's absolute monarchy. The alliance with Stalin's Soviet Union—perhaps the most diabolical regime in human history—was necessary for victory in World War II. Today the wide range of US security, economic, and environmental interests around the world necessitates diplomatic engagement with autocracies.

Nonetheless, American policymakers can conduct relations with their counterparts in autocratic regimes, while simultaneously pursuing policies that might facilitate democratic development in these same countries. US foreign policy officials must reject the false linkage between cooperation and silence on human rights abuses whenever autocrats make it a precondition of engagement. Few friendly autocratic regimes have ever stopped working with the United States on a strategic issue of mutual benefit because an American official criticized their antidemocratic practices.

When it comes to autocratic regimes with which the United States is friendly, American leaders have real leverage to press for evolutionary change, especially over countries dependent on US military protection or economic assistance. Rather than coercing them, US officials must first try persuading our autocratic friends that they can ultimately best protect their material and security interests by proactively leading a process of evolutionary change rather than by reactively resisting an eventual process of revolutionary change. American officials did exactly this, when they helped coax allies in South Korea, Chile, and South Africa into embracing democratic change. Careful diplomacy in the Philippines also helped keep the end of the Marcos dictatorship peaceful.

Paradoxically, the same logic of engagement applies when considering the promotion of democracy in dictatorships hostile to the United States. Attempts to isolate or sanction these regimes have rarely worked. Sanctions against the apartheid regime in South Africa only succeeded because the United States, Great Britain, and other European countries had developed deep economic ties beforehand. South African democrats, unlike the leaders of the democratic movement in Iran today, also wanted these sanctions. Because the United States does not have significant trade with or investments in Iran, Cuba, or Burma, sanctions against these autocracies do little to help the prodemocracy forces inside these countries. However, diplomatic relations with these regimes creates a more hospitable environment for internal democratic development.[14] In the USSR, for instance, democratic forces gained strength in the late 1980s when US-Soviet relations were improving, not earlier in the decade when tensions were high. With rare exception, policies that open societies and economies up to international influence have helped spur democratic change while policies that isolate societies impede such progress.

Reorganizing Democracy Assistance

For most of American history, US foreign assistance did not explicitly aim to promote democracy. President Kennedy created the US Agency of International Development in 1961 to counter communism and Soviet foreign assistance, but the focus was economic development. Twenty years later, Ronald Reagan made democracy promotion a central objective when he worked with Democrats in Congress to create the National Endowment for Democracy (NED) in 1983. At the time, however, NED's budget was a fraction of total foreign assistance. Importantly, NED also was not constituted as an organ of the US government. While receiving its budget directly from Congress (and not through the State Department or USAID), NED established its own board, its own procedures for disseminating money, and made its own decisions about whom it would and would not support.

With the creation of NED came four affiliated organizations: the National Democratic Institute for International Affairs (NDI), the International Republican Institute (IRI), the American Center for International Labor Solidarity (ACILS, formerly the Free Trade Union Institute [FTUI]), and the Center for International Private Enterprise (CIPE). These organizations all had ties to US nongovernment institutions: NDI to the Democratic Party, IRI to the Republican Party, ACILS to the AFL-CIO, and CIPE to the US Chamber of Congress. The idea behind these affiliations was that organizations with democracy as a longstanding element of their missions could set their own agendas.

Over time, however, the US government has increasingly become a direct provider of democracy assistance. With the announcement of its "Democracy Initiative" in December 1990, the US Agency for International Development (USAID) made democracy promotion a core focus and soon became the main source of funding for many nongovernmental organizations (NGOs) in the democracy promotion business, including NDI and IRI. As USAID funds for democracy assistance increased in the 1990s primarily in response to new opportunities in the former communist world, several for-profit contractors joined the democracy promotion business as well. Eventually, tension developed between USAID's leadership and USAID's nongovernment grantees. Over the 1990s, USAID employees—that is, government officials—gradually assumed greater responsibility for crafting democracy promotion strategies and treated the NGOs as merely "implementers" of their ideas. The recipients, and especially the NGOs, resisted the label of implementer and instead tried to preserve their identities as independent actors. The lines between government and nongovernmental actors, already blurred, became even more ambiguous.

After September 11, President Bush to his credit increased general foreign assistance funding, including support for democracy promotion. Within the State Department, the Bush administration established the Middle East Partnership Initiative, which became a new funding source for democracy assistance programs, among others. At State, the Bureau for Democracy, Human Rights, and Labor Affairs received major increases in its democracy assistance budget. The Department of Defense also has become increasingly involved in democracy-related activities in Afghanistan and Iraq. To coordinate civilian, military, and intelligence operations in post-conflict settings better, the Bush administration established the Coordinator for Reconstruction and Stabilization, a new office within the State Department but staffed with personnel on loan from DoD, USAID, and other parts of the executive branch. Most dramatically, under Secretary of State Condoleezza Rice's new trans-formational diplomacy initiative, the department is trying to reform the way in which foreign assistance is funded and delivered. The reform aims to consolidate the funding accounts and to make strategic planning about assistance the purview of the State Department. As a first step, Rice created a new position within the State Department: the director of Foreign Assistance, who also serves as administrator of USAID.

This focus on how the government is organized to provide democracy assistance is badly needed. The reform ideas to date, however, have not been ambitious enough. Any strategy for more effective democracy promotion must include significantly greater resources as well as a reorganization of all US government bureaus and agencies that are tasked with providing democracy assistance. A new Department of International Development must be created, and its head must be a member of the Cabinet. All foreign assistance resources currently funneled through other agencies and departments—with the exception of military training and assistance—must be transferred to this new department. This new department would largely absorb USAID, as well as DoD post-war reconstruction operations, rule of law training programs currently housed in the Department of Justice, agricultural aid now located in the Department of Agriculture, and the Millennium Challenge Corporation. It is absolutely crucial that this department be, and be perceived as, autonomous from both the Department of State and the Department of Defense. The mandate of this new department would be very different from the traditional missions of the military and diplomacy: not regime destruction, but regime construction, including nurturing improved governance, economic development, and democratic consolidation. This separation of departments to fulfill different missions will help each to deepen expertise in its respective field, and also clarify to the outside world which arms of the US government are doing what. Soldiers should not kill terrorists one day and teach Thomas Jefferson the next. Diplomats should not negotiate a basing agreement with a government one day and then turn around and fund an opposition leader to that same government.

Once constituted, the new Department of International Development should direct and administer all assistance that is delivered *directly* to foreign governments. When the US government does provide direct assistance to a foreign government through this new department, it must be firmly conditioned on pursuit of development objectives. There will be situations in which the United States has a national security interest in providing an autocratic regime with military aid or antiterrorist assistance, but this aid must not be called *democracy* assistance or development aid.

At the same time, no democracy assistance to nongovernmental organizations should come from this new department—or from any other branch of the US government. Even if a new Department of International Development is not established, this firewall between state-to-state assistance and the aid given to nongovernmental actors should become a guiding principle for democracy assistance reform. For instance, it is appropriate for the USAID or some other part of the US executive branch to fund a technical assistance program for a justice ministry in a foreign country under the rubric of a bilateral government-to-government agreement.

Inevitably, conflicts of interest and misinterpretations of motives arise when the State Department provides direct financial support to an NGO in another country. Is this money provided to aid democracy? Or is it given to advance a concrete US economic or strategic interest? Non-American NGOs, especially those working in autocratic societies, are increasingly reluctant to accept American assistance for fear of being labeled a lackey of the Bush administration or a spy for the United States.[15] Such questions come up regardless of the exact origin of US funding. Increased separation between the US government and American funders of nongovernmental actors thus can only be for the better. This money for direct assistance to NGOs also must be protected from any punishments or conditionalities directed at the government of that country. When the White House decides to cut foreign assistance to a country in order to change its behavior at home or abroad, US funds earmarked to promote democracy through nongovernmental actors must not be part of the conditionality.

A vastly expanded NED would be one model. To assume this role, NED would have to provide direct grants to all American providers of technical and financial assistance for the nongovernmental sector, which will loosen its connection with its four main grantees and require more involvement with for-profit contractors. NED would also need to open offices around the world. Because both of these changes might dilute NED's current mission, an alternative model would be the creation of a new foundation, modeled after NED, but with a wider mandate and a different mechanism for providing grants to both American organizations in the democracy promotion business as well as direct grants to local NGOs around the world.

Democracy promotion should be placed in a broader context of promoting economic development, reducing poverty, and furthering good governance. The four objectives are interlinked in multiple ways: good governance is widely accepted as a requisite for economic growth, widespread poverty undermines democratic legitimacy, growth reduces poverty, democratic accountability is often required to combat corruption and poor governance, and growth creates a favorable climate for democratic consolidation. Good governance in recipient countries is also critical to maintaining congressional and popular support for assistance programs. Nothing undermines support as much as the perception that US taxpayer dollars are going into a proverbial Swiss bank account. The United States cannot limit itself to the promotion of democracy; it must also use its leverage to promote development and good governance. These connections need to be reflected in how policy is articulated as well. Senior foreign policy officials in the Bush administration rarely invoke values such as equality and justice; yet historically, American leaders have considered these ideas fundamental to shaping our own government.

Enhancing and Creating International Institutions for Democracy Promotion

After World War II, the visionary American internationalists spearheaded the creation of a military alliance—the North Atlantic Treaty Organization (NATO)—to contain the Soviet threat in Europe, and crafted bilateral security pacts with Japan and South Korea to thwart the communist menace in Asia. American leaders also launched the Bretton Woods agreements and its institutions, the International Monetary Fund and the World Bank, as a strategy for maintaining an open, liberal capitalist order and avoiding a repeat of the protectionist-driven meltdown of the 1930s. Democracy promotion was not an explicit objective of either NATO or the International Monetary Fund. Member states in these institutions did not even have to be democracies. Nonetheless NATO's security umbrella, combined with American assistance through the Marshall Plan and other subsequent programs, did help prevent communist coups in Western Europe; keep the peace between formerly hostile countries within the alliance; and contain Soviet military expansion in Europe, which surely would have undermined democratic institutions.

The stable security environment was conducive to the deepening of democracy within member states and for increasing economic and political cooperation among those states, later culminating in the creation of the European Union. This regional community in turn helped inspire Eastern European dissidents to demand recognition of their human rights as outlined in Basket Three of the Helsinki Final Act. NATO expansion after the collapse of the Warsaw Pact offered Western multilateral connectivity to the new democracies in East Central Europe and served as a bridge as they prepared bids to join the European Union. The gravitational pull of the European Union may be the most powerful tool of democratic consolidation in the world today. The US security umbrella in Asia provided a similar facilitating condition for democratic development first in Japan, then South Korea, and eventually Taiwan. More intermittently, the United States has also used its leadership within the Organization of American States to encourage democratic development in Latin America.

Given the success of these multilateral institutions in promoting democracy, it is striking how little effort President Bush has devoted to creating new multilateral institutions or reforming existing ones to advance freedom. Since September 11, 2001, not one new major international organization has been formed to promote democratic reform. Nor has the Bush administration devoted serious effort toward boosting existing international organizations' focus on democracy promotion. This neglect of multilateral institutions must end.

More than any other region in the world, the greater Middle East is devoid of multilateral security institutions. The United States, Canada, the European Union, and other consolidated democracies should partner with their Middle Eastern counterparts to establish regional norms, confidence-building measures, and other forms of dialogue and political reassurance. The goal should be to establish a regional architecture that will affirm human rights and promote regional security based on the model of the Helsinki process in Eastern Europe, which gave rise to the Organization of Security and Cooperation in Europe and extensive human rights monitoring within and across borders.

The impetus for creating regional structures must come from within the region, but the initiative should also be supported from the outside. Such efforts can draw inspiration and lessons from past experiences in Europe and elsewhere. At the heart of the Helsinki process was the recognition that true security depended not only on relations between states but also on the relationship between rulers and the ruled. Many Middle Eastern governments have signed statements committing themselves to democratic reform, yet the Middle East lacks a regime that can help empower citizens to hold their rulers accountable to such pledges at home and in their relations with their neighbors.

Beyond the Middle East, an expanded NATO could be an important, stabilizing force in uniting democracies around the globe. ASEAN is a regional organization that seems ready to adopt more rigorous norms about democratic government and human rights. The recently created Community of Democracies got off to a bad start by extending membership to nondemocracies. But the idea of a new multilateral organization committed to advancing democratic practices, be it a revamped Community of Democracies or a new "League of Democracies," is needed.[16] More boldly, American leaders must embrace new modalities of strengthening ties within the community of democratic states, be it through a new treaty or a new alliance.[17]

Even the World Trade Organization (WTO) and other trade agreements must be viewed as levers that help open up economies, which in turn fosters democratic development. Excluding countries such as Iran from the WTO only hurts the democratic forces inside Iran who favor more, not less, integration of their country into the world system. In some rare circumstances such as South Africa under apartheid, economic sanctions have effectively pressured autocratic regimes to liberalize. The list of failures—including decades-long sanctions against Cuba and Iran—is equally striking. As a rule of thumb, the world democratic community should take its cues about sanctions from the democratic opposition in the target country.

Strengthening International Norms

The collapse of communism ushered in a giddy era for democracy promotion. Because so many autocratic regimes disappeared at the same time, new post-Communist regimes welcomed Western democracy promoters into their countries with few restrictions. Today the atmosphere for democracy promotion is markedly different. The allegedly easy cases of democratic transition in East Central Europe have consolidated and require no further assistance from democracy promoters. Autocratic regimes, at first weak after communism's collapse, have themselves consolidated and now have the means to push back. Finally, the war in Iraq has greatly tainted the idea of external regime change and put under suspicion all foreigners working to promote democratic change.

This new context requires a new strategy for bolstering the legitimacy of democracy promotion and the defense of human rights. Governments must come together and draft a code of conduct for democratic interventions in the same way that governments and the international human rights community have specified conditions in which external actors have the "responsibility to protect" threatened populations. A "right to help" doctrine is needed. A starting point for this new normative regime would be the "right" to free and fair elections, which in turn would legitimize international election monitors and international assistance targeted at electoral transparency. At the other extreme, a new international code of conduct could include strict prohibitions on direct financial assistance to political parties, yet affirm the legality of foreign assistance to nonpartisan NGOs. Once these rules of the road are codified, signatories to such a covenant would be obligated to respect them. And if they did not, then the violation would serve as a license for further intrusive behavior from external actors.

An internationally agreed-upon code of conduct for democracy assistance will constrain the activities of some US actors. But it will also enable other kinds of activities and interventions. But in the long run, the United States and other democracies will only be effective in promoting freedom abroad if we develop international institutions that enhance mutually beneficial cooperation, and then abide by the rules of these institutions in the conduct of our foreign policy.

In highlighting the moral and strategic imperatives for promoting democracy abroad, President Bush has continued a longstanding tradition in US foreign policy that has deep roots in both the Democratic and Republican parties. Declaration of any important objective, however, must be accompanied by a realistic and comprehensive strategy for achieving it. Simply trumpeting the importance of the objective over and over again is not a substitute for a strategy. The tragic result of the gap between objectives and strategies is that many Americans are starting to view this goal as no longer desirable or attainable. The next American president must do better. A more effective strategy for promoting democracy and human rights is both needed and available.

Notes

1 *Freedom in the World 2007*, selected data from Freedom House's annual global survey of political rights and civil liberties (Washington: Freedom House, 2007), p. 1.

2 For elaboration of this logic, see James Goldgeier and Michael McFaul, "What To Do about Russia," *Policy Review*, No. 133, October–November 2005, pp. 45–62.

3 David Adesnik and Michael McFaul, "Engaging Autocratic Allies to Promote Democracy," *The Washington Quarterly*, Vol. 29, No. 2, Spring 2006, pp. 7–26.

4 Robert Barro, *Determinants of Economics Growth: A Cross Country Empirical Study* (Cambridge: MIT Press, 1997) p. 58.

5 Ronald Inglehart, "The Worldviews of Islamic Publics in Global Perspective," in Mansour Moaddel, ed., *Worldviews of Islamic Publics* (New York: Palgrave, 2005), p. 16; James Zogby, *What Arabs Think: Values, Beliefs and Concerns* (Washington: Zogby International, 2002); Mark Tessler, "Do Islamic Orientations Influence Attitudes Toward Democracy in the Arab World? Evidence from Egypt, Jordan, Morocco, and Algeria," *International Journal of Comparative Sociology*, Vol. 43, Nos. 3–5, June 2002, pp. 229–249; and the cluster of articles under the rubric "How People View Democracy" in *Journal of Democracy*, Vol. 12, No. 1, January 2001, pp. 93–145.

6 Samuel P. Huntington, *The Clash of Civilizations and the Remaking of World Order* (New York: Simon and Schuster, 1996).

7 Henry A. Kissinger, *A World Restored: Europe after Napoleon* (Gloucester, MA: Peter Smith, 1973).

8 Natan Sharansky, *The Case for Democracy: The Power of Freedom to Overcome Tyranny and Terror* (Balfour Books: 2006).

9 Francis Fukuyama, "Identity, Immigration, and Liberal Democracy," *Journal of Democracy*, Vol. 17, No. 2, April 2006, pp. 5–20.

10 Jack Snyder, *From Voting to Violence: Democratization and Nationalist Conflict* (New York: W. W. Norton, 2000); and Jack Snyder and Edward D. Mansfield, *Electing to Fight: Why Emerging Democracies Go to War* (Cambridge, MA: MIT Press, 2007).

11 Samuel P. Huntington, *Political Order in Changing Societies* (New Haven: Yale University Press, 1968).

12 Fareed Zakaria, *The Future of Freedom: Illiberal Democracy at Home and Abroad* (New York: W. W. Norton, 2003).

13 Thomas Carothers, "The 'Sequencing' Fallacy," *Journal of Democracy*, Vol. 18, No. 1, 2007, pp. 12–27.

14 McFaul, Milani, and Diamond, "A Win-Win Strategy for Dealing with Iran," *The Washington Quarterly*, Winter 2006–07.

15 Akbar Ganji, "Money Can't Buy Us Democracy," *The New York Times*, August 2, 2006.

16 Senator John McCain proposed the idea of a new league of democracies in a speech at the Hoover Institution on May 2, 2007.

17 On these other modalities, see Tod Lindberg, "The Treaty of the Democratic Peace," *The Weekly Standard*, February 12, 2007, pp. 19–24; and Ivo Daalder and James Lindsey, "Democracies of the World, Unite," *The American Interest*, Vol. 2, No. 3, January–February 2007, pp. 5–19.

10

In Defense of Values

Derek Chollet and Tod Lindberg

Is idealism dead? Should the promotion of American values of liberalism, democracy, human rights, and rule of law be a core element of US foreign policy? Where to strike the balance between principles and interests is one of the most enduring debates about America's role in the world. But since September 11, this question has become intensely contested and deeply controversial. It has emerged as one of the central divides between the political right and left—in large part because of the history of the past seven years, the Bush administration's rhetoric, its strong association with the "freedom agenda," and its actions justified at least in part by democracy promotion (namely the war in Iraq). Yet it is also becoming a sharper division *within* each end of the political spectrum.

Of course, the choice between realism and idealism is a false one: US foreign policy must be firmly rooted in both national interests and values. But now, after two successive presidents of opposite political parties (Bill Clinton and George W. Bush) have argued that the spread of American values is itself a vital interest, there is growing skepticism in many quarters about whether trying to do so is worth significant costs, or even a true interest of the United States at all. Facts matter, and after several difficult years of pursuing a foreign policy framed as a fight for American values, more are wondering whether the sacrifice is worth it. In the view of many policymakers, politicians, analysts, and average citizens, the time has come to have a more realistic foreign policy—scaling back the United States' global ambitions, respecting the limits to America's capabilities and will, recognizing and embracing the constraints of the international system, and maintaining a healthy skepticism about the broad applicability of American values.

But if the values agenda has been discredited among many on both the left and the right, and a greater realism is the preferred alternative, what would such a strategy look like? Moving beyond the slogans, would a truly values-free foreign policy really secure US interests, strengthen US power, and draw the sustained support of the American people? We think not. American values are an indispensable component of the US role in the world—they are a key part of what unites the United States to allies in Europe and elsewhere and distinguishes the United States from countries like China. Instead of dividing conservatives and liberals, American values in foreign policy can in fact translate into a set of policies that both sides can rally around. In the current political environment, as we approach the first post-9/11, post-Bush election, building such a policy bridge will be difficult. But given the stakes, it is imperative.

Skepticism on the Left . . .

The emphasis placed on promoting liberal values internationally has drawn increasing hostility among traditional liberals and within the Democratic Party. Many of those who once embraced the proud liberal tradition of Woodrow Wilson, Franklin D. Roosevelt, and John F. Kennedy find themselves questioning their assumptions. And for those liberals who still embrace the importance of values, their numbers are fewer. According to a June 2006 poll commissioned by the German Marshall Fund of the United States, only 35 percent of Democrats said that the United States should "help establish democracy in other countries"—whereas 64 percent of Republicans responded favorably.[1]

This skepticism is driven by several factors. First, and most fundamentally, is the fact that this approach is so closely identified with President Bush and his administration's policies. In the wake of 9/11, Bush tapped into many common (and bipartisan) themes about the enduring importance of American values, but his vision is infused with a religiosity that leaves many liberals nervous. Yet, even when he got his rhetoric right—for example, many liberals admired statements like his November 2003 speech at the National Endowment for Democracy—the means he chose to implement policies, such as the war in Iraq, have proven very costly. The result now is that for many on the left, efforts to pursue policies largely rooted in values, especially democracy promotion, have become discredited and are increasingly unpopular politically.

For some liberals, the political difficulty of supporting a values-based foreign policy stems from a second factor: the structural incentives of the current political environment. Because an unpopular president has so closely identified his policies with the promotion of values, liberals are driven to oppose him. In fact, the president's leadership style has offered very little in return, even to those liberals who might agree with him. So for many on the left, if Bush is for it, they must be against it—even if this means embracing the cognitive dissonance of turning away from long-held beliefs and traditions. For many liberals, it has become politically incorrect to admit when Bush has actually gotten something right. With Democrats in control of the US Congress, these incentives of opposition are now also institutional. This creates a similar dynamic to that of the aftermath of the 1994 congressional elections, when the new Republican majority turned increasingly inward in opposition to the internationalism of the Clinton administration. Whereas the Bush team came into office in 2001 with an "ABC" policy—anything but Clinton—the Democratic Congress today, and a possible Democratic president in 2009, will be tempted to do exactly the same: anything but Bush.

But liberal skepticism is more than structural or institutional—it is also internal to the debates among different camps within liberal politics. The history of the past seven years—and the consequences of a policy perceived as driven more by values than interests—has been sobering for a number of left-leaning members of the foreign policy establishment. Many supported the 2003 invasion of Iraq for the same reasons that they supported confronting Saddam Hussein during the Clinton years. And many applauded President Bush when he talked about the importance of democracy promotion. Yet, now that the costs of such policies are apparent—whether in terms of political capital, US global prestige, or blood and treasure—many in the foreign policy elite have become more cautious, scaling back ambitions and endorsing more realistic goals. For many mainstream foreign policy liberals, the downfall of Britain's Tony Blair—who championed values-based concepts like "humanitarian intervention" during the late 1990s—is a stark warning about the costs of embracing such policies too tightly.

The intellectual and political disconnect between the liberal establishment and the liberal grassroots activists is growing, especially over US foreign policy and the purpose and use of American power. The convulsions within the political left that began in the late 1990s—illustrated by the rise of the antiglobalization movement and division over the Clinton administration's military interventions in Bosnia, Kosovo, and its 1998 air strikes against Iraq—have only become more severe and divisive. To be sure, this reflects anger with President Bush. But it is more than that. When it comes to national security issues, the left has become splintered in a way not seen since the 1970s, when Vietnam split the Democratic party and ruined the post-World War II liberal establishment. A similar dynamic is at work today, as a new generation of liberal activists (fueled by the power of the blogosphere) rages not just against Bush, but against a Democratic foreign policy establishment they perceive as aiding and abetting the Bush agenda—central to which is the promotion of American values. If this divide deepens, it will become very difficult for Democratic leaders to embrace explicitly values-centered policies even if they wanted to.

. . . and Wariness on the Right

The growing discomfort with the promotion of American values in foreign policy is felt not only by those on the left. Increasingly, conservatives are having second thoughts about the extent to which US foreign policy should be driven by ideology and the promotion of values ahead of interests. Since the Bush administration still dominates conservative politics, the right remains more strongly identified with the values agenda and the wariness among conservatives is more muted than among liberals. But the recent rise of "realists"—as illustrated by the personnel changes at the Defense Department and the US Mission to the United Nations, greater pragmatism at the State Department, and the return to prominence of figures like former Secretary of State James Baker and Brent Scowcroft—has been heralded as a rebalancing away from what many argue were the ideological excesses of the president's first four years in office. Like liberals, conservatives are contemplating their future beyond the Bush presidency—and this debate will intensify as the focus turns from the current administration to the one that will take office in January 2009.

In several respects, the factors driving conservatives' frustrations with the values agenda mirror the frustrations on the left. The first issue is a practical one: the American people's deepening disillusionment with the Bush administration's policies are raising the political costs of supporting the Bush agenda. Bush's growing unpopularity makes supporting his policies risky. Put another way, the president's success at branding his administration's actions as part of a values-based policy is directly related to the political efficacy of supporting it. When it was seen as working, the bandwagon was enthusiastic and big, but the more it is perceived as a failure, many of the president's political allies are more than happy to let him ride alone.

Like liberals, conservatives also face a structural challenge that will only increase as the 2008 election draws closer. Any Republican presidential nominee will seek to differentiate himself from his predecessor. And since more conservatives are reading the Bush years as a caution against an ambitious, values-based foreign policy, stressing realism might be the way to distinguish oneself. In this sense, one can foresee a replay of the early 1990s, when the lessons drawn from George H. W. Bush's electoral defeat in 1992—that his presidency was too focused on foreign affairs at the expense of domestic issues—caused many conservatives to move away not only from a values-based policy but from internationalism itself.

Moreover, the events of the past several years, especially the war in Iraq, have thrown much of the conservative foreign policy establishment into a crisis of confidence. Like many establishment liberals, conservatives in and out of government are questioning not only the capabilities required to implement values-promoting policies (and whether the United States can ever develop such capabilities) but the underlying assumptions of the policy itself. Such self-doubt is especially acute because many of the officials so closely identified with these policies were once heralded for their national security experience and acumen. Expectations were high, so the results of their time in office—a major crisis for America's role in the world—have been sobering.

The neoconservatives—those most closely identified with a foreign policy based on promoting American values and bold interventionism—have come in for the most criticism, and not just from the left. The internal split reemerging within conservatism over ideals is the fourth driver of wariness. During the 1990s, neoconservatives saw themselves as insurgents, agitating against both the creeping isolationism within the Republican party and what they considered the feckless policies of the Clinton team (even if most neoconservatives agreed on actions like intervention in the Balkans). But for several years after 9/11, their agenda wielded great influence over the direction of the Bush administration's policy, especially its focus on spreading American values. Six years later, neoconservatives again find themselves largely on the outside looking in, as many mainstream Republicans seek a return to the kinds of policies then-Governor Bush articulated during the 2000 presidential campaign: a foreign policy based on humility, skepticism about the United States' interests in "nation-building," and the limited applicability of American values to regions like the Middle East.

So for political and intellectual reasons, the role of values in foreign policy is now in retreat domestically—liberals are increasingly skeptical and conservatives having deep doubts. One must also note the suspicion (or worse) with which many in other countries view a values-based US foreign policy. In the first place, many around the world are disinclined to take Americans at their word on the principles they claim to be promoting. Many hear rhetoric of principle as nothing more than a cover for the raw assertion of American power. Some world leaders hear the rhetoric of democracy promotion and take it seriously, and for that very reason regard it as dangerous, a threat to their own claims of legitimacy. One could probably break this category down further, into those hostile to any threat to their personal prerogatives on the one hand, and on the other those generally sympathetic to liberalization, but worried that too-hasty movement in that direction might tear their societies apart. Finally, the promotion of American values opens the United States to charges of hypocrisy: Does American conduct actually live up to the values America espouses? Many have found the United States' actions wanting in areas ranging from Guantanamo and Abu Ghraib to the US relationship with Pakistan and the House of Saud, and would urge that the United States tone down its complaints about others until it removes the log in its own eye. By these lights, the promotion of American values should begin at home (a view that also has purchase both on the left side of American public opinion and, to a degree, on the libertarian right).

The "Acirema" World

But if a foreign policy that promotes American values is the problem, what is the solution? In considering this question, it might be helpful to ask: what would US foreign policy actually look like if it were somehow stripped of its "values" component? It's worth trying to conjure such a vision, not only as an intellectual exercise but also because there is no quicker way to see exactly why such a policy would be a nonstarter for the United States.

As a point of departure, we might look to the assumptions about the character of the international system embraced by scholars in the "neorealist" school of international relations, on the grounds that neorealists regard such considerations as morality as largely epiphenomenal in explaining the behavior of states. Since one key neorealist assumption is that the internal characteristics of states don't matter (or matter much), we find a more or less explicit attempt to write moral considerations out of the rules of statecraft. What they posit, then, is an anarchical international system—no authority higher than the state. Each state wishes to be entirely free to make its own judgments about the conduct of its internal affairs. These judgments, insofar as they implicate events outside the state's territory and thus beyond its uncontested authority, yield a set of national interests in relation to other states. Because any state's supreme vital interest is self-preservation, each state's first priority is to ensure its security. The only means of achieving security is self-help. Unfortunately, the actions states take in pursuit of their own security and national interests tend to bring them into conflict with other states. Some structural configurations of the international system are more conducive to peace and stability than others, but no structure is impervious to internal stresses that may cause it to collapse or change convulsively as states act in pursuit of security under shifting perceptions of national interest.

How might this abstract description of state action in the international system translate into policy choices for a state in the position in which the United States finds itself today? For purposes of our investigation, we will call this state "Acirema," which is "America" spelled backwards. We do this for two reasons. First, by speculating in accordance with this "values-free" scenario, we do not want to be taken to be proposing what follows as a genuine alternative to US policy; on the contrary, the speculation shows how far removed from the realm of possibility and desirability such a neorealist scenario would be. Second, "Acirema," strikes us as capturing just how radical an inversion of American priorities and traditions the pursuit of such a values-free policy would be.

In the first place, Acirema is the dominant military power in the world, and it would certainly make sense to try to maintain that dominance. This is not a judgment alien to existing US policy: The Bush administration's 2002 National Security Strategy (NSS) pledged not to allow a "peer competitor" to its military power to emerge. The Bush NSS, however, justified this policy as a way to encourage peaceful relations among states. State-on-state conflict, for example the attempt to conquer territory by force, would be discouraged by overwhelming US power. But it is by no means clear, from a values-free perspective, why we should be attached to a principle of peaceful relations among states and the illegitimacy of aggressive war or conquest. True, Acirema does not want to be attacked, and would seek to maintain sufficient power to deter and if necessary defeat any potential aggressor. But why Acirema would care if Iran attacked Iraq, or China attacked Russia, or France attacked Germany, is entirely a question of whether Acirema's aims would best be served by peace or war between any given two states.

Acirema would pursue an overall strategy of maintaining its dominance. Again, this is not foreign to current US grand strategy. But the United States has welcomed and encouraged modernization, economic growth, and globalization not only in order to enrich Americans but also according to a theory that greater and greater trade flows and economic interdependence make for a more peaceful international environment and are good in themselves. Neither of the latter two justifications would matter to Acirema.

There is danger in an Acireman policy that encourages other states to become rich: with riches come the capacity to develop military power that in turn might challenge Acirema, or covertly fund challenges and challengers. Acireman policymakers would want to examine the trade-off between the economic benefits of an open trading system and the potential danger in allowing others to enrich themselves, thus potentially increasing their power. An Asian economic flu might be a bad thing, but it might also be a good thing. China's modernization might yield cheap goods, but if the price is a more formidable military challenge to Acirema, the price might be too high. The best way to deal with China's self-professed desire for a "peaceful rise" might be to disregard the rhetoric of peaceability and act to prevent the rise. Acirema might want to identify potential vulnerabilities in the Chinese economy and try to exploit them to undermine Chinese economic growth. The collapse of central authority in China would be destabilizing—but primarily for the Chinese, who might then be too preoccupied with their internal turmoil to pose a threat.

More generally, the stability Acirema would seek would be the stability of its own position. The stability of other states and relations among other states is of concern only insofar as it impinges on the stability of the Acireman position. Indeed, a subsidiary strategy of preserving dominance might be to maintain a *fragile* international stability, one in which all other states felt themselves to be constantly *at risk* from instability without actually sliding into it, with a potentially adverse effect on Acirema.

Under this scenario, one would have to reject engagement in the Middle East, except with regard to securing Acireman energy needs. To the extent that support for Israel arouses hostility from Israel's neighbors, Acirema should cease such support, unless Israel is capable of providing a benefit to Acirema sufficient to offset the damage—a tall order. Meanwhile, however, it is not solely Acireman support for Israel that antagonizes certain elements in the Middle East and, to the extent that funding for these elements comes from governments that have grown wealthy from oil revenues, it may be best to go directly to the source and deprive the funders of the revenue. Acirema might seize and hold sufficient oilfields to see to its needs and then destroy the capacity of others to exploit the resources on their territory.

In the event that the negative repercussions of such a move might be deemed too costly, then Acireman disengagement from the region might work—provided it is accompanied by an unambiguous warning from Acirema to states in the region about the unacceptability of funding terrorists, their ideological supporters, and their sympathizers. Acirema would have to make clear that regime elimination awaits any states that fail to accept that their continued oil revenue depends on their refraining from harboring, funding, or supporting anti-Acireman terrorism. The credibility of such a policy would likely require a demonstration. A policy of regime elimination would differ from "regime change" in its rejection of Colin Powell's "Pottery Barn" principle: you break it, you own it. On the contrary, any state foolish enough to provoke Acirema to forcibly remove its regime, with all the risk and expense that would entail for Aciremans, would be on its own to sort out what comes next. Acirema wouldn't care, though it would certainly hope that whatever regime emerged had learned a lesson from the experience of the toppling of its predecessor.

The policy of Acirema toward Israel is a specific case of what would be a more general revision in alliance policy. The essential question for Acirema with regard to any ally is whether Acireman security is improved, on net, as a result of the alliance. The notion of an alliance as an all-purpose mechanism for securing the cooperation of others in mutual pursuit of security objectives would need to be reassessed. What, specifically, is the value of "cooperation"? Needless to say, Acirema will harbor no prejudice in favor of cooperation or multilateralism, instead asking whether cooperative or multilateral means would bring a benefit that Acirema cannot obtain on its own. Acirema need not be especially concerned with the opinions of states that lack the capacity to make a difference. There will be no free-riding on the provision of security, because Acirema will not enter into alliance relationships except with partners whose tangible assets improve Acireman security.

Needless to say, any assistance Acirema would choose to provide to other states would be tightly tied to the tangible benefit received, either economically or in terms of security. The notion of "humanitarian" aid or "humanitarian" intervention of any kind is self-evidently meaningless to a foreign policy free of moral consideration. Acirema might have a concern with averting refugee flows toward its shores, but only if the cost of action abroad to prevent the flows exceeds the cost of turning away those attempting to enter.

Local disputes in faraway places would not necessarily bother Acirema. There is nothing historically unusual about violent contests for power within states, and Acirema would not worry overmuch about the outbreak of such conflicts. They have disadvantages in terms of disrupting commerce, but they have advantages as well, in that those engaged in fierce local conflict are unlikely to have the surplus capacity to threaten Acireman national interests. Even intense local conflict, with civilian deaths running to hundreds of thousands, would have to be assessed through the prism of whether it poses any sort of threat to Acirema that might warrant intervention.

It is difficult to see what gain Acirema might get from raising the issue of "human rights" with other states. Doing so would come at the cost of pressing other, more useful demands upon weaker states and would needlessly complicate relations with stronger states. There might be advantages to be gained from fomenting internal dissension and rebellion within stronger states, in accordance with a general strategy of fragile stability, and this provocation might be couched in terms of "human rights" in the event that doing so would be efficacious. But the use of "human rights" would be entirely instrumental, and Acirema would have to refrain from establishing any sentimental bonds with those it was encouraging, since the likelihood is that the state in which they are rebelling will move to crush them if the crisis becomes serious, and of course Acirema would have no reason to assist them at that point.

The strongest states will be those with nuclear weapons, and the impulse of states to acquire them would undoubtedly be very strong. Needless to say, Acirema would have to be very wary of states already possessing substantial nuclear arsenals. Freedom of action against Russia, China, Great Britain, France, and Israel would accordingly be constrained. As for those newly seeking to acquire the technology of atomic weapons, Acirema might choose to acquiesce, provided it was confident that its own arsenal was deterring any aggression against Acirema. This might be true of some but not all states. On the other hand, possession of a nuclear deterrent by another state might embolden that state to act against the national interests of Acirema. It might be necessary to take preemptive action to establish that mere possession of a few nuclear weapons is not sufficient to deter or coerce Acirema. Acirema might have to launch a nuclear attack first. Of course, there would be some risk of nuclear counterattack if the other state had the means to deliver its nuclear weapons. On the other hand, Acirema could withstand such a small strike, whereas its antagonist would be obliterated.

Yes, we have wandered into the bizarro territory of *Dr. Strangelove*, and the scenario described above is both monstrous to contemplate and impossible to envision actually coming to pass. But why is that? In the first place, can anyone—liberal or conservative—plausibly imagine the United States electing a president on such a callous "Acirema First" platform? Patrick Buchanan tried a slightly attenuated version of the Acirema project and was unable to win the Republican nomination, let alone seriously contest the general election. During the 2000 election, the platform of Ralph Nader's Green Party shared many aspects of the Acireman program but garnered little support (yet just enough to help determine the outcome). The closest a Democratic presidential nominee has ever come to the Acirema agenda is probably George McGovern's disastrous 1972 campaign, in which his slogan "Come home, America" was taken as a call for broad-based disengagement and dramatic reduction of defense spending, not just an immediate end to the Vietnam War.

Disband NATO, abandon Israel, destabilize China, welcome wars when useful, disregard genocide, and wage preemptive nuclear war? While such views are consistently found in certain small segments of the political spectrum, there is, thankfully, no plausible passageway from America to Acirema.

Some have claimed—and indeed the 2002 National Security Strategy and other statements of President Bush flirt with—the notion that US values and interests are quite closely aligned or can be so. Such an argument effectively dodges the question of which should take precedence. And indeed, it may be that "failed states" are something the United States should take action to prevent because of the potential for danger where no one is adequately in charge. We disagree on the relative magnitude of the danger there.[2] We agree, however, that US action to prevent the failure of states is morally good. The point is that without the moral frame of reference, one could imagine having a debate about whether the collapse of a state into civil war, warlordism, and genocide is good or bad for the United States—and that such a debate would remain imaginary, because it can never occur in the real world.

Moreover, it is a conceit that this "values-free" *machtpolitik* or *realpolitik* is truly free of moral considerations. Even the proposition "look out for No. 1" has a moral aspect. Why should you look out for No. 1? Because you place a value on No. 1 and think it is morally good to seek the benefit of No. 1. Indeed, there may have been a time in human history—perhaps in Hobbes's state of nature, the "war of all against all"—when moral considerations, though hardly absent, involved calculations no more complicated than this.

But the United States was founded not as a "values-free" rational calculator of what's good for No. 1, but as a nation embodying certain values or principles that justified rebellion against its lawful sovereign. While, to this day, the United States has been accused (often with justification) of failing to live up to the values of the Declaration of Independence, the United States has never been able to or seriously attempted to expunge those values from all consideration in the conduct of domestic or foreign policy. This seems unlikely to change. And rightly or wrongly, Americans demand consideration for those principles not simply because they are "ours"—and no one has the right to interfere in our affairs by telling us anything different—but because of our belief that they are true.

Toward a New Consensus on Principle in Foreign Policy

While the place of American values in foreign policy endures, questions remain about how such policies should be implemented and how the inevitable trade-offs should be managed, especially in the current political environment. The Bush legacy casts a long shadow. During the past several years, intellectuals and policy analysts have offered numerous grand strategies as a corrective to Bush, rebalancing foreign policy between realism and idealism. Some stress one perspective more than the other, and they usually combine some version of both words in their titles: Francis Fukuyama offers "Realistic Wilsonianism," Robert Wright proposes "Progressive Realism," John Hulsman and Anatol Lieven describe "Ethical Realism," Charles Krauthammer espouses "Democratic Realism," and John Ikenberry and Charles Kupchan outline "Liberal Realism" (we could go on).

Instead of adding yet another grand strategy slogan into the mix, we believe that it is more important to describe a set of principles and priorities that should guide US foreign relations in the challenging years ahead. Below we outline six principles, each rooted in American ideals and serving American interests. This is not an exhaustive list (additional policies are described in other chapters in this book), yet it shows that it is possible to construct a common agenda between liberals and conservatives that is firmly built upon a commitment to uphold—and promote—values.

Standing Against the Conquest of Territory by Force

The United States must continue to uphold one of the most basic norms of international relations: preventing and when necessary reversing the conquest of territory across an international border by military force. While support for this principle may seem self-evident—after all, it is at the heart of the UN Charter and the underlying rationale of the world's most important security organization, NATO—it is in fact a value that the United States must choose to defend. As made clear by the alternative Acirema world described earlier, a great power like the United States could decide that upholding this norm is too costly or outside the bounds of its core national interests. We believe that since preventing territorial conquest by force remains a keystone of the international system and a driver of its enduring stability, this must remain a core value of US foreign policy.

Such a commitment entails certain responsibilities around the world and, fundamentally, demands an interventionist foreign policy—preferably as an active partner through international institutions, but if necessary alone. The means that are required will depend on the specific situation and the other US interests at stake, such as alliance or other security or political relationships and the potential for wider violence. Yet the full range of tools—from diplomacy to sanctions and political isolation to military force—must always be available.

Sometimes this might require active diplomacy to prevent one state from threatening another with force, such as the United States' repeated efforts in recent years to reduce tensions between India and Pakistan. Other instances will require US leadership to try to negotiate an end to conflicts after they have broken out. For example, this is what the Clinton administration did when it hammered out the Dayton Peace Accords in 1995, reversing Slobodan Milošević's aggression against the newly independent Bosnia. And on some (and hopefully rare) occasions, the United States will have to use military force to reverse aggression, as George H. W. Bush did in 1991 when he created and led a UN-sanctioned international coalition to kick Iraq out of Kuwait. Today, looking into the future and the probability of a smaller American presence in Iraq, the commitment to territorial integrity will be critical insurance against potential incursions by neighbors such as Iran.

Of course, another way of describing this is that by valuing the protection of territorial integrity from threats of force, we are valuing the defense of sovereignty. That's correct to an extent, but we do recognize that under certain circumstances this value can be trumped by other values, such as the responsibility to defend the rights and lives of people living within a state's own territory. We discuss this in greater detail below, but suffice it to say that the United States should not allow any leader to hide behind one value (the right not to be invaded) in order to violate another (his people's right not to be brutalized).

Defending Liberal Regimes

The United States should be prepared and willing to help any and all democratic governments that come under challenge internationally or from internal anti-democratic elements seeking to overturn liberal political and social order and the rule of law. This is a basic principle of *democratic solidarity*, according to which the most secure, established, and stable liberal democracies, the United States above all, should acknowledge a responsibility to come to the assistance of democratic governments that are threatened, that have yet to become fully consolidated and mature, or are subject to forces of internal instability.

Liberal democracy, in the view of most of those who govern themselves according to its principles, is not merely a matter of sovereign choice—just one among many options. Rather, citizens of democracies tend to regard their form of government as the *right* or *best* choice, at least for them; they would not consider trading their form of government for autocratic or totalitarian or theocratic government,[3] and would rightly consider any force in favor of such a change in governance as a serious threat, one to be challenged and defeated—*not* by whatever means necessary, such as abandonment of liberal principles for the sake of security, but by any means legitimate *within* the horizon of liberal principles.

If citizens of democracies view their system as the right or best choice for themselves, those citizens and that state ought to be willing to acknowledge the rightness of the choice of liberal democracy among the citizens of other states. They have a stake not only in their own domestic political arrangements but in their view of the rightness of liberal democracy, which does not end at their borders. A threat to liberal democracy elsewhere is accordingly a challenge, and one which any democratic states with the means to do so should be willing to meet head on.

The United States has a number of alliances with democratic states, including several with allies that were not democratic when the alliance relationship began but became so, perhaps partly as a result of the security provided by the United States. These alliance commitments remain fully in force, but they are only a beginning. The United States must recognize that it will not sit idly by as nondemocratic states try to undermine or even overturn democracies or fragile liberalizing states. On the contrary, the United States should step up, together with other democratic states, to provide all the support or assistance possible.

The correct response when a powerful nondemocratic state tries to coerce a weaker democratic state—such as Russia has tried with Ukraine and especially Georgia—is not to temporize out of deference to the power of the strong but to speak up unequivocally in defense of democracy under threat. To stand aloof or to appease the stronger power would be to embolden antidemocratic forces, and not just locally. Some argued that extending the NATO alliance to the Baltic States was foolish because of the military difficulty of defending Estonia, Latvia, and Lithuania against attack and because extending the Atlantic Alliance onto the territory of the former Soviet Union would unnecessarily antagonize Russia. We strongly disagreed at the time and believe we were correct. In our view, the newly won freedom of the Baltic nations and the establishment of liberal, democratic governments there *already* created obligations for the United States and NATO countries. NATO accession did not create, but ratified and codified that obligation toward these peoples. The process was exemplary in warding off any urge to interfere with and disrupt democratic development and consolidation there—and elsewhere in Central and Eastern Europe, in our view.

A principle of democratic solidarity is not only good in itself, it makes external threats to democratic governments less likely by demonstrating that making such threats will have adverse *global* consequences for anyone inclined to pursue such a course. It would be a mistake to view the principle of democratic solidarity as a military doctrine; its main components are political, diplomatic, and social.

There are some instances in which democratic solidarity comes with conditions. For example, US willingness to defend Taiwan against Chinese attack depends on Taipei not taking the provocative step of a declaration of independence—to which China would respond militarily, according to Beijing's declaratory policy. This is a reasonable codicil given local circumstances. There may be others (though Taiwan is arguably the most neuralgic of such at present). An absolute *military* doctrine of democratic solidarity would create moral hazard, since a state might conclude it could act as provocatively as it wished in response to local circumstances and still receive the backing of the United States and other democratic states. That is not the deal. Such a state, by taking action other democratic states would regard as unreasonable, would itself be breaking from democratic solidarity. But with such nuances always in mind, a principle of democratic solidarity should guide US policy, and the United States should encourage other democratic states to embrace it.

Promoting Liberal Governance

If a principle of democratic solidarity makes sense at the level of state-to-state relations, it also makes sense for the United States in relation to people working toward liberalization and democracy in their own societies. This is not likely to be especially controversial as a matter of principle among democratic allies. Opinion surveys in Europe, for example, show large majorities in favor of promotion of democracy by peaceful means.[4] And it seems likely that a substantial part of the lingering opposition is a product of concern that democracy will not be liberal, but rather will bring to power illiberal elements. Our discussion should be understood to refer to the promotion of liberal democracy, in which the two components are a liberal social order based on principles of freedom and minority rights, as well as popularly elected governments followed by peaceful transfer of power.

Nevertheless, it cannot be denied that a principle of democratic solidarity—even if broadly accepted by and among, and in application to, democratic states facing external threats or internal challenge, and even if accepted as the rightness of supporting development of liberal democracy in principle—will surely be controversial when considered in application to supporters of democracy in nondemocratic states.

We think that the United States should, as far as possible, provide whatever help aspiring democrats and liberalizers seek. The United States should also encourage similar support among fellow democratic states—an extension of democratic solidarity. But considerations of prudence, national interests (such as access to energy resources), and *force majeure* will inevitably weigh into such decisions.

What we propose is the imperative of *balancing prudential considerations and principle*. It is not enough to take note of Saudi oil fields and declare, therefore, that Saudi Arabia is off limits for criticism and promotion of reform of its extraordinarily repressive regime. Similarly, China is big, powerful, rising—and undemocratic (indeed, increasingly openly antidemocratic). We must deal with the fact that China is a vast and increasingly powerful country; it would be madness to try to deny it. But we must also deal with the fact that China is undemocratic.

The United States can and must pursue dual-track policies in such cases, as Francis Fukuyama and Michael McFaul argue.[5] One track will address exigency, the other the moral case.

On the moral track, rather than a one-size-fits-all model of democracy promotion, we propose a method, a way of thinking about and acting on the problem that does not pretend to a greater degree of generality than is appropriate. The objective, in each country in which liberal democracy has yet to take hold, or take hold fully, is to identify *next steps*. What is the next plausible step for the expansion of the liberal and democratic space? Conversely, what is the next plausible step for the constriction of the space in which authoritarians or antidemocratic elements operate? The United States should then work vigorously to promote the next step, applying pressure for reform against the authoritarian element (typically, the government) and assistance to the democratic element to help achieve measurable progress. Once the next-step objective has been achieved, the United States must immediately move on to the *next* next step. Pressure and assistance must not let up following interim successes; on the contrary, it should increase.

We agree that the key failure of the Bush administration's democracy promotion policy in Egypt, for example, was overeagerness to claim credit for progress in response to small positive steps. Yes, it was consequential that the Mubarak government decided to allow other parties to compete in a presidential election. But it was hardly the birth of liberal democracy on the Nile Delta. Mubarak deserved congratulations for taking the step he took—followed without pause by the demand that he take the next step of moving toward a free and fair election.

With this next-step policy of constant pressure to expand the liberal space while contracting the authoritarian space, the United States will be in a position to say it is keeping faith with the forces of democracy and liberalization in every country, even in the face of inevitable practical constraints.

Enforcing the Responsibility to Protect

Liberal democracy, in which people choose their leaders in free and fair elections and in which political and human rights are secure, including for minorities, stands at the pinnacle of human political achievement. For some states, such as the United States, the most urgent political task lies in helping others achieve this great end while being ever mindful of and seeking to address the imperfections of its own governance. For others, the consolidation of transition to democratic governance is the key political task, and it can often be one of life and death, as in the case of the assassination of reformist Serbian Prime Minister Zoran Djindjic or the dioxin poisoning of Orange Revolution leader Viktor Yushchenko in Ukraine. For still others, the political challenge is to pry open any space at all for the opposition in an authoritarian country.

But for the worst off of all, such as the Tutsi minority in Rwanda or the Kurds of Saddam Hussein's Iraq, the essential political challenge is survival—against the wishes of the government or the mob in whose midst they have the misfortune to live. Surely, it cannot be right to embrace a principle of democratic solidarity and democracy promotion for those relatively high on the social ladder while offering nothing to those in greatest peril of losing the most basic human right: the right to live.

At the United Nations' 2005 World Summit in New York, the world's leaders embraced for the first time the doctrine of *The Responsibility to Protect*. It holds, briefly, that with sovereign rights come sovereign responsibility, and the primary responsibility of a government is to protect the people who live within its territory. In the event that a government is unable or unwilling to provide protection for its people from would-be perpetrators of genocide or mass killing and ethnic cleansing—or worse, is complicit in such crimes against humanity—the international community must take upon itself the responsibility to protect. No government that fails to protect its people may legitimately assert a right to noninterference in its internal affairs.

The responsibility to protect is a transformational concept in international relations. Previously, the victims of the worst sort of war crimes and human rights abuses on a mass scale had no recourse, trapped as they were behind a curtain of sovereign right. The adoption of the responsibility to protect grants them an appeal to the international community.

This is often construed solely through the prism of military intervention and, in some cases, the only way to stop determined genocidaires may be by force. But it is wrong to think that military means are the first or main recourse. The international community needs to take active measures in terms of monitoring and applying diplomatic and other forms of pressure (such as sanctions, diplomatic isolation, and negotiations) to avert mass killings and ethnic cleansing whenever possible.

Of course, there is much dispute over how the "international community" may act. We agree that the United Nations Security Council is the best venue, not because we think that the United Nations is the only path to legality and legitimacy, but because so many other states take this view, and their wishes deserve respect. However, in the event the Security Council fails to take timely and effective action as a human rights catastrophe unfolds, the United States must not stand on the sidelines. In the case of Kosovo, when the Security Council was blocked, NATO stepped up to take decisive action, thereby preventing a genocide. Some still question the legality of that action. We take the concern seriously coming from those who were willing to act; we do not take it seriously coming from those who were prepared to let hundreds of thousands fall prey to ethnic cleansing and genocide. When necessary, the United States must lead or be willing to join others to mobilize an effective response to mass killing and widespread repression.

Addressing Global Hardship

As the world's most powerful country, the United States has the capability to help address the challenges stemming from poverty, hunger, disease, and lack of opportunity for billions of people in the developing world. We believe that leadership in these areas is not just something the United States can do—it is what the United States *must* do.

While these issues were once only considered "humanitarian" or "soft"—implying that they are always elective or secondary—there are instrumental reasons why the United States should focus on them. If one accepts the argument (and we do) that threats emanating from weak or failed states can endanger US national security, then it is in America's interest to help these states stabilize. Some describe this as part of "draining the swamp" of desperation and hardship that radical jihadists and other extremists thrive in by reducing extreme poverty and replacing the extreme fundamentalism taught in some madrassas with basic education. As evidence of the growing consensus on the relationship between these issues and national security, the Bush administration justifies many of its efforts along these lines—and when it is criticized, it is usually for not doing enough.

But US leadership in these areas is about more than protecting security. America's actions in the world are a powerful demonstration of what it wants to accomplish with its power and the values it wishes to uphold. In this sense, the United States should embrace humanitarianism, and not consider it optional or of minor importance. To do so is both the smart and the morally right thing to do for our security.

This is also an area where there is significant common ground between the political right and left. Liberals have long argued that addressing issues like poverty and disease need to be a core part of US foreign policy. Many conservatives have as well, especially among the evangelical community (as exemplified by the work of Franklin Graham and Rick Warren). Spurred in part by evangelical advocates, the Bush administration has made positive strides in this direction, increasing assistance to Africa by 67 percent and boosting spending for programs to fight HIV/AIDS. Meanwhile, three of the major Democratic candidates for president have talked about the importance of fighting global poverty and making a major push to improve education throughout the developing world.

Looking ahead, both conservatives and liberals should embrace an agenda centered on stronger American leadership in these areas—in fact, one valid criticism of recent US policy is that it too often cedes the initiative to others. For example, greater resources should be put behind combating poverty and disease, and a broad recognition that free trade is critical to helping the developing world advance economically. And we should consider fundamental reforms in the way the US government is organized to implement such policies, including ideas like establishing a Department of Global Development (along the lines of that in the United Kingdom) and replacing the Foreign Assistance Act.

Strengthening Alliances and Institutions

Any discussion of implementing the principles outlined above begs a fundamental question about means: how should the United States work with other countries? Throughout American history, the subject of whether the United States should tie itself to the fate of others abroad—or work with others to solve problems—has been hotly contested. This has been especially true since the end of the Cold War and the apogee of US primacy, when we really didn't *need* others to solve most problems. While this tugging between unilateralism and multilateralism is often seen as concerned solely with efficacy and instrumentality—sometimes it is better for us to share the burden, sometimes not—we believe that it is in fact a debate about what kind of global power America should be and what kind of international system we should support. It is not about instruments; it is about principles.

As Ivo Daalder and Robert Kagan argue, it is important for US policies to be seen as legitimate both in the eyes of the American people and the world.[6] That is a value that other countries—certainly Acirema—might not necessarily care about. America does and should. But the question is how best to uphold this value, and what institutions (whether existing or new) or multilateral arrangements are the best means to do so. As discussed earlier, when it comes to implementing values-based policies like defending liberal regimes or enforcing the responsibility to protect, working through alliances and international institutions should be as important to the United States (at least as something to aspire to) as it is to others.

The challenge has been that for many conservatives and liberals, the unilateral vs. multilateral discourse has framed these ideas as an either/or choice. The right has focused too much on the constraints of multilateralism and maintaining US freedom of action. We agree that the United States always reserves the right to act alone if the circumstances require, but this should not be the preferred option. In this sense, the Bush administration's substance and style—exemplified by its "with us or against us" statements or rhetoric about preemption—has prompted international skepticism about whether the United States genuinely wants institutions like the United Nations to function, or even exist at all.

Yet too many liberals slide into the opposite problem: upholding multilateralism for its own sake. This has only intensified during the Bush years, when support for the United States around the world has reached alarming lows. If the United States is unpopular, some believe that it must be solely our fault and make no judgment about the behavior of our allies. The remedy among many on the left seems to us to be overly simplistic: defer at all times to the collective decisions of institutions. This confuses the reality that international organizations are stages, not actors. They are simply groupings of other sovereign states, and while organizations can help facilitate decisions for states, they cannot make choices for them. They can neither prevent internal disagreements nor force free-riders and buck passers to act.

Recently we've seen signs of greater nuance in the unilateral/multilateral debate between left and right. For example, in his second term President Bush began working through institutions like the UN Security Council to deal with problems like Iran and Darfur, and with an ad hoc coalition to negotiate with North Korea. Even his rhetoric is softening: when asked recently what he has learned from his European partners, he said that "I have come to realize that other countries do rely upon the United Nations, and I respect that a lot. So there's an area, for example, where I have been taught a lesson by my allies and friends."[7] And among liberals, there is greater recognition that the multilateral route often can frustrate rather than facilitate action. For example, the longer the Security Council's divisions prevent strong action to end the genocide in Darfur, the louder the calls become for a NATO response or even unilateral US military intervention.

This bolsters our belief that a new consensus can be formed in support of seeking the broadest possible coalition to pursue US foreign policy goals. This means working through alliances and institutions, but also ensuring that these organizations work. The United States should have high expectations of its alliances, and in turn it should have high expectations of its allies. It should be an active and energetic partner, recognizing that getting something done through a coalition often requires the same kind of daily politicking, strong-arming, logrolling, and handholding used every day in working with the US Congress. And while the United States should seek to make existing institutions like the United Nations and NATO stronger and more effective, it should also work to build other organizations like the Alliance of Democracies.

The conclusion we come to is that while an idealistic foreign policy has become harder to defend politically, it is possible to construct a forward-looking, values-based agenda that both liberals and conservatives can support. In fact, such an approach should garner more than just passive support—the policies presented above can actually serve as part of the foundation for US foreign policy in the years ahead. Neither sentimental nor coldly aloof, these values comprise the core of the rules-based, liberal international order that the United States should aspire to achieve. This is about more than what we want; it is about who we are.

Yet because the political incentives against an approach to foreign policy that promotes American values remain so powerful, as we described at the outset, such a policy will not emerge on its own. Even with greater clarity about what values we want to uphold and promote, difficult questions will remain about how to do so. There will always be debates about acceptable costs and the trade-offs involved. So success will require sustained attention and steadfast leadership. With both, the American people will rise to the challenge.

Notes

1 *Transatlantic Trends 2006*, The German Marshall Fund of the United States, 2006, p. 16, *http:// www.transatlantictrends.org/trends/doc/2006_TT_Key%20Findings%20FINAL.pdf*.

2 Lindberg tends to the view that failed states mainly pose a problem for those directly affected, who have their hands full trying to survive the local crisis. Chollet is more concerned about spillover effects and broader destabilization.

3 There is, of course, a substantial amount of disagreement over the extent to which conservative evangelical Christians in the United States seek, ultimately, the enactment of their religious views into law. Chollet sees this as a potentially serious threat to liberal constitutional principles and minority rights. Lindberg does not consider it as serious of a threat, viewing the political activities of even those who would wish to see their views enacted in such fashion as circumscribed by a liberal, democratic political order out of which they are unwilling to break.

4 *Transatlantic Trends 2006*, The German Marshall Fund of the United States, 2006.

5 See Chap. 9 of this volume.

6 See Chap. 1 of this volume.

7 See Bush Press Conference with German Chancellor Angela Merkel, January 4, 2007, *http:// www.whitehouse.gov/news/releases/2007/01/20070104-2.html*.

Contributors

Kenneth Anderson is professor of law at Washington College of Law, American University, and a research fellow of the Hoover Institution, Stanford University. A former director of the Human Rights Watch Arms Division and former general counsel to the Open Society Institute, he is a member of the editorial board of the journal *Terrorism and Political Violence*, legal editor of the book *Crimes of War*, and frequent contributor to scholarly journals on the laws of war, human rights, terrorism, and international law.

Stephen E. Biegun is vice president of International Governmental Affairs for Ford Motor Company. Prior to joining Ford, he served as national security advisor to the Senate Majority Leader. He worked in the White House from 2001 to 2003 as executive secretary of the National Security Council. Prior to joining the White House staff, he served for 14 years as a foreign policy advisor to members of both the House of Representatives and the United States Senate. During this time, he held the position of chief of staff of the United States Senate Committee on Foreign Relations.

Peter Brookes is a senior fellow at the Heritage Foundation, a Washington, DC, think tank. He is also a weekly columnist for the *New York Post*, a contributing editor for the *Armed Forces Journal*, a commissioner with the US-China Economic and Security Review Commission, and the author of *A Devil's Triangle: Terrorism, Weapons of Mass Destruction, and Rogue States*. Previously, he has served as a Deputy Assistant Secretary of Defense, Capitol Hill staffer, CIA operations officer, and naval officer.

Derek Chollet is a senior fellow at the Center for a New American Security and a non-resident fellow in the Brookings Institution's Global Economy and Development Program. Previously, he was foreign policy adviser to Senator John Edwards, both on his legislative staff and during the 2004 Kerry/Edwards presidential campaign. During the Clinton administration, he served in the US State Department as chief speechwriter for UN Ambassador Richard Holbrooke and special adviser to Deputy Secretary of State Strobe Talbott. He is the author of *The Road to the Dayton Accords: A Study of American Statecraft.*

Ivo H. Daalder is a senior fellow at the Brookings Institution in Washington, DC. From 1995 to 1996 he was director for European affairs on President Clinton's National Security Council staff. Daalder has authored eleven books, including the award-winning *America Unbound: The Bush Revolution in Foreign Policy* (with James M. Lindsay). His forthcoming books include (with James M. Lindsay) *Restoring Trust: How to Reverse the Bush Revolution in Foreign Policy* (John Wiley, 2008) and (with I. M. Destler) *In the Shadow of the Oval Office: The President's National Security Adviser and the Making of American Foreign Policy* (Simon & Schuster, 2008).

Andrew Erdmann is a management consultant. His client experience includes work in the retail, energy, high tech and public sectors. Between 2001 and 2005 he served with the US government as a member of the secretary of state's policy planning staff; senior advisor to the Ministry of Higher Education & Scientific Research with the Coalition Provisional Authority and, lastly, director for Iran, Iraq, and Strategic Planning on the National Security Council staff. Trained as a historian of US foreign relations, he has also taught international affairs at Harvard and George Washington University.

Francis Fukuyama is Bernard L. Schwartz Professor of International Political Economy at the School of Advanced International Studies (SAIS) of Johns Hopkins University and director of SAIS' International Development program. Dr. Fukuyama received degrees from Cornell and Harvard. He was a member of the Political Science Department of the RAND Corporation and a member of the Policy Planning Staff of the US Department of State. From 1996 to 2000 he was Omer L. and Nancy Hirst Professor of Public Policy at the School of Public Policy at George Mason University.

Frederick W. Kagan is a resident scholar at the American Enterprise Institute, specializing in defense transformation, the defense budget, and defense strategy and warfare. Previously he spent ten years as a professor of military history at the United States Military Academy (West Point). Kagan's 2006 book, *Finding the*

Target: The Transformation of American Military Policy (Encounter Books), examines the post-Vietnam development of US armed forces, particularly in structure and fundamental approach. Kagan was coauthor of an influential January 2007 report, *Choosing Victory: A Plan for Success in Iraq*, advocating an increased deployment.

Robert Kagan is senior associate at the Carnegie Endowment for International Peace and Transatlantic Fellow at the German Marshall Fund. His most recent book is *Dangerous Nation: America's Place in the World from its Earliest Days to the Dawn of the Twentieth Century* (Knopf, 2006). His previous book was *Of Paradise and Power* (Knopf, 2003), an international bestseller that has been translated into more than 25 languages. Dr. Kagan writes a monthly column on world affairs for *The Washington Post* and is a contributing editor at both *The New Republic* and *The Weekly Standard*.

Mark P. Lagon is Ambassador-at-Large directing the Office to Monitor and Combat Trafficking in Persons at the U.S. Department of State. At the time of writing, he was Deputy Assistant Secretary of State for International Organization Affairs— with responsibility for policy at the United Nations on reform, management, human rights, humanitarian affairs, and public diplomacy. Before joining the Bush administration, he was a senior staff member with the Senate Foreign Relations Committee (for Chairman Helms). He has been a Council on Foreign Relations International Affairs Fellow at the Project for a New American Century and an aide to Ambassador Jeane Kirkpatrick at the American Enterprise Institute.

Tod Lindberg is a research fellow at the Hoover Institution, Stanford University, and editor of its bimonthly journal, *Policy Review*. He is the author of *The Political Teachings of Jesus* (HarperCollins) and editor of *Beyond Paradise and Power: Europe, America and the Future of a Troubled Partnership*. He is a contributing editor to *The Weekly Standard* and has frequently appeared as an analyst on National Public Radio. In 2005 he served on the expert staff of the United States Institute of Peace's Task Force on the United Nations (the Gingrich-Mitchell Task Force), for which he coordinated the working group on responding to genocide and major human rights abuses.

Elisa Massimino has been Washington Director of Human Rights First for more than a decade, where she is responsible for the organization's overall advocacy effort with the United States' government. She testifies frequently before Congress and writes extensively for legal and popular publications. Prior to joining Human Rights First, she practiced law in Washington and was pro bono counsel in many human rights cases. She holds a master's degree in philosophy from Johns Hopkins University and a law degree from the University of Michigan. She teaches human rights advocacy at Georgetown University Law Center.

Michael McFaul is the Peter and Helen Bing Senior Fellow at the Hoover Institution, where he codirects the Iran Democracy Project. He is also the director of the Center on Democracy, Development, and Rule of Law at the Freeman Spogli Institute and professor of political science at Stanford University. He is also a nonresident senior associate at the Carnegie Endowment for International Peace.

Suzanne Nossel founded the Democracy Arsenal weblog and writes a column on foreign policy for *The New Republic* online. She has served as a senior fellow at the Center for American Progress and the Century Foundation. During the Clinton administration she was deputy to the ambassador for UN Management and Reform under Ambassador Richard Holbrooke. Nossel has also served as masthead vice president of Sales Strategy and Operations for *The Wall Street Journal*, as vice president of Strategy and Business Development for Bertelsmann, Inc., and as a consultant at McKinsey & Company. She currently serves as chief of operations for a large global NGO.

Michael O'Hanlon is senior fellow and Sydney Stein Jr. Chair in foreign policy studies at the Brookings Institution, where he specializes in US defense strategy, the use of military force, and homeland security. O'Hanlon is coauthor most recently of *Hard Power: the New Politics of National Security* (Basic Books), a look at the sources of Democrats' political vulnerability on national security in recent decades and an agenda to correct it. He previously was an analyst with the Congressional Budget Office. Brookings' Iraq Index project, which he leads, is a regular feature on *The New York Times* Op-Ed page.

Michael Schiffer is a program officer at the Stanley Foundation, where he works on Asia programs and a range of other US national and global security issues. Before joining the foundation, he was a Council on Foreign Relations International Affairs Fellow at the National Institute of Defense Studies in Japan. From 1995 to 2004, Schiffer worked on the staff of US Senator Dianne Feinstein (D-CA), where he was her senior national security adviser and legislative director. He has also managed a bed and breakfast inn in Hawaii.

Gary Schmitt is a resident scholar and director of the American Enterprise Institute's Program on Advanced Strategic Studies. He has worked both on Capitol Hill as the minority staff director for the Senate Select Committee on Intelligence and in the White House as executive director of the President's Foreign Intelligence Advisory Board. Dr. Schmitt has written extensively on national security issues and

American politics. His most recent publication, with Tom Donnelly, is *Of Men and Materiel: The Crisis in Military Resources* (AEI Press, 2007).

David Shorr is a program officer for policy analysis and dialogue at the Stanley Foundation and managed extensive consultations that were convened in support of the UN High-level Panel and in the run-up to the 2005 UN Summit. Shorr previously spent many years in Washington working for policy research and advocacy organizations such as: Human Rights First, Refugees International, Search for Common Ground, British American Security Information Council, Arms Control Association, and Physicians for Social Responsibility.

Julianne Smith is the director of the Europe Program at the Center for Strategic and International Studies. She is the author or contributor to a number of CSIS books and reports, including *Transforming NATO (. . . again): A Primer for the NATO Summit in Riga 2006* and *America and the World in the Age of Terror*. She also coedited and authored a chapter for *Five Years After 9/11: An Assessment of America's War on Terror* and served as one of the lead investigators for a CSIS project on European Defense Integration. Smith codirects the Transatlantic Dialogue on Terrorism, which examines US-European disagreements over the root causes of terrorism.

Jon B. Wolfsthal is a senior fellow with the international security program at the Center for Strategic and International Studies. He worked in the 1990s for the United States Department of Energy on a variety of nuclear security and non-proliferation programs and served as the US government's on-site monitor at North Korea's Yongbyon nuclear facilities in 1995–1996. He is the coauthor of *Deadly Arsenals: Tracking Weapons of Mass Destruction*. He served as the chairman of the nonproliferation advisory team for the 2004 Presidential Campaign of Senator John Kerry and as a nonproliferation advisor on the 1992 Campaign of then Governor Bill Clinton.

Index